The *Changing* Humanities

The
Changing Humanities

AN APPRAISAL OF OLD VALUES
AND NEW USES

BY *David H. Stevens*

FORMER DIRECTOR FOR THE HUMANITIES
THE ROCKEFELLER FOUNDATION

"Animosities are mortal,
but the humanities live forever." *Noctes Ambrosianae: 1834*

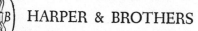
HARPER & BROTHERS

Publishers, New York

To *Ruth Davis Stevens*

Contents

Preface

My purpose in this book is to give the general reader an image of the humanities in American colleges and universities. The impressions underlying it were drawn from experience as a teacher and administrator in the United States and from my visits to foreign countries. A central theme is that all humanistic research and teaching must be international. There is no nationalism in learning or in the arts.

Many persons who live with the means and ends of learning, or by expression through the arts, may not agree with all that is here reported of them. I hope, however, that some will be led to make more intelligible what I have written of their special interests, and that all may discover here new signs of unity among the humanities.

No formal recognition can be offered to the persons and institutions that have benefited my studies. Much of their help was given unawares as they talked with me—administrators over budgets, students on courses of study, and teachers regarding positions in colleges and universities. All have contributed toward my assumptions and beliefs on the place of the humanities in American life.

Advantages have come in these years of uneasy peace out of discussions with younger men returning from war duties and with teachers who, while abroad, have changed their views on the nature of higher education at home. My cordial thanks are extended to all such individuals and to the publishers who have granted permission to quote from their works. My greatest debt is to the University of Chicago, the Rockefeller Foundation, and the Henry E. Huntington Library and Art Gallery. A period of reading in this library gave me much of the background material for this commentary. Its general sources, however, were in my forty years of active duty, which were evenly divided between the other two institutions. Each gave access to countless persons and so developed my appreciation of the role of the humanities in maintaining and improving this world of free men.

Acknowledgment of permission to quote copyrighted materials is made to individuals and to publishers as follows: the American Council of Learned Societies—*Bulletin* of March, 1952; Chatto & Windus, *A Critical History of English Poetry*, by H. J. C. Grierson and J. C. Smith, for rights exclusive of the United States; the University of Chicago Press, *American Diplomacy, 1900-1950*, by George F. Kennan; Harper & Brothers, *Creating an Industrial Civilization*, edited by Eugene Staley, and *Philosophy in American Education: Its Tasks and Opportunities*, by Brand Blanshard *et al*; Harvard University Press, *Virgin Land: the American West as Symbol and Myth*, by Henry Nash Smith; the University of Kansas Press, *The Humanities for Our Time*, by Walter B. Agard *et al*; Alfred A. Knopf, Inc., *Marvelous Journey: A Survey of Four Centuries of Brazilian Writing*, by Samuel Putnam; The Macmillan Company, *History of the United States of America*, by Henry William Elson; Methuen and Company, Ltd., *On the Writing of History*, by Sir Charles Oman; *The Modern Language Journal*, two articles in Vol. XXVII (May, 1943); University of Oklahoma Press, *The American University as Publisher: A Digest of a Report on American University Presses*, by Chester Kerr; Oxford University Press, American Branch, *A Critical History of English Poetry*, by H. J. C. Grierson and J. C. Smith, for rights in the United States; The Philosophical Library, Inc., *Essays in Science and Philosophy*, by Alfred North Whitehead; Princeton University Press, *The Reinterpretation of Victorian Literature*, by Joseph E. Baker; The Ronald Press Company, *The Poems of John Milton*, edited by James Holly Hanford (1936); Mrs. Annette L. Thorndike, *Literature in a Changing Age*, by Ashley H. Thorndike; and the executors of the estate of Mr. H. G. Wells, through the courtesy of A. P. Watt & Son, *The New Teaching of History*, with a Reply to Some Recent Criticisms of the "Outline of History," by H. G. Wells.

D. H. S.

Ephraim, Wisconsin
March 15, 1953

Introduction

The humanities have two distinguishing marks that are clearly understood by any who look upon education as a part of life, not as an experience of their first quarter century in a particular environment. These are the same identifying qualities as each of us would name first in a definition of civilization; like man himself, the humanities are out of time, but always timeless and changing.

It is true that men have used this term "humanities" in order to distinguish one form of higher education from the parts known as sciences and social sciences. They have done many things that give the humanities institutional settings, such as the creation of libraries and university disciplines of teaching and research. But the humanities are not confined within these formal limits. They do not belong to any class or profession of men. Rather they are the embodiments, in forms that all can understand, of the learning, experience, and expression of humanity. The school boy, as truly as the scholar in his university or the artist in his studio, possesses the values that the humanities hold and give.

We should begin, therefore, to identify their meanings and uses more constantly with people. Like ourselves, they depend on what is past and follow opened paths into the future. They put upon every individual a compulsion to use whatever he gathers from humane experiences in his every act and expression; this natural necessity of personal identification with what we learn of mankind, creates new life out of the old. The humanistic way is always out of what was past and what is present. That it leads through schools and universities is only incidental to its existence, for the way of the humanities existed long before our institutions and will outlast them. Each person enters into that way when he realizes that he himself is part and product of all that the humanities signify.

The mind of every reader turns to what it has known. The meaning, by way of familiar experience, that comes from a printed page to meet an individual gives him a part of the definition of the humanities. The other part he finds for himself, within himself.

These two forms of personal experience have become separated by custom. The scholars of the Renaissance were unconscious of that blend of learning and of self-expression which gave their works a temporal immortality. It was much later in time when the humanities became something in scholarship and something quite different in the daily experience of men. The scholars have told us this, and have demonstrated it themselves. Yet out of our own lives, and from what we read in the histories of the arts, we know the two experiences to be indivisible.

The scholar in his university discipline and the expressive artist at his desk or in his studio work with identical purpose—to give themselves and others the sense of belonging to mankind. Each gives something of himself as he recalls in his own way the ideas and desires of other men. To succeed in his purpose the scholar keeps alive his vision of the past for the benefit of after ages. The expressive artist adds his own increase to the great tradition. Each of us, as receivers and givers, does a little of the work of both. As we do that, we identify again the scholar and the artist in the mind of man, for we are proving that all rely on the same universal elements throughout life.

We shall be helping toward the recovery of that unity if we will but remember that in origin and by their nature the humanities are out of man's inner self. For these reasons a commentary on their place in higher education should be in terms of human spirit rather than of function. They move and have their being within the organic forms of institutions, but how they do so may be left to the descriptive historian. He will find his evidence in the catalogs resting quietly on library shelves of American colleges and universities. The way is less than the life, as is the body less than the spirit within it.

Through people all humanistic disciplines have influence upon individual men and women, and so upon their conduct in life. What the scholar and teacher give and do is influential in world affairs, by example and by guidance toward the humane values of all time. Their usefulness in that world is a matter in need of study and description. Humanists will carry on their refinements in methodology and their reviews of change in scholarship, over long periods of time; they can also render great service by turning their minds, and so the minds of all, toward the constant, universal values in their substances. Time is the soil of the humanities, but they are not buried in it. Through growth and adaptation they live and produce for the benefit of every individual of any nation, race, or creed.

Today, with a world-wide opportunity for the increase of cultural and personal contacts among all men, they have new, universal responsibilities. The narrower channels of humane studies today have been widened to carry the flow of fact and meaning at full tide and are waiting to be filled.

The great traditions of learning are not exclusive possessions of scholars. They never have been, any more than are the ways of expression in the arts. In our time both learning and the arts have come to greater influence in the day-by-day life of the people. This is true in spite of mechanized amusement and political misuse of the arts and artists by dictators. Denial of freedom of thought, by either expedient, has not stopped men from creative effort and self-expression in any but the captive countries. Such sweeping denials of human rights as do exist today will not in the end overcome the rights of citizens to learn and of artists to create. Meanwhile, promise of finer and fuller development through the arts is foreshadowed by the strength of the humanistic disciplines in this country and by the lively attention of the American public to all new ideas in education.

For their part, the humanists in and out of universities have two obligations—to increase the body of learning and to interpret human values for the benefit of the public mind. When they do both, they are at their full task. They will not want for followers so long as they demonstrate in practice the interplay of research, teaching, and interpretation dealing with the personal values in life.

Perpetually the humanities, as disciplines to maintain knowledge of the part of man in his universe, face a single question that bears on every individual act and judgment. They deal with the "why" in human existence. The sciences, in a myriad of ways, work to determine the "how" and the "when." Between the two, and helpful to both, are the social sciences seeking after limited proofs according to approximately scientific standards. They cannot reduce their conclusions to laws, because by definition they deal with living people instead of with inert matter. At the end of their interpretations, both social sciences and humanities make room for the personal equation. One might say that the former do so in spite of themselves, and the other gladly.

The humanities deal primarily with the individual rather than with masses of men in any social structure past or present. Masses of matter are for science, and statistical data for social science. Yet the humanities function through processes of highest technical quality. Though employing methods that in part are also those of the sciences and the social sciences, with respect to function they are unique: by interpreting a galaxy of human acts and aspirations, the effect upon individuals of all types of experience throughout recorded time, and the concern of Man with God and Nature, they reveal the range of individual choices in all environments. Their function is not to discover so much as to show the ways to self-discovery.

To bring that opportunity within the reach of literate persons everywhere is the function of the humanist in society. Only the professional workers in humanistic disciplines know how slow and methodical must be the advance toward goals of scholarship. The meaningful end product is often a result of scores of investigations. A definitive edition of an early poet and even passages of Biblical text most familiar to all, are fair copies from hundreds of studies that lay scattered over centuries of time before these classical forms came into being.

For his own enjoyment and profit the scholar constructs retrospective reviews of what has been done in his special field. It is hoped that he and the general reader may be moderately satisfied with a much less ambitious account of changes in humanistic studies during the short span of fifty years within a single country.

The specialist and the general reader have in common their exposures to daily life, no matter how far apart their routines of living come to be in working for a livelihood. Both had the same kinds of teaching in school and college of what, to the time of that generation, the humanities had yielded by research. Both had similar tasks in finding how to educate others, in their own families if not in classrooms. Both constantly feel the same uneasiness in deciding what to read and what to reject out of the towering mass of current print, how to nourish the arts, and what is the aim of higher education in a democratic society.

The second of these perpetual questions—how to nourish the arts— has more precise answer on a national scale in other countries. Great Britain ranks high among the nations of Europe for its recognition of this responsibility of government, and for its success in bringing the arts to the people through their own powers wisely stimulated. Canada is today going more deeply into possibilities of the same nature. Meanwhile the United States has traversed many fields of artistic expression, to find few lasting solutions to the problems of administration and maintenance. The one great experiment, under the Works Progress Administration during the thirties, succeeded in spite of the Congressional voters making the appropriations. Most of them understood the relief phase of that compulsory act and very little beyond. The credit goes to devoted individuals from our colleges and universities and to other talented, idealistic persons from the country at large. The judgment and vision of Harry L. Hopkins made their work possible. In spite of that demonstration, this country still counts on the private donor and on the teacher in school or college to foster these natural resources of humanistic change.

But a new period is at hand. The American public schools have opened the way, particularly in the larger cities, while the colleges and universities are realizing their need to guide our practice in the arts of expression. They are developing an American history of trial and error in these matters, from which expert minds can draw valuable conclusions. Twenty years hence demonstration and definition will have yielded a body of sound proof, as is not the case today. We know that here the humanities are regaining lost territories. Enough has been accomplished to prove this true. Though the present statement contains too little of the story to form a record of that advance, it has sufficient detail possibly to forecast the future cultivation of the arts in American institutions of higher education.

The influence of the humanities upon individuals and through them upon society at large, is great. Now more than ever before they enable one to influence others effectually and on a world-wide scale. By virtue of the helps from science and invention, the humanist can reach any point where print or controlled sound waves now travel. More realistically, he himself can go out to interpret the values in his professional discipline, or where he cannot go he can see to it that others go. In the maze of university duties and studies that hold him in an agreeable captivity, he still can direct younger scholars toward their future choices from his point of vantage midway between past and future opportunities.

Fortunately at this time in human affairs the demands put upon professional humanists are so great as to do away with needless attempts at self-justification. They long since learned to value science instead of resisting it, as in the windmill contests of religion against science and of science against religion. Humanists and scientists now see that their paths lead to identical destinations of proof and belief. Humanists have now no arguments with social scientists over differences in aim and treatment of their disciplines; they realize that reliance of one on the other is mutual. Scholars who once lamented that the humanities had lost their "time-honored place" in sustaining the true values of liberal education, now see that their service is given to all branches of learning indirectly, while as disciplines of learning they are as always near the sources of all knowledge. They have not lost their place.

By every practicable means, our nation should be using its cultural and spiritual powers to increase good will among men. The first step toward that limitless horizon is to show the professional humanist himself what he and all his colleagues are now contributing to human welfare within their own country. He is not one to profess much openly, but instead lets the quality of his performance as teacher and scholar be felt and valued. He believes as much in the followers whom he develops as in himself, for he sees the faults in his own incomplete interpretations of values. To him, and to the public at large, should be made known what constant benefits derive from his work. This cannot be done by talk of the dominance of science and technologies, but by discerning how scientists and technicians rely upon the humanists to give better balance to their loads of social responsibility. Nor can it be done by criticising adversely the use of public and private funds for other kinds of research. The good to be done is by setting forth positive truth regarding the humanities themselves.

Benefits to mankind from the humanities have been accepted as customary and, like daylight, to be remarked on only when lacking. So just is that observation, that man's constant reliance on them is their surest source of security and increase. They do not need the dramatic announcements of discovery in science or of new invention. They do, however, need to be constantly at hand to meet man's daily needs and so, like wind and rain, to keep him in contact with his universe.

The *Changing* Humanities

ONE

Patterns of Humanistic Research and Teaching

I

As choice of weapons is the preliminary to duelling, so a statement concerning the humanities in present time should open with a definition of its terms of discourse. This is especially desirable because of the many changes in their meaning since the Renaissance. Also, since other words of diverse kinds have grown from the same root, the reader may need to have the word "humanities" placed in its academic setting.

The humanities are distinct from sciences and social sciences in being centered about the meanings of life to man as an individual. Their disciplines of research and subjects of teaching deal with his experiences and his expressions of self. His ideas and feelings are made known articulately in language, symbolically through all the arts, and with philosophical or historical concern for values as he turns toward the inner or outward meanings of human existence. All recorded signs of what man has found in himself and in the world about him are brought within the disciplines of the humanities, to be given form by scholars and teachers for use by all men in present and in future time.

What these disciplines and subjects are today, is partly a consequence of description given to fields of study under different environments. Their place in American life at the halfway mark of the twentieth century is different from what it was a hundred years ago. A backward look toward their form and influence at that time will show that the humanities have grown logically out of what they then were but have also added to themselves new fields of interest in keeping with contemporary circumstance. Research has pushed further the boundaries of knowledge to bring in the story of civilizations that were unknown a hundred years ago, and has made familiar to all, ideas and values that were then realized only by scholars.

What the humanities were in this country a hundred years ago owed much to the great traditions of learning and of religious thought that started in the Renaissance and Reformation. The Europe of the fifteenth, sixteenth, and seventeenth centuries set patterns that are still of high influence; from these, and others more widely drawn into the American tradition during the eighteenth and nineteenth centuries, came the earliest forms of Oriental and Asiatic influence. Advance into new territory has been constant. The background, therefore, is one of change in definition of the humanities through an increase of subject matter and of improved techniques for both research and teaching.

Initially, secular studies were separated from knowledge of contemporary affairs and from belief in the field of religion, to be denoted by the word *humanus*. Thereafter, in the early stages of the Renaissance, these elements took on individual forms that were brought into unity as the humanities. During medieval times appeared those terms which are still familiar in scholarship—grammar, rhetoric, philosophy, arithmetic, geometry, astronomy, and music. These seven original disciplines were long in power, but by the nineteenth century they were considerably changed and commonly stated in this order— philosophy, history, ancient and modern languages and literatures, mathematics, physical science, and natural history. A hundred years ago these were counted as forming the body of liberal studies. By that time the original division between religious and secular had been dropped. The later break between sciences and the humanities still lay ahead.

Fifty years later, at the beginning of the twentieth century, the *Oxford English Dictionary* provided a definition that shows a real advance toward modern usage. It also gives a landing stage in the survey of what went on during the growth of the humanities into a closely related group of disciplines in institutions for higher education. This definition, brought into print in 1901, reads: "Learning or literature concerned with human culture: a term including the various branches of polite scholarship, as grammar, rhetoric, poetry, and esp. the study of ancient Latin and Greek classics." The scientific elements of a liberal education are here no longer included, but the notion of "polite" scholarship is still there and becomes a hindrance to the widest usefulness of the humanities through all the channels of research and teaching.

For present times, these are abstract and undeveloped terms of reference. That deficiency is partly due to currently accepted connotations for words that had earlier a wider application among humanistic scholars and their colleagues. It is proper to believe that teachers of a century ago had clear and concrete ideas of the content of teaching; of that fact their writings give good evidence.

A little later than a century ago, a notable advance beyond such limiting description was made in this country. In 1878 the third annual report of the Johns Hopkins University contained a statement that gave formal patterns to humanistic studies. These were for both undergraduate and graduate levels of teaching and investigation. Resistance to the elective system that became open and constant afterwards had its frank statement in the formula of what, in this new university, would be the patterns of study.

From that year the practice grew in American universities of combining several "subjects" under formal groupings, in order to increase effectiveness of research. Fields began to take the place of subjects. Terms now familiar, as "combination of courses" and "relationships," appeared. In contrast to the elective systems on the extreme left and of fixed curricula on the right, "liberal education" took on a form implied by the literal meanings of the words. Undergraduates had put before them several varieties of prescribed patterns, their choices limited to selections from among a few organized groups with closely interrelated parts in each grouping.

They saw their choices of direction for studies in the old classical course; in modern languages; chemistry, mathematics and physics; history and political science; and in certain subjects fixed as preliminary to study of medicine, as history and political science stood ahead of work in law. The contest among departments for advanced students was lessened, presumably, and a few professors could offer work at Johns Hopkins for future humanists under a flexible but always purposeful pattern. By present standards, the offerings were limited and the treatment of them as well, but the interchange of students among departments was a marked benefit for faculty and students toward a wider, deeper approach to the humanities than had existed earlier.

For example, the group requirements placed Latin, Sanskrit, and German in one unit, with German, English, and Sanskrit in another. A third unit that was to persist for several decades in American graduate schools had in it English, German, and Old Norse. German as the constant factor in these triads was not long lived, and shortly the movement toward English studies brought a reorientation toward the relevant languages and dialects of Western Europe. At the moment, the benefit lay in a new unity among faculties, even though there was a lack of formal work in history, literature, and philosophy. The few graduate students obviously were destined to be taught by a small group of professors. Any explanation of this controlled direction of humanistic studies is not in criticism of quality of work, but rather gives supporting proof of a determination to establish high standards of performance in fundamental subjects. Unquestionably, from the results, one knows that the type of teacher so produced was superior, in scope of knowledge and in ability to give guidance to younger men, to the product of the loosely fashioned methods previously favored.

This pattern of group arrangement was not a borrowing from Germany, even though in 1876 scholars as well as scientists and physicians were returning in goodly number from their studies in that country. The crossing and turning back home during the nineteenth century had its least lasting effects on the humanities. This has seemed on the surface to be untrue, by reason of dominance of German method and concept in a few subjects. Instead, one should marvel at the freedom of choice in matter and method soon to appear. The records show that in 1876 nearly all of the fifty-three professors in the Johns Hopkins faculty had studied in Germany. Certain fixations were naturally passed on by them to their students. These were most evident in metaphysics, in philology, and in that sense-of-fact kind of history that was the product of the German school. Nonetheless, a spirit of independence was at work and the patterns of humanistic studies began taking on an American quality.

Many forces were then at work in this country to make the humanities more intimately individual and so not confined in spirit by a detached, analytic attitude. It is true the sciences were giving to the humanities an incentive toward exactness, but at the same time original concepts at home were displacing the rigid metaphysics of German thought. The social sciences had not been thought of, much less established; typical of the times was the conflict between religion and science in the universities, with no intervention of social formulae in the arguments.

The humanists had in this situation a double function, to serve the demands of man for an individual right to religious freedom and to make the humanistic traditions of religious history support their claims to a hearing. Then, too, the cultivation of literary studies in the universities was beginning without disturbance from philology. There was place in faculties for men using both kinds of humanistic discourse. The critical writing on literatures then produced now seems light, but original and natural in treatment. It showed a great deal about its author in almost every instance, and brought into the universities a human element that changed the formalism of advanced studies. The American college, intent on production of lawyers, teachers, and clergymen, showed its greatest originality in what it granted to the humanities of freedom and of general influence. The effect was to be felt in all liberal educational practice and so in society as a whole. Within the quarter of a century after the Johns Hopkins definition of higher studies, this country possessed a national ideal guiding those who were responsible for college and university education.

By 1900 the streams of humanistic thought were entering American life out of every country in Europe. German techniques and concepts had never become dominant for any considerable time, even in studies in philology and in metaphysics. Through Britain came those scholarly and religious values of the Renaissance and Reformation that have marked the course of American cultural history down to the present. Their literary manifestations in the works of writers of Western Europe became basic in higher studies, along with the literatures and histories of the classical originals of Greece and Rome and of all that followed them in later cultures. The mosaic of forms and substances prevented any attachment to one source. American philosophy, history, and letters grew out of European origins, clearly enough, but with a natural, national way of expression and adaptation. The diversity of American life was such that any other course would have been unlikely, while the variety of sources opened such a wealth of new materials that imitation of any one tradition became unattractive if not literally impossible.

II

Humanists properly ask for heavy stress in graduate schools upon research, and that it be scrupulously conducted by staffs of the various disciplines under their care. Yet in fact graduate work in all the humanities is given over as fully to teaching through lectures and discussion as is true in the undergraduate colleges; today discussion is far more general and the contacts of master and learner much closer among humanists in graduate schools than in any other part of the modern university. Only the honors work in college gives an undergraduate student a comparably intimate contact with his fellows and teachers.

The greatest advance toward unity of all undergraduate studies in humanities has come through the divisional organization of subjects. Students are led to see relationships and to move freely among the departments. They thus become aware of methods and aims of higher studies in a manner that opens more easily the way into graduate work or original productive activity.

From several causes, therefore, the humanities have now a more highly developed unity than before. Research, as organized curiosity, appears in undergraduate critical and creative writing, to match in attractiveness the customary modes of intensive digging after new data on literatures, languages, or historical backgrounds. There is still a useful distinction between undergraduate and graduate school terminology, of "subject" to denote a department in a college and "discipline" to signify the wider range of values and kinds of requirement in a professional school for the humanities. Though the ways of work are similar, these are useful distinctions. A subject is that area of learning wherein the learner gains familiarity with a language and literature, or with a sequence in history or philosophy. A discipline is indicative of what a graduate school means by way of ranging power in a broader field of concentration, with the aim of directing the scholar toward some mastery of cultural tradition and a use of his own inventiveness to design new patterns of definition and criticism. In every advancing stage, the learner is led to appreciate the closeness of all languages, literatures, histories, and philosophies to one another. He discovers the unity of humanistic learning.

Approach to that unity is by any one of the four avenues: languages, philosophies, histories, or literatures. Languages and philosophies lead more quickly across national boundaries. They are as closely interwoven in the web of human existence as speech and religion. Histories are more bound by time and nationalism. Literatures are commonly thought of with no sense of national origin at the levels of attention in childhood. In later school years and in college they develop international stature. Through literatures, undoubtedly, the humanities first open the minds of learners to their timeless, intimate meaning for every man.

What they are is best seen in the lives of those who, as teachers and research workers, have a professional concern to foster the humanities in higher education. These men and women are as individual as their special subjects and disciplines, but all alike in purpose. A community of scholars in a university is held together by the same relationship of master and disciples as is revealed in the beginnings of Christianity. Earlier, in Greek philosophy, the strength of learning grew out of the same close intimacy of minds. Printed pages have not replaced this essential contact of living persons intent on higher spiritual and intellectual pursuits. By the time of the Renaissance, *humanus* stood as counterpart of religious, a division of substances that led to the establishment of separate disciplines in the field of learning. With refinements of specialization, these disciplines of the humanities exist still as ways of mutual understanding among scholars and their masters.

Our times have made three general delimitations for all disciplines. The sciences, social sciences, and the humanities are academic headings for their grouped disciplines, which in each of the three have fairly close organic relationships; yet the interplay among all disciplines is constant, as from the first has been true of humanities.

One living outside the university looks on these issues as trivial, but they are not so. The unity of science is being demonstrated endlessly in these recent years, and is being proved realistically in action to be essential. The greater coherence of humanistic studies is due to another cause that may be appreciated from recent changes in work with literatures. Imperative need to defend the individual against aggression touching all his higher attributes is reason for these changes. The scholar turns more to critical interpretation of content in all literary works, including modern ones. The teacher of teachers leads their minds toward the humane values in their materials, exemplified by individuals in fact and story. The motives underlying action are brought to a reader of all literatures, including his own, that he may sense the forces at work in the world today among peoples of all civilized countries. Through literatures men reach quickly into the psychology and temperament of other cultures, to discover that all peoples keep their likeness to others in their own literatures and through these arrive at quick understanding of the life and feeling of all men.

How much the humanist has at stake in this situation appears in his outlook on life. Scholars and scientists in universities mark off areas of knowledge with the greatest care. Among themselves, they are as precise in their differentiations as are specialists in the higher brackets of medicine. The differences among them appear in their attitudes toward nature, man, and society. A humanist, in a modern university, is the one to deal with all the higher needs of man. His responsibility to mind and spirit is that of the general medical practitioner. His sense of exactness is not paramount in all that he does; he regards equally, with that, his breadth of understanding, touching all manifestations of humanity. This is as true of him, one may hope, as of the general practitioner whose concern is also with the individual, in physical respect; both must think of man as an individual.

Viscount Bryce once remarked on the differences of this order between the scientific and the humane spirit, saying that "no one at a supreme crisis in his life can nerve himself to action, or comfort himself under a stroke of fate, by reflecting that the angles at the base of an isosceles triangle are equal."[1]

Had he gone further in explanation, he would have signified as sources of such needed strength the concepts at the center of the humanities. He would have had something to say of the four elemental sources—languages, histories, literatures, and philosophies. Out of these come meanings which have been of help in emergencies to generations of men, each of the four in its own way being a contributing force in religion and in the daily conduct of life. To meet the universal needs of mankind the scholar works in his academic discipline. By a precision that is exact in its kind, and with a desire to interpret values of human history for understanding use in his own time, he draws from the past, gives present meanings to old truths, and places man above nature. The four primary origins of the humanities are the same as they always have been, and the scholar today has the same spirit of inquiry into their uses among his fellows as had the scholars of two hundred or five hundred years ago. Of the four, literatures are the most active and general transmitters of the humane spirit.

From histories come personal, racial, and national records around which are written the interpretations of human living. These are out of present life, as well as from earliest times, and each item of human evidence is open to an interpretation beneficial to all whom the scholar as interpreter influences. From languages, for these interpretations, the scholar draws a world of meanings and sorts out those suited to his purposes—the exact, figurative, and abstract uses of words in every tongue and every time of man. Out of philosophies he derives those standards of value that characterize entire nations and individuals, typical and exceptional in their human qualities. Philosophies and literatures contain what all men seek to know of one another, and do this in forms that display the fullness of intellectual, imaginative, emotional, and spiritual attributes of man, in individual examples. All this the humanist brings close to his contemporaries. To gather his evidence he will leave the strict boundaries of his discipline, in order to attain his particular end. In this he may differ from the social scientist. He is under no obligation to deal with society at large, for he is uninterested in social trends and the practices of formal living. His aim is to demonstrate how at all times the nature of man is revealed through those substances which make up the humanistic disciplines. His work is to give the key to man's past, as benefit to the present time and as guide to the future of humanity.

Here the substances of literatures are excellent to illustrate the peculiar quality of the humanities, which is the revelation of individual characteristics shown by man as person, not as one of a typed group or mass of people. The social interpretation of literatures has been tried; that, at times, has been deforming of taste, in that social evidence when taken as primary makes students fact-minded. Purposeful searches for evidence on how men live in social groups will never strengthen a reader's sense of the infinite variety in human nature. To gain that, he needs the four sources of the humanities, and must learn to use them in harmony. Only the humanists can show him the way, with any systematic plan. The journey is slow but rewarding, and increasingly so.

Through languages, the learner discovers the theory and description of linguistic analysis; definition and grammatical change in words; idiomatic and rhetorical effectiveness, with figurative and semantic insights; and, finally, the varied ways of learning to control languages, the preparation of dictionaries, and the fullness of meaning hidden in words concerning other lands and strange peoples.

As man's strongest and most flexible mode of self-expression is by language, it opens a direct path into his own personality. The vocabulary of an individual tells at once who he is in point of thought and total experience, as his pronunciation tells where he is from. These evidences lead on into studies of dialects, and most fundamentally into clear appreciation of all literatures. Without languages the humanist is unable to move freely into the thought of all men and in all times. Even though he pursues his studies in them but moderately, turning to other fields, he will always appreciate their place in his pattern of studies.

Histories, also to be discussed in detail, are without exception humanistic when used to develop meanings of man in his relations to the total world of fact, imagination, and feeling. The most mechanistic records of occurrences, in time, have in them these values of personal reaction in the individual, in the mind of the critic observing the past events or present circumstances of human existence. These are the substances out of which the humanist makes his interpretative constructs and his imaginative creations that take on literary or philosophic form. "History" implies movement and change through time, as determined by the field in which description is to be attempted. It may be geological change, as in earth strata, or the evolution of a theory in the mind of one man or in the minds of many working on an idea at widely separated periods of time. The humanist enters into historical studies only to interpret selected evidences of man's place in the world. If a student of literature, he follows fairly definite patterns of historical criticism. These have been set by practice, as in characterizations of periods of literary history; yet in all humanistic interpretation he will deal with historical data in a way that helps him establish within the lives of individuals certain specific humane values.

All literatures are socially definable in relation to the cultures that produced them. Each rests on the inheritance it has of ancient, medieval, and modern literatures; these are universal properties, but open only as scholars make them so by constant study and interpretation. All literatures, present ones included, must be made known through scholars fitted to keep alive the story of man's past greatness in life and learning. They surround their editions of important literary monuments with the essentials of explanatory matter to place a work in its relationships with remote and immediate times. The critical writing in an edition, or in a separate study, engages a scholar in more discursive surveys of similar works written in other periods and in other countries; so a lifetime of research may at length yield a definitive study for his own generation of readers and possibly for many more to come.

At that point, possessing a wide range of related facts and some assumptions of his own, the scholar consolidates his years of research in a work of literary and critical importance. His journeys of mind may have traversed writings in many languages, and his physical travels have been repeatedly across wide spaces. His product will bear his own mark and that of the age in which he lived.

So much may suggest the historical time and variation of subject that any humanistic discipline opens before the scholar. Broad lines of inquiry are set for him by kind of approach. His term of reference may be a national one, or an arbitrary grouping of works and writers under such universal indicators as classical, romantic, or naturalistic. With names of countries to set up convenient boundaries, and with time spaces for further limiting of research, the scholar enters upon his task. He will do far more than reconstruct the spirit of the age in which historical time places his studies; he will work forward and backward, across national boundaries, and in every one of the four fundamental sources of humanistic development.

Such is the range and diversity of his inquiries that he soon loses sight of any disciplinary limitations of research or interpretation. The most formal definition of his discipline will not keep a scholar within it. He may profess to do so, professionally, but he will forage in every direction for evidence on the task in hand. For social sciences and the sciences, the unities may be demonstrable in some style—by use of fundamental laws, mathematical and statistical data, and kinds of interaction proving them bound together in their very natures. The humanist possesses a different kind of unity, the individual one of personal evaluation; he adds to whatever he has taken from the external world, in time and place, that personal unity of individual outlook. Scientific work in the most objective forms is necessary to advance the humanities in every one of the four major categories, languages, histories, literatures, and philosophies; yet their real unity is that of the individual employing these as he will for extension of learning and refinement of cultural appreciation.

III

Among the strongest influences toward a "new humanities" in American colleges and universities has been an unbroken succession of great teachers. Masters of their disciplines, they have brought that added power of personality to create enthusiasm and devotion among their followers. It was natural that some should be perverse, dogmatic, and downright amusing at times; also, it followed that their mannerisms intrigued some into oddities of imitation. But such idiosyncrasies have been forgotten, apart from anecdote, to leave a fine residue of influence upon the humanities in the United States derived from great teachers in past decades. These men have created a native American tradition in the humanities in this half century, and others today maintain it.

Since 1900, the leadership of these individuals has passed from one to another field of inquiry, to arouse new interests in younger men throughout the nation. First philology was dominant, and succeeding it we now have varieties in linguistic research, theoretical and applied, that reach to all quarters of the globe. Folklore and balladry are now only elements in a schematic survey of folk literatures, reaching from primitive backgrounds to highly cultivated types in existing societies. Historical studies for literary interpretation have followed a time scale from medieval to modern times, successively enlarged in scope and depth. Old stocks of fact and criticism are being constantly refreshed, as the younger generation of scholars brings into use areas of world culture unrecognized in this country fifty years ago. One such newcomer is our own culture, in all its variations and in its current development through all the arts of expression.

Some of these men have been originators in methods of research, others of new schools of philosophical thought and criticism. Illustrations might be drawn from all fields—from linguistics, history, philosophy, literature, aesthetics, and religion. Some few have so completely identified themselves with the subjects and geographic areas of their investigations that their names stand among professional scholars as descriptive of scholarship in their fields in their time. Not all have been of American birth. This half century has had a counterpart to the familiar story of many men going abroad for their training, in the more recent trend of foreign scholars to this country to be temporary or permanent members of humanistic groups in universities.

One obvious source has been Europe during the Hitler regime, and a rich source that has been; the United States has gained greatly in classical studies and in philosophy from that single cause. Yet none would say that this coming has altered the native traditions, but only enriched them. Nationalism is least thought of by these newcomers or their hosts, for the humanities are international in spirit at all times unless under such political compulsions as have appeared in random instances throughout human history.

One of the finest tributes that can be paid to American humanists is full credit for freedom from nationalistic, self-glorifying cant about themselves or their country. Rather than that, one finds repeatedly how they have sought after foreign specialists to establish here some of the badly needed forms of certain disciplines and to strengthen many others—musicology, classical and Biblical exegesis, archival administration, philosophy, and art history. These five headings could be increased to many, for the added personnel are in virtually every humanistic field. In consequence, this country is today most favored of all in the variety and strength of its staffs, and thereby is made more responsible than ever before to maintain all work in humanities.

It takes time to develop new personnel and to secure establishment of chairs in universities. So many are the forces working today to make war rather than wisdom, that the chance to have new scholarly foundations created by these foreign scholars is a great gift from fortune to this country and, in time, to the entire world. As their best disciples come on into maturity, they will be leaders in the tradition of American learning and founders of new schools of humanistic studies. Even so far in the story, the evidence is clear. The gain in variety and power of humanistic studies is, as scientists and social scientists would say, "measurable" and is likewise gratifying. We have added to our rosters such men as Panofsky in art history, Turyn in classics, Curt Sachs in musicology, and Tillich in philosophy and theology. This short list could be lengthened to a total of not less than two hundred principal persons out of Europe and many more out of Latin America and the Far East who have brought us permanent increase.

For our part, we have moved more and more heavily into international exchange of persons. Some of this increase has been fortuitous, out of war's aftermath since 1945. Yet though the Fulbright amendment to the Congressional Act of 1946, setting up funds abroad from sales of war surplus, has fortified plans on a large scale and for many years, there are many other sources—government departments, special aid programs, and American foundations. Our largest contingents of teachers and scholars yearly go to Western Europe and the Mediterranean, but likewise nearly everywhere else overseas. They are to be found in Latin America, the Near East, the Far East, and at least in the fringes of the Slavic world.

This two-way traffic is still to be increased by the visits of scholars who will come here for study in libraries, galleries, and museums as well as in universities. In spite of war and threats of more wars, this country is nearing the ideal goal of Francis Bacon, with missions sent abroad to foster international trade in learning which, as he called it in his *New Atlantis*, is still "God's first creature, which was light."

To trace the changes in these relationships, and the lasting gains, one goes to the new works of scholarship that come from American presses; to the international bibliographies of separate subjects; and to the book reviews in scholarly journals. The learned societies of this and other countries are other sources of proof that the gains of humanities have been so intelligently planned as to make them lasting and the quality of the work of highest order. Such are among the more quiet, fundamental values of the humanities in society that must be pointed out for the benefit of the layman. He has some of the harvests daily, but rarely sees the fields from which they come and does little to help in the planting.

The great teachers have always been at work. It would take a long account to deal moderately with the persons who have benefited international ties while creating this new American standard for the humanities. One example, from the earlier part of the fifty-year period, is typical of the many that might be cited. In two sentences is a sufficient biography, for this purpose, of Francis B. Gummere: "At Haverford he maintained the tradition of teaching established by his father and grandfather, giving courses in early English literature, Chaucer, Shakespeare, Milton, the popular ballads, and Goethe. Meanwhile he became known as a scholar throughout the United States and Northern Europe." This brief valuation is from the *Dictionary of American Biography*.[2] A more sensitive one, characterizing the writer and many others of his own time, was from John M. Manly, who wrote of him in 1919 as "the creator of that kind of scholarship which is far more than erudition and a source of that kind of culture without which the achievements of science are delusive and vain."[3]

In many instances, as with Gummere, this growth of strong individuals came in an independent, private college. Posts in universities were still few, and in the period before a rounded program of research had grown in the state universities the humanities were at some disadvantage in many newer centers. This was not true of the private colleges, where for many years of this century the humanities flourished alongside the sciences before the social sciences had proliferated their types of inquiry into the ways of men in group, national, and international environments. Changes due to enlargement in number of disciplines have benefited the humanities, while increased contacts with sciences and social sciences have intensified the usefulness of all three categories of higher education. Professional schools share in these benefits. As fully as any, the future doctor and man of business affairs are receptive to values from the humanities; today, as fifty years ago, the teacher as much as his subject draws such followers for whatever time they can take outside of professional requirements.

It would seem to be laboring this point to assume that humanists are more consistently good teachers than others, or that in fact they themselves are conscious of any special influence upon their followers. Every discipline in the university calendar has its listing of great names. All who teach and do research wholeheartedly impress on learners the spirit of their professions. It is given, however, to the humanist to deal constantly with what are the human manifestations of individuals, regardless of lacks or peculiar merits, real or fanciful, that they had in life; many of the most noteworthy never have existed outside the mind of a writer or other artist, and still they are supremely important in the lives of generation after generation of learners. This appeal of the emotional and artistic forces that surround the rational forms of knowledge raises the humanities to unique place. They cannot fail to affect those who work in them throughout a lifetime of teaching.

During one of his visits to the United States, Wells was asked how an instructor in an American public school can hope to teach municipal government realistically, using case histories from surrounding life. His reply was that every teacher has an unequalled chance to do what he wishes, in limits; for daily, during three-quarters of an hour, he has a classroom filled with listeners unable to leave, and the rest of the world cannot interfere. In short, the teacher is a highly favored individual in a democracy. He has responsibilities of first order, in consequence. He probably likewise has as great satisfactions as any citizen out of his work. It is his fortune to watch changes in outlook of those still systematically endeavoring to widen and deepen their experiences under the guidance of a specialist whose interest is disinterested and lively.

These benefits are common to teachers, and all are heightened for humanists by the nature of the materials they work in. Inevitably, they should become exceptional teachers if they unceasingly read their texts and do their own thinking.

Enough has been said of the materials and the men who use them. A great deal more might be set down regarding public ignorance today of that distinction which humanistic studies held in this country during times of restricted opportunity to attain to higher education. Gains in one form have brought loss in others, until now the college graduate is less notable for his peculiar possessions in humanistic values than was his forerunner of fifty years ago. He is likely to be one of the millions having less regard for the lawyer, the minister, and the man of letters than for some political figure, a columnist using space on an inner sheet of his newspaper, and for writers of comic strips. Yet such changes are not matters for lamentation, but rather for a study of causes.

The single source of valuable information is the student himself.

As wise physicians look backward for the history of a malady, seeking habits that may have modified bodily function, so the search of the professional humanist after causes of faulty attitudes of young persons toward his work must be in their personal histories. He will begin to go further back than to their grades in fifteen school subjects taken as warrant for a college admission. He cannot change these oncoming learners, nor can he decisively reject them from studies for which they were ill prepared. He must use them as his case histories, to demonstrate to school boards and boards of teacher certification that the product has been damaged too often long before he was called in as consultant and prescriber of a new way for the individual mind and spirit. Selfishly, to mature a following of promising scholars for the humanities, he should know what to demand for the exceptional learner and then have ready his clearly drawn program suited to the individual.

The American public has learned its lessons of this kind with respect to professional and technical education. They see to it that aspirants to a lifework in medicine, engineering, or law are led steadily towards their ultimate hopes. Moreover, the students themselves know and accept these directives; they give up what would divert them or fill the time spans essential for preparation in advance of a following need. It is in precisely the same manner that the humanities will secure their new leaders in time to come, when many more people and a greater variety of training will be demanded in their services.

It seems to be a nonsense question to ask why the American public has substituted something easier than reading and reflection, when we see all the variants of diversion now drawing men away from these sources of self-development. Nothing is gained by pointing at ill effects in matured personalities from such substitutions. Much is possible, however, through a study of early symptoms of deforming habits that will affect permanently a person's spiritual and mental potentialities. Preventive treatment near the origin of illness is as necessary, in these two respects, as in physical growth.

Here we are considering why the youth entering college is often weak in power of attention and scant in tastes. At that point the humanities have their opportunity to define their meanings in individual lives. This opportunity they are using admirably, to the limit of what is practicable in allotted time. Some of the most discerning and skillful instruction in American colleges is done by humanists. Even so, they make their own tasks more difficult by failing to look back to the causes of loss and of lack in all but their best learners. They also can elevate the quality of later work by these few, by concentrating earlier upon those points of promise in each individual. They can make clearer, earlier in the college period, what are the ways to distinction.

When professional humanists prove to their students that many now come too late, even at sixteen or eighteen years of age, to make up lost chances of success in the particular modes of humanistic activity, the gains will be great. It is idle to permit to grow without comment a false hope of becoming a significant writer, critic, or teacher by such as have evaded all the preliminary stages of development. These stages are well known. It is as impossible for a college student to read intelligently and rapidly without training with varied kinds of material, as for one to manage higher mathematics without the rudiments of arithmetic, algebra, and trigonometry. The humanities have their own laws of progression. Indistinct by reason of the nature of the materials, these nevertheless are positive laws controlling the advancing change in powers of attention and that basic ability to see the relationships of things. "Things," for the humanities, are all those forces of language, history, and cultural expression that carry an individual further into discriminating experiences mentally and emotionally. His plan of development can be charted.

These few instances show that the patterns of humanistic teaching and research in American institutions have had changing outlines, drawn again and again to conform to the known laws of learning and the recognized needs of the times. Certain of these patterns appeared in our graduate schools before the beginning of this century, and were adapted in one university after another to conform to a changing national outlook. New disciplines were added, and more interrelationships among fields of knowledge were established. The departmental control over a student's time lessened, to the advantage of everyone, wherever a divisional development of the humanities was genuinely sustained by the administration. Thus all subjects of the humanities, sciences, and social sciences came into closer divisional unities, and the last two years of the undergraduate colleges attained a new authority. Every department was more truly organic in reference to every other composing the total humanistic program, and produced students in consequence with finer preparation for graduate studies.

The changing patterns were to serve a broader purpose than improvement of the processes of higher education. They were devised also to bring in new substances and procedures to meet the needs of the people. That generalization rests on true though scattered evidence. Its clearest proof is in the printed records of courses and professed aims of the American college and graduate school from 1900 to 1950. Every well-developed college and university in the country illustrates this way of natural progression.

It would be impossible, and wholly beyond desire, to write a formula for humanistic education on a national scale. That would, if attempted, deaden the spirit that animates all learning and expression through the humanities. Yet one who would chart the facts of progress need only take a backward look over the printed announcements of a few representative institutions for these fifty years. He will uncover facts as encouraging as those offered him more freely from the field of elementary and secondary education, to prove that the individual has been placed above the system in our national practices. Within that pattern of enlightenment the humanities have given and have taken benefits that will endure.

IV

During the twenties the survey concept began its influence in colleges, under the idea that an introduction to liberal studies could be attained through one or a series of fine general courses giving balance and perspective. The earliest sweeps across the history of civilization were of two kinds—either to determine the outlines of the contemporary or to contrast a contemporary pattern with an old one of high distinction. During the thirty years now past, the survey has had many forms, usually as a requirement of earliest years in undergraduate colleges and occasionally as a concluding view back over the four years of study. This shift of emphasis from the particular to the general had its sources in the events opening into much wider responsibilities than in years before 1918. The colleges moved toward new and necessary duties.

Simultaneously a greater enrollment of students steadily increased the burden put upon the colleges and graduate schools. The humanities were affected as deeply as the sciences and social sciences, though less harm was done to standards of these areas than to the professional requirements embedded in college curricula as preliminary to medicine, law, and technical subjects. The important matters for the humanities were in the gains structurally under survey work in the colleges, and by virtue of closer attention to planning of advanced studies in the college and the graduate school. It was during the thirties that the disciplines of the humanities became interrelated in greater degree and so more and more effective. In all the changes caused by larger enrollments and wider world views of interest, they benefited.

Benefits at the undergraduate level were mixed with unfavorable effects, as those putting foreign languages at a disadvantage as options alongside the heavier requirements of the first two years. It was in the advanced work of departments that the humanities profited from planning of another kind. Urge was put upon students to go forward into graduate work without the long lag so common with all except those early dedicated to professional studies in medicine or law. This may have had a practical basis too in the demand for teachers to meet the increasing college enrollments, and in the desire for better unity in humanistic programs.

As the spread of graduate work into institutions lacking staff and libraries for humanistic studies changed the surface of higher education, with more and more degrees given at the master's and doctor's levels, the quality of college instruction was simultaneously hurt by enlargement, into four-year colleges giving liberal arts degrees, of institutions having no traditional interests beyond applied and vocational studies. Junior colleges also altered the nature of the work in the two years beyond preparatory school, to give a terminal training that experimentally at least is now being fashioned into something comparable to a limited form of liberal education. The two-year college and the unified "general education" bridging the secondary school–college relationship are both valid outgrowths of the demand for a consolidated and descriptive approach to the modern world by way of survey courses in the first part of a college experience.

One tangle still not resolved resulted. Admission to colleges was put upon several footings. Certificates and examinations were still widely in use, but individual trial under observation during a first period became almost compulsory to meet the needs of students asking admission at irregular times. The terminal examinations of "general education" are valuable means to solve this perplexity, which is partly due to the number of students coming from other countries. In the exchange programs set up by governments that bring many undergraduates as well as graduate students into the United States, have appeared the most difficult problems of adjustment in admission requirements. With the best efforts at judging the quality of work in any institution, at home or abroad, the transfers of persons must always be on a conditional basis.

There is a decided benefit in this unsettled state of methods of admission to colleges and graduate schools in the arts. The staffs for humanities are made free to set up their own standards of study, advancement, and graduation, for variations are so constant among applicants for admission as to throw the burden of proof upon the faculties instead of upon admission officers. At the college level, part of the responsibility already has been shifted to the faculties, by set requirements in survey courses before admission to advanced departmental subjects. The points of actual trial are the examinations in survey and of proficiency in a foreign language. As for the graduate schools, faculties in social sciences and humanities have two ways to control values by limitation of enrollments; they start their entering students toward clear admission by enrolling all in general courses to test ability and promise, and they make the master's degree a "difficulty test" as well as an educational objective in order to discourage less able persons from work toward a doctorate.

The graduate schools in humanities are setting greater store by their own testing of applicants than by college reports showing that applicants have completed numerically the proper fractions of a total score to secure degrees. Applicants are benefited quite as greatly as the institutions that require more than that kind of evidence of merit, because their aptitudes for successful activity in humanistic teaching and scholarly studies are tested at the most critical point in their careers. To dissuade and to encourage are equal responsibilities of professional humanists in graduate faculties, quite as surely as is true in recruitments for any other service. They must be far more inquisitive concerning personal background of an applicant, his scope and originality of outlook, and his ideas and ideals with respect to conduct of life.

At the college level, such matters are open to solution of some sort through guidance and arranged requirements of study, but to make the choice of graduate students in humanities a responsibility of the faculties rather than of administrative officers is imperative if there is to be a high standard of work, and of potential usefulness, among new entrants into the profession. Of all the matters involved in higher education, none is so completely dependent for its future as the humanities upon the quality of the individual. Unless he has spiritual, intellectual, and emotional balance, his imaginative and factual qualities of mind will be misapplied.

All this leads back into the life of the colleges. It is there that the pointing toward careers in the humanities is to be done by discerning teachers. The errors in judgment will be few on the part of students if their teachers have applied common sense in periodic canvassing of what is being demonstrated month after month under their teaching and questioning. A college degree is not true evidence of readiness for advanced studies, and no fixed examinations at the day of application for admission can give to graduate faculties in humanities a clear proof of capability. Interviews are important, but hard to arrange on an equitable basis. Recommendations from college staffs whose standards are durable and high seem far more valid, provided these recommendations carry down into the background of childhood and youth of candidates. It is true that a person often seems transformed by his graduate studies into a true teacher and scholar, almost suddenly in certain instances; yet even these exceptional individuals surely must have given some signs of future growth during their years of relationship in college with observing and discerning professors.

An admitting officer may be entrusted with the duty of judging the record of an applicant. He would be instructed to look for achievement of some basic work in modern science, in part by experiment, and for a like demonstration of theoretical and applied abilities in one of the arts. The student should show views on the taste and public interests of his times, some reading in literatures of European and eastern Mediterranean cultures, and at least some familiarity with critical terminology in the various arts. Basic courses in history, political economy, and economics will have given him enough experience to understand where are the best sources of more current information. Particularly in some forms of history the learner will have intimate acquaintance with those forces always at work in society to produce individual values and cultural patterns. He will have had at least ten year-hours of directed study in one foreign language, with the time fairly distributed in compact periods of school experience so that he will be able to apply his sense of structures in his study of any other one. Above all, home and school will have supplied out of ample libraries the resources for intellectual freedom and the play of mind over unfamiliar ideas, and at least a few teachers will have brought to reality in mind and spirit of the learner some part of the lasting values that are contained in the arts of the humanities.

Ideally, such a train of experiences leads back into a childhood of wide reading in translation from other literatures and a constant, highly varied experience in the use of English words. "Semantics" may be a mystic term to adults who late in life discover the infinite varieties of language, but as an indicator of a learning process for those who have loved the sounds and significations of words from childhood a formal introduction to semantics is unnecessary. Another source of all humanistic strength and sensitivity is balance of values coming through experience in religion. A learning of precepts is not what is wanted, for the form is not sure to bring meaning. Religion is to be realized as a force touching the individual. An atheistic person is not a humanist. Religion in some form must be a personal influence in the life of a man if he is to appreciate humane values; it cannot be simply a matter of objective study. Its force in all cultural history is great, and understanding of its influence imperative. But this is not enough. The teacher in humanities is, by the nature of his commitments, bound to possess a faith out of experience. In technical skills he is to be compared to a mathematician or a surgeon, but beyond that men will judge him for his awareness of the intangibles of existence.

Graduate schools should take more care to determine the qualifications of any learner seeking the fullest acceptance as a future leader in the humanities. Discussions have been cluttered with critical words for "remote" scholarship, and for one whose sense of exactness in minutiae apparently carries him away from the humanities of the spirit. The double rejoinder to such judgments is that the critic usually is repeating a comment that is as traditional as comic opera character lines for the professor on stage, and that he has no understanding of the essential uses of detailed evidence in scholarly affairs. Yet a third comment, one that the profession itself makes in a self-critical mood, is that too little care is shown for humane values when choosing those individuals meriting full development for a life work in important posts.

One entering the community of scholars is first to be judged on his total experience in the substances of humanistic learning and appreciation, as sign of fitness to progress steadily in higher studies. He then is to be judged on the indications of individual capability to respond normally to ideas and ideals that are intrinsic in a cultivated and spiritually elevated society. A personal sense of man's aspirations and humane interests will do more than make him a sensitive student of the arts and of their relevance to life about us; it will permeate all that he does from then on through life as teacher of new followers in the humanistic traditions of learning and of interpretation.

No two patterns of humanistic teaching are identical. They are not fixed by descriptions or techniques, but are set by living individuals who give out their own interpretations of man's place in his universe. Constant reliance upon learning is not to obscure their unchanging interest in man as individual, and their following in customary channels of humanistic disciplines is not to subdue their personal freedom in choices from the total of human knowledge and experience. It is this freedom of choice that makes the matured scholar unlike all his predecessors and the student in turn unlike his master. As in all creative expression through the arts, the scholar as teacher makes himself known through the materials that he works in, and then leaves for others of later time some increase in the body of human learning and of interpretation of man's creative powers.

V

In a mood of weary desperation over the mass of humane learning faced by the student, whatever his age or earlier training, some guides have pointed the way out of perplexity with a simplified proposal that interests the humanist particularly. They have denoted certain books of high merit in their own times, and still standing as landmarks in man's progress. In only one respect can such simplifiers of learning justify themselves; they have asked the individual to do his own thinking. Their limited lists of master works are arbitrary, and for good reason their arbitrariness is questioned. They do not intend that any should assume these to contain all of useful knowledge; their plans would have been as feasible with the Harvard Classics. They intend, however, that the learner shall submit to active discussion what truths for present time these favored works contain. Here they are on sure ground. No two persons can fail to benefit mutually and separately through serious, sincere discussion about anything that touches conduct of life. Yet this supposed newly discovered method of personal advancement in learning—by discussion and by reasoning in areas of unfamiliar sort—is not new; nor do its protagonists profess it to be. They, and all humanists, are simply asserting the old laws of individual development that are constantly at work wherever the humanities are seriously considered.

This relationship of student and teacher, or master and disciple, is as old and well tried as any in man's experience. The "great books" pattern is not a discovery, but only a medium in which people may endeavor to think. Those who take the listed titles as something oracular in value, defeat the sound purposes of the scheme. By going on, they may well arrive at points of disagreement with the devisers of the list of contents—as have many professional humanists. That may be a value unexpected by any who begin the program of reading and discussion. In fact, unless that outcome appears eventually, the plan may be as empty as a calm acceptance of the monthly selections of books, by a group of critics, as authoritative guides to appreciation. The book itself is nothing until the one holding it in his hand is ready for understanding of ideas and of emotions at its level. He benefits most when an understanding mind, with wider experience in both thought and feeling, is beside him as guide.

Simplification of tasks is dangerous in itself, simply because tasks of individual development are not simple. This is the reason why higher education in college and graduate school opens new paths to learners with the foresight of men who travel the old paths of formal disciplines. The evolution of their procedures has taken much time and much thought. Each master of his discipline adds something that makes an experience in learning, under his care, a greater experience than any learner could possibly have alone or with a less knowing guide. The great teachers are those who have learned the processes of their arts and the substance of their disciplines; they do this by years of devoted study which heighten their enthusiasms and strengthen their abilities to communicate to others.

No one will assert that such analysis and teaching are the sole possessions of colleges and universities. They are more commonly to be found there, and the growth of learning among followers of a master teacher is more sure than in any other place. An institution produces precisely as a manufacturing establishment through the continuous and organized nature of its operations. Though the comparison is particularly infelicitous when made for the humanities, nothing in all learning profits as do they from wisdom and personal quality of excellence in their expositors. Silent reading of literary works as prescribed by special lists and occasional discussions in study groups as organized for adults are not substitutes for participation in formal courses under deeply informed and inspiring teachers who know how to arouse fruitful discussion of central ideas in their fields.

In contrast to the irregularities of most study groups for adults, we have formal planning for the use of "great books" by small numbers of persons. Each has his own copies of all the texts, in a uniform edition, so that reading before free discussion in a group meeting is easily done and with an immediate placing of the passage—or even word—under scrutiny. Also, a leader is assigned to develop a dialectical approach to these unfamiliar writings, so that there may be some progress in the art of reasoning about matters of opinion. Mere give and take of assertions, whenever facts are not useful, is thereby lessened. These study groups, randomly organized of people from varied types of intellectual and social background, possess one constant virtue; in all their varieties of intensity and of method, they have the great fundamental relationship of master and disciple, to be followed by a relationship of one to another within the small group that creates human understanding. Yet these are not substitutes for the reading, discussion, and reflection based upon clearly charted lines of thought and interpretation as laid down in daily meetings with a professional teacher.

We now have courses for the first year of college that teach dialectic analysis apart from any fixed list of "great" books, but instead out of a group of eight that are selected for a given year. The assigned readings are to create freedom of thought by analysis and steady discussion. This form of basic experience in learning to reflect as well as to read, is the most significant to be set up in colleges of our time. Adopting it amounts to admitting past errors in the use of anthologies of literature in English as introductory to more intensive work. The snippets tossed to untrained readers in old-fashioned historical surveys do not hang together. They have too little relevance to immediate affairs of life. Assorted samples of fine literature need an excellent teacher if they are to bring to the learner an appreciation of literary differences. A learner should find himself first, using the stronger and simpler vehicles of thought and imaginative power; he then may discover the finer, more artistic values in literatures developing into a mosaic of meanings that are ceaselessly suggestive and compelling to attention.

Students have insights that are lacking among older members of faculties in at least one respect; they know the tempo of their own times and its meanings for young people. Fortunate the teacher who stays young spiritually so as to be with his followers in this respect. In the nineteen-twenties an undergraduate at the University of Chicago would listen patiently or otherwise through his hour of formal work with a period of literature or on a single significant author. He then would talk earnestly between classes with his classmates on what then gripped the attention of them all—the work of the living writers in the Chicago groups; the ideas of Mencken; the poems of Millay, Teasdale, and Wylie; and the new fiction making literary history that the undergraduates often recognized as such before their professors.

In determining what persons among entrants deserve most careful attention from the humanists of college and university, we must establish patterns for individual growth of talented, idealistic, and responsive students. Also, it is essential to listen to the students themselves as they advance stage by stage in learning. If the humanities are to attain again the social and intellectual influence of their greatest periods, it will be by the consonant action of masters and disciples, teachers and students, researchers and interpreters. The only essential is an unceasing concern with the individual, to draw out his unique and his universal characteristics from the mass of human records and direct expressions of personality, for the use of all men.

The beginning is in what the humanities give to society through liberal education. The constant enlargement of what these disciplines have to give is by way of research, all of it relevant to some part of that total human story. What must be realized is the part of research in all liberal educational practice, even though to the layman the changes it brings may be imperceptible. Languages, histories, literatures, and philosophies are all brought to finer usefulness in living societies because of meticulous care in pursuing ideas and theories to useful conclusions.

As elective systems and fixed prerequisites of departments fall before the broader divisional schemes of a college, the balance of studies is again stressed. It is more than a survey pattern, introductory to all the usual opportunities of three or two years of intensive work; it is a developed program that ties the separate values into a unity of meaning. The social, scientific, and humane elements in that education are all in proper balance when the special and preprofessional requirements are held in check and the fullest possible chance is given for individual growth. That is done successfully in humanities—with honors work and interdepartmental plans that are effectual toward comprehension of values and appreciation of mankind on a universal scale.

Much is written regarding the ways to liberal education, and much of the best is from humanists. Among these, Sir Richard Livingstone[4] is eminently able in commentaries on university life in Great Britain and in the United States. His long view is valuable to all teachers and administrators. In active examples, Canada is a tonic source for those of our humanists who are nationally provincial; the classics and the ways of building a spirit of humanism into a people are kept alive there, in living institutions. The future there is clearer than in Great Britain, where the difficulties ahead and about are touched on uneasily by many writers. Among these is the variously valued work of Sir Walter Moberly, *The Crisis in the University*,[5] which since 1949 has made impressions on the thinking of professors, perhaps of administrators in higher education, on both sides of the Atlantic.

Here at home, the writing of Fred B. Millett in *The Rebirth of Liberal Education*[6] has had since 1945 the salutary effects which as teacher he continues to achieve. In these matters—the place of the humanities in life, as in higher education—he who runs cannot take profit if he runs while he reads. He must learn to sit down and reflect on what education is for him and his children and children's children, aside from its incidental contributions to making a living.

In the end, the scholar will have his say, and perhaps his way, inside the university, on what the humanities are to be. His outspoken utterances are few. His signs of attention to the demands of life about him are encouraging. His concern that the patterns of humanities cover the living needs of mankind is now clearly evident. At the same time, he is not one to forego the old traditions in method and his private devotion to significant sectors of cultural history.

One who has spoken for the scholar after studying him well, has the following to say of him:

Scholars like to think of themselves as individualists driven in their investigations by their own intimate and personal curiosity. If this were a complete description of them, it would be very difficult to make any roughly valid generalizations about their way of conducting the study of man. But it is not a complete description of them. They have also accepted, like scientists, a large measure of discipline—self-discipline to be sure, derived from an accumulating body of scholarly convention—with the result that there are established ways of pursuing the study of man so clearly defined as to constitute what might be called the technology of learning.

Though there are some uniformities in the world of learning, one must not force this reference to the *pattern* of the study of man to the point where it implies the existence of a rationally ordered coherent plan in which the several parts fit together into a neatly ordered whole. The most obvious characteristic of the study of man is indeed the way in which it is split in a disordered fashion among a variety of disciplines which have come into existence as a matter of historical accident and which are certainly not attributable to any logical plan. Some are fairly old as self-conscious, organized disciplines: for example, Greek and Latin languages and literatures, philosophy, law, and theology, arts and music, the last two being old as objects of professional interest but less firmly established in academic institutions. Other disciplines are the result of splintering from, or adding to, older disciplines, such as the modern languages and literatures added to those of Greece and Rome, history derived from literature, political science and economics derived from history, and psychology derived from philosophy. Still others are more independent creations, like sociology and anthropology.

Each of the self-conscious disciplines devoted to the study of one or another facet of man, his activities, and his creations has had its pioneers and propagators, its inventors of improved methodology, its recognized high priests to set or maintain standards, its routines for developing trained adherents in the oncoming generation, its own sense of importance and dignity and, lamentably, its tendency to jealousy of other disciplines. These disciplines tend to live in isolation, despite the fact that they often deal with common materials, employ similar methods, and respond to more general fashions or ideas in the scholarly world. With each of the disciplines driven by its own inner dynamic, preserving its traditional content and purpose, organizing at the university level into departments, and at the national level into societies, it is no wonder that the whole study of man appears planless, that there is so little evidence still in the colleges and universities of a paramount concern with identifying better ways to achieve a rounded and full study of man.[7]

This passage from the 1952 report of Director Odegaard to the American Council of Learned Societies has much of the fact and spirit of present-day humanities in the United States.

The "self-conscious" characteristic of the several disciplines, on which he remarks, is the product of intensity and definiteness in research. It also is the mark of distinction setting apart from others each individual aspect of investigation. In kinds of specialization, the classics show a varied array which is unequalled elsewhere. The age and fruitfulness of a discipline are natural causes of such differentiation in the humanities, as in the sciences. No single pattern serves even a single discipline for long. The sign of growth is in change, also, of the fields having intensive cultivation. New ones are added, and new leaders in them must develop by the processes of the old. It is by accumulation of essential materials that the way is made ready for entry into undeveloped areas of the humanities. Those that have been long under cultivation continue to yield, under the intensive work of specialists. Through constancy of effort suited to the levels of development and of need, the humanists of this country have met these new and changing demands from their disciplines. During the first half of the twentieth century they have kept alive the values of their old traditions while they were preparing for forthcoming requirements of research and teaching.

Despite satisfying development within institutions, the humanities must fully serve their purposes beyond those boundaries. The service may be long deferred, for the scholar is like the scientific investigator in his need of protracted periods in isolation. It may also be occasional service, through encouragement or participation that gives to the public mind something wanted and wanting. Whatever the cause or the time of action, the humanities gain whenever brought to use in the daily life of the people. Nothing could be more fruitful for them today than the full recognition of this self-evident truth.

Our colleges and universities can, and generally do, hold to that ideal of accomplishment; they achieve this by production of material and by development of persons to illuminate and enlarge the humanistic tradition. They alter their formal patterns to match changes in demand and opportunity, but meanwhile hold to standards and aims within their fields of interest. At their best, these institutions give to the individuals within them that first essential of all humanistic advancement, opportunity for self-development and self-expression. Then, in human forms, the humanities take on patterns as actual as man himself. They return to their sources and reappear in new yet familiar manifestations.

NOTES

The quotation on the title page is from John Wilson (Christopher North), *Noctes Ambrosianae*, August, 1834, ed. R. S. Mackenzie (5 vols.; Widdleton, New York, 1863), V, 290.

1. Quoted in *The Humanities for Our Time*, by Walter R. Agard *et al.* (University of Kansas Press, Lawrence, 1949), p. 2.

2. *Dictionary of American Biography*, VIII, 48.

3. *Modern Philology*, XVII (1919), 57.

4. Two of Sir Richard Livingstone's valued works are *The Future in Education* and *Education for a World Adrift*, now issued in a single volume with the title *On Education* (x+158; The University Press, Cambridge, and Macmillan, New York, 1944). A third is his group of lectures delivered in 1945 at the University of Toronto, *Some Tasks for Education* (viii+98; Oxford University Press, Toronto, 1946).

5. Published for the Christian Frontier Council (316 pp.; SCM Press, London, 1949).

6. Published three years after a national survey, of six months in time, given to visits in a large number of colleges and universities where work in the humanities was experimental or otherwise of particular interest (xii+179; Harcourt, Brace, New York, 1945).

7. American Council of Learned Societies, Bulletin No. 45 (March, 1952), pp. 2–3.

TWO

Languages

I

Active communication with other minds by means of words or other symbols is the first concern of the humanist. He is a voluminous reader in his own language, and to this one-way communication he adds a good deal by silent translation out of others. He moves in a world of words. If he reads ancient manuscripts, or print in any tongue except his own, he makes the transfer of thought from one set of symbols to another with as little marring of the original idea as possible. His success depends upon control of thought patterns in both languages, his own and the original, and on his skill in bringing ideas into speech or written form.

This seems simple, at least to the scholar: other persons are more likely to put it down as an exercise of formal education which is difficult but happily ended on leaving college. Yet these two different conventional views are now changing. War sent and sends millions of younger Americans beyond sound of English as customary speech; they return home with smatterings of strange languages, many of them convinced that they must become bilingual. Second choices for some few will be outside the familiar triad of German, French, and Spanish. Notions of future living overseas will lead to the study of Chinese, Japanese, Russian, Turkish, or Arabic—five of the languages that will be used increasingly to meet future American responsibilities abroad in trade, politics, education, and unhappily in war. As for scholars and teachers, war's aftermath is already affecting them in two ways. It is sending thousands overseas under special subsidies, and is bringing here large numbers of foreigners who have only a little English on arrival.

The issues involved in these movements of minds across borders are as vast as the more familiar ones of international exchanges in money and goods. One can foresee a time when the outlook internationally, through command of foreign languages, will be so far improved in this country that the contrast would be beyond the imaginative reach of persons in present time. Scholars and teachers are enlisted in this effort. They will determine how soon the United States begins to meet the world instead of facing it.

The scholar who has learned to bring ideas out of foreign languages for his personal use in the humanities is not for that reason able to teach others the four ways of communication in a living language— through speech, hearing, reading, and writing. In fact, as will be seen later, he has been reluctant to give serious attention to the colloquial forms of any tongue, and has concentrated all effort on the literary and historical uses of words. It is rather the teacher of modern languages who must carry further current research into methods of instruction, production of materials fitted to learners of all ages, and the creation of an environment for American students that is most like that in which a particular language is acquired by native speakers.

What the task is, will appear from a survey of what has been accomplished through scientific study and testing during the past fifty years. Much of the advance in learning other languages than one's own is due to research into the manner in which language grows out of rudimentary to complex form. The changes over centuries are as those in a bare shoot that becomes a massive tree, with root systems and branches forming a typical unity of its kind and different from every other in certain characteristics. The scholar knows the unique characteristics of a given language that set it apart from others. He masters its rhetoric, grammar, idiom, and allusive usages. He benefits from all the labors of his predecessors, and in turn gives the learner who follows him the advantages from previous analysis and description.

He does this partly by use of likenesses. For example, he shows the person whose native tongue is English, what are the similarities in Spanish. The student from Latin America has these same aids during his first weeks of English. But the discerning teacher soon turns from similarities to the characteristics of the language which is being taught. He brings habit into play, and applies the customary methods by which anyone gathers an understanding of his mother tongue. This total approach to a foreign language follows systematically the stages of study needed for the understanding of a complicated machine with a great number of interrelated parts, none of which mean a great deal until known through their relationships to other functioning elements in it. Every language is a self-contained but slowly changing system of symbolic communication. When the teacher makes this concept clear, he awakens the student to the realization that his native tongue is a unique structure, deserving of constant, systematic scrutiny; that every living language possesses peculiar merits; and that his own country is but one among many. Through studies in language, it appears, a person discovers a great deal about himself and about others in a diverse, global pattern of peoples.

That revolutionary change in American outlook will come to something fundamental in value when the humanist makes generally known our deep dependence on language power. He will do this by stressing the simple facts first, and then the more significant ones. He will point out that at the lowest levels of description, differences of one language from another are on the same plane as those of dress and diet. To sense this much is informing but not enlightening. More significantly, a particular language, as our own, is part of a legacy from forbears to be passed on to posterity fundamentally unchanged. At its most important functioning, it is related to a philosophy of existence and so can be made to reveal the most intimate truths and beliefs of those people who have inherited and used its symbolic system with ease. To know a man or a nation, first learn enough about the language that they use in order to learn more and more.

For the American mind, that attitude toward the rest of the world has not come to being through a voluntary process. It has been forced on this country. Had foresight led to sound preparation for universal changes, much loss and devastating misunderstanding among all men would have been avoided. The purblind politician would have recognized scholars possessing unique insights into foreign cultures as protectors of this republic. The university administrator, more often, would have been among those setting language and other humanistic disciplines on an equality with the sciences. The scholars themselves would have been more zealous in urging protective cultivation of exceptional languages, for the sake of national security and a cosmopolitan outlook on living cultures.

The backward glance is not more profitable in these affairs than in any others of mankind, unless as warning against continued neglect and similar shortsightedness. Direct view of what today is proved and practicable, gives two clear facts for remembrance. Every matured civilization, including our own, can produce masters of language. There is no racial block to winning linguistic abilities. Also, we live in a period that demands easy use of languages, not of "a language," in order that international communication may be accomplished in every tongue and at every level of discourse. Each race and nation needs to think not after but with all others.

II

At first thought, the watcher of change in world affairs will think that simpler expedients might be found for bridging the gap between races of men than by teaching them to communicate in the languages of one another. One ready solution often proposed is that all men be brought to use easily my language—whatever that happens to be—and so, though differing in many of the attributes of my humanity, every man anywhere will respond to the same words with identical reactions in idea and in feeling. This is a self-evident fallacy.

Ignoring the facts of inefficiency of any single language being used freely today in world-wide communication, one must agree that three or four have had very general acceptance at specific levels of use. These are the ones established by more formal dealings in diplomacy and trade, or by those literary and scholastic readers who have at least the ability for silent reading in other languages than their own. Spanish, German, French, and English have now such international standing. Some fortunate few have ability in North European and Mediterranean tongues.

The real test comes when attempts are made to give power in the four kinds of ability in a second language to any population in a wholly different environment. No "living" language is genuinely alive beyond its natural borders of constant use. A sign of what to expect is in the record of attempts to teach English, on a national scale, in totally different environments. Teaching the English of Great Britain, of the United States, or of any other English-speaking nation by the standard methods of classroom instruction has failed in Latin America, in the Far East, in India, and in South Africa. The exposure of mind is too spasmodic and too much in conflict with thought in the native language. Also, the chance to use immediately what has been added daily is ordinarily lacking.

The real obstacle, however, is in the lack of teachers able to think and so to speak idiomatically in the two languages that contend with one another in the mind of the learner. Until fluency in thought is at high level in both idioms, the teacher is incompetent to lead other minds across gaps between the familiar and the foreign. This has been proved, however, to be a possibility under favorable conditions. Young children, leaving their homes with nothing but Spanish as their medium of communication, have had their instruction for several years from teachers highly developed bilingually in English and Spanish, and for every subject of their curriculum. They have developed in three years actual ability to think in both languages, spontaneously and without the confusion usual among pupils who had an immersion in English simultaneously with a complete break from Spanish. These favored few moved in thought along two lines interchangeably, with their teachers, until the assimilation within had become an accomplished effect. They had moved from familiar patterns to new ones. Success in the four forms of expression had come easily because what was known had not been discarded but had been utilized in this new experience.

For adults, the difficulty is much greater; for them, exposures to a second language must be devised in every possible way. Practice in speaking and hearing must be parallel to reading and writing, with stress on habits of use rather than upon mechanics of structure. At earlier stages, the process is to be as close to normal for the adult, as for the child in customary methods of acquiring his mother tongue. The task involved in doing so much for an adult population, even in the native speech of a country, is well understood. National "literacy" campaigns have proved its difficulty. Adults do not easily change: they only grow older. The four ways of communication in a second language are obviously much harder to learn. Presumably such a revolutionary change in an adult population is not worth what it costs. Adults, beyond school experience, will not and cannot give up their ways of life in order to succeed—unless under a rigid compulsion for some immediate advantage.

The simpler trial in Ireland—to re-establish an older native speech as secondary, on national grounds—has had its misfortunes. At best, such attempts can bring useful returns throughout a population only where the second language has daily usage in active discourse.

A plan for China was devised in 1937 that was to give an elementary command of English to the greater part of the people in that large land area. This was possibly the most comprehensive of modern programs of this kind. Work in schools was to be with scientifically constructed texts, to give normal growth in reading. News print and posters put up in villages were to bring familiarity with English in print, and loud speakers in the streets were to bring in broadcasts. The practice of teaching informally was thus to be carried around the clock, in school and out, in ways to stimulate adults in all their daily routines. They also were to gain steadily through contacts at home with younger members of the family who could transfer some part of their formal learning as supplement to what was acquired from street signs, broadcasts, and simple reading.

This plan fell before the war that began in 1937 and has since continued; so the work in China of Richards and his followers never came to fruition. Had fair trial of this scheme been made, two favorable circumstances would have supported the plan—the widespread use of English in China as the acceptable second language and its complete difference from written forms of the native speech. The Chinese learner would have had help from some understanding of oral English, and the benefits from expert handling of the materials for print.

Other efforts to make English a strong second language in important areas have been made under governmental favor, as in Japan, in the Philippines, in India, and in Malaya. Russia, with its Litvinov plan, once set courses in the elements of English for four million men in arms, and for many years the armies of India pursued regular studies of similar kind. Through the two world wars of this century foreign minds, in the Near East, Latin America, and all of Europe, have been trained to understand English in the limited vocabularies of technical and engineering operations. Yet responses to wartime demands have no effect in years of peaceful change, unless there has come out of emergency a lasting sense of the necessity for understanding day by day, in a wide variety of associations.

The supposed ready solution of the person wishing all men to take his language, if judged by large-scale attempts with English, is no solution. He must be satisfied with seeing a slow penetration of this or any other into comprehension, by the applying of scientific processes in classroom instruction and by the preparation of texts, dictionaries, and speech records. Though English print and sound waves carrying spoken words circle the globe, they will not create a four-way use of the language around the world nor be of much help to the Western mind toward discovering what the other man is thinking about or intending to do.

These scientific processes are so well accepted that work with words to carry pupils through their first stages of formal training in language is on a high level of efficiency. This is an accomplishment of less than fifty years, based upon frequency studies of usage, word order, and grammatical forms as these appear in masses of current print. The work of Thorndike on English was followed by similar analyses of other important modern languages. Texts are, in consequence, now constructed to teach important matters first, and to create a scale of progress based on the evidence from research. Dictionaries and word books bearing the names of Thorndike, Ogden, Barnhart, and Collins[1] are examples of the efficient new tools given in recent years to beginners. Such texts and dictionaries give proof and promise of solid progress in teaching all children their mother tongues with less effort, and in leading every youth and adult to realize the inner meanings of another language far more deeply and usefully than hitherto.

If the Western mind could become master of other languages than those native to its particular environment, the West would be ready to think and to plan comprehensively toward the needs of mankind. The greatest hope toward mastery of French, German, Spanish, or English, by natives of the countries using any one of these four tongues, lies in future production of such teaching materials for beginners as are coming to use in this country. As matters stand, few today operate mentally with any ease in more than one of these four other than his own. All will be called on to ask help of others whenever they cross the shadow line beyond simple communication in speech and silent translation to themselves. This predicament seems to block the assumption that two widely employed international tongues might be spread with some symmetry over the land areas where these are now current, one in full use and the other partially so. Many smaller nations, we know, have attained that facility internally. But the "dead end" is that each of two language areas may send its print and sound waves to good effect into the spaces of the other unit, and still continue in fairly complete ignorance of what is in the minds of those who read and listen. This is proved by the status today of even the most favorable American contacts.

The search for a way through has led devisers of artificial languages to press hard for attention, and with some success in small cross sections of business or with formal bodies naturally in steady communication by means of limited vocabularies. Science has found its way by such media, requiring of all a steadfast use of arbitrary symbols for formal ideas. Beyond any fixed framework of arbitrary assignment of meanings, as in coded messages, an artificial language could have only a small "moving" vocabulary, meaning a working body of words that gathered fresh meanings as inventive minds began turning them to metaphorical and idiomatic applications. Always, the "road block" to thought in an artificially constructed language would be precisely this limit in vocabulary, and in man's inability to operate creatively in the four essential ways of normal communication against the tide of formed mental habits that earlier had been created by artificial designations of symbols.

Use of translations is proposed as the third solution. If we cannot have a second tongue made equal in value to the native one of a given language area, and if no artificial language can even approach general usage because opposed by all the habits of words when in lively process of change, may we not do a fair job of it by massed translation? This has its appeal, assuredly to UNESCO, which can confine its directives toward specific ends and achieve them.

Assume that this task of translating is to be confined within the bounds of creditable literary and historical selections from twenty to thirty languages that possess cultural traditions of universal importance. Such an operation could be brought off successfully in due time, at high cost. Conceivably, in a reasonable term of human history enough people would learn to appreciate the backgrounds of several such cultural records by reading these translations. They still would be outside the zones of the contemporary, unable to exchange a few ideas with a native of another country who also stands apart as an "operator" inside a single form of language. The world would have arrived at a goal only to find it an unsatisfactory one for purposes of mutual understanding and self-expression to opposite minds across the boundaries of what stood in print. Translations can be fundamentally useful, but need human contacts to become effectual in men's lives.

These reminders of the ineffectiveness of translations for general communication are not to detract from the great value they have in disseminating ideas for special purposes. Dependence upon translations, in print and by interpreters, has increased tremendously since the close of the First World War. They are giving to the public mind something that before was possessed only by scholars and a modest group of readers in almost any cultivated nation.

Cultural history is being made in present time by methods close to those for translation now in use generally. The United Nations and governments working for their own ends issue news bulletins that contain much information on the arts. Summaries on public events and epitomes of new literary works enliven their pages of economic and political information. Translations also appear, but the significant substitute for full length, literal translation is the digest. Often overlooked by general readers are the issues of the *Current Digest of the Soviet Press*. A weekly of sixty-four or more pages giving a great deal of first-hand information in accurate reporting of what the Russian authorities permit in print, this product of American scholarship is more effective than any other digest in current circulation. It presents true and professed aspects of Russian culture that are highly revealing.

Other works of the American Council of Learned Societies are in a series of full-length English translations of books from Russian, with many reprints in original texts that are wanted by Western scholars and scientists. The initiative of humanistic societies in these matters brought support from those working in social studies, and also from the greater news services. No better example, historically, can be found to show the dependence of all men upon bilingual scholars. For valid representations of the minds and purposes of those using other languages than English, our world must rely on its humanists to produce digests and translations on every conceivable subject.

One would be thoughtless and unobserving if he overlooked the important rivals of print for giving to the world its current translations and digests from foreign languages. The development of radio broadcasting and of television could be responsible in future for the abandonment of printed pages, except for transfers of classic works in literatures, encyclopedias, and comparable standard items in cultural history. It is now feasible to take out of thin air what the printing press can produce for laborious distribution, at high costs in foreign exchange, to be read long afterwards. A phonographic record has some special advantages over print, as has that other source of direct transmission of ideas—the land telephone—of which all radio and television channels are offsprings.

It is useful to reflect a moment on the changes in speedy transmission of ideas that have come from modern invention during our century. The story, in incomplete form, will convince anyone of the revolutionary consequences still to be expected, in the best sense of these two words, from refinements in the applied uses of what even today is known. The dreamers who fancy the future to hold for us a translation machine, operating independently of human minds, are no more exciting than their realistic forerunners. The men who brought electrical transmission of sounds to its present level affected the lives of all, and involved this generation in schemes of propaganda, evil and good, that touch the existence of every individual. The humanist is deeply concerned with what has been and may be in this change from a slow-moving process of thought transfer. He stands close to the center of all communication, as always.

Fifty years ago two persons could talk back and forth over a single strand of wire in a common language. Soon a series of connections on the same wire brought several more into contact, with some loss in privacy but with considerable increase of communication—still at short range and therefore usually restricted to conversation on local matters. Soon the network spread over the continent, next across national boundaries, and finally through the air around the world instead of by the intermediary of cabled codes. It still was only by such symbols as the Morse code that contact was made outside the limits of a single language at both ends of the system; there translation came into play, from code into local speech or from one tongue into another, usually a slow operation from received sound into writing. The climax of transmission came with transfer by a bilingual person so highly trained in the thought processes of two languages that he could deliver orally, with slight delay, the content of the message to listeners who could understand only his translation.

Today, in sessions of the United Nations, auditors receive in the language of their choice from a battery of intercommunicants what some bilingual expert has transformed into that language with accuracy in idea and idiom at the moment after his contact by telephone with the spoken words from the speaker's desk. All who work in this corps of translators achieve the feat of thinking out loud, literally and rapidly, from any one of several spoken tongues into all the earphones connected to their desks as translators for those who listen, at their own selection, from any place in the audience. One highly trained mind almost immediately can carry part of a listening world across any barrier of language.

All this is a commonplace of communication, well known but also slightly appreciated as a potential asset for international understanding beyond the limits of such significant congresses. Such instantaneous reception of ideas around the world in appropriate languages for general understanding can be achieved by radio and telephone, if not by television, and can lessen the influence of all other media having slower contact—as print, which, by slowness in travel and a lack of exactness in expression of feeling, limits the power of words as symbols of thought.

III

Rapid changes in the foreign relations of this country since 1945 have brought on a great increase in the American need of persons highly qualified in a second language. The other language alongside English may be one that is common in any quarter of the globe, but that does not mean of necessity that the user must live in the native location in order to be of service. Probably a call for men by any branch of the government, for work with other nationals than American citizens, would imply residence abroad, and yet there are abundant domestic opportunities. Expert bilingual persons who have likewise other special training and experience are greatly needed everywhere. All kinds of contact with incoming foreigners start at customs ports and continue on up through graduate studies in universities to operative and training posts in large industries, and to all commercial, social, and cultural dealings at international levels. Diplomacy is but one branch of public affairs, though the first thought of, for which a broad and deep knowledge of foreign languages is imperative.

The extent of this demand is not properly realized by most persons outside the inner operations of a few government departments. For the most part, members of Congress are lamentably insensitive to such nonphysical facts of preparedness; being able to get on within the narrow zone of English as the one language essential to common contacts, they are apt to be unappreciative of those few specialists who are the intellectual armory of the nation. Also, the slow, hard way to attaining this kind of preparedness is beyond comprehension of the inexperienced observer. A bare beginning has been made when many individuals, wholly acceptable in other respects, have acquired fine competences in any of the twenty languages essential today in world intercommunication. They must also attain clear insights into the relevant histories, literatures, and philosophies of the people who speak them; must know their cultural possessions and their physical resources; and particularly be fit to make close friendships at virtually all social levels—the fullest test of applied uses of a second language.

Of these matters professional humanists have full appreciation. They know what it costs in time and money to develop men and women to such high levels of competence, even in modest numbers; yet as a class they do little to relieve American shortages, because they are too deeply involved in their own designated duties. The humanist, too, lacks that urgent searching drive for scientific discoveries of use in peace as in war, and misses too often its striking counterpart in his own work—the call to new cultural opportunities. He does not realize that the recent expansion of American obligations to cooperative action has opened limitless ways of work in the humanities. Formal diplomacy, military affairs, export and import of goods, and the total medley of human interests overseas are duplicated by what might be done here for incoming foreigners. Out of these insistent and immediate needs grow the cultural values that the humanist is fitted to develop later. His discoveries can be in minds and spirits of persons rather than in physical matter, provided that he has devoted himself to those new areas of study opened for him by world events.

This responsibility is at the doors of universities. Out of their teaching and research must come the personnel and the materials for use by private and governmental agencies to foster internationalism of mind and spirit. During the nineteen forties that pattern of American procedure carried the "good neighbor" program into the other Americas. Universities, foundations, and governmental agencies joined in a single plan. It was well conceived, genuine, and fairly disinterested; yet its maintenance became uncertain and finally limited because of too little long-range planning.

One need not try to judge the issues on a world scale, but only as something met constantly on the American continents. To simplify still further what is lacking to create international sensitivity in American life, the observer needs only to ask how appreciative the public mind is of the cultures of our two nearest neighbors, Canada and Mexico, and how intelligently this country is being expressed culturally to their peoples. The American record of isolationism is as easily read by those who look for it in cultural affairs as in the widely publicized political poses common to certain sections of the United States. Nowhere is this blind Americanism more evident than in an indifference to processes of understanding that are based upon a command of "foreign" languages and cultures by both contacting nations.

In 1918 the government bureaus in Washington were far less competent to handle foreign languages, even in print, than those in the capitals of any power in Western Europe. In 1953 our political and diplomatic officers and our military representatives are relatively better fortified in ability to use the four or five primary international languages, but our comparative ratings on unusual languages would be perhaps as strikingly bad as thirty-five years earlier.

Though such comparisons have no meaning except in the context of contrasting conditions there and here, perhaps one can draw deductions of value from the facts faced by the United States since 1917. In that year this country entered into war communications lamely, trying to use the four or five primary international languages alongside its European allies. By 1938 it was only a little better prepared for its use of German, French, Spanish, Italian, and Russian—least of all in the last named. Again it relied on its allies while at last striving to make up its long arrears and to capture the many less familiar vocabularies and less used languages that were being drawn into daily demand by contacts around the world. Thereafter gains were painfully slow, but slightly systematic in technical respects by reason of help from our allies, as previously, and also from universities and colleges.

A few of the stronger humanistic universities of the United States have now worked out internally a revolution in administrative and scholarly outlook toward the use of national, not foreign, interpreters of our ideas and of those prevalent in important nations with whom we must deal daily. Planning and expenditures are being done wisely. Such centers can be intellectual intermediaries at other levels of comprehension than the highly cultivated ones fostered by the "pure" humanism, confining formal study to literary texts and to languages whose literary and scholarly vocabularies open the meanings of so much and no more than higher levels of interpretation.

These minor gains are opening the minds of students to cultural histories other than those commonly offered in colleges and graduate schools of the United States. These, traditionally, are confined to the areas of Western Europe, the Mediterranean Basin, and the continent of North America. Realistically, in terms of American necessities and the fresh curiosities of its young people returning from overseas, future teaching and research in cultural histories must be world-wide. At the base of every such structure must be the footing of language.

Fortunately, out of the Second World War came enough talented teachers of cultural history to bring the marginal areas of the world into reach of American students. A new stock of American specialists had been started, and younger scholars from other nations have been brought to several centers to work alongside them. Finally, after a half-century of lagging behind European nations, because no force was driving us into learning the languages and customs of other peoples really well, the United States has a few promising beginnings.

Colonial obligations were partly responsible for the wisdom that Europe gained regarding traditions and peoples of the Far East, Near East, Africa, and the South Pacific. France, the Netherlands, Germany, and Great Britain have led the way there. Today the United States is moving outward toward these same areas, finding the signposts in foreign tongues slightly less hard to read. At the same time, there is realization that the actual living cultures of Western Europe and the Mediterranean Basin are lacking in our higher studies. American scholarship is on new ventures in unfamiliar areas of humanistic study: it is also due to bring down to modern times its surveys of those areas long taught and studied here with such success. Again, languages are proved to be basic for contemporary cultural understanding, as for all the customary requirements of day-to-day existence.

Today the pressures on this country to have an adequate control of all modern languages are as great as they have been in Europe. For over half a century national interest has suffered, not only in political and commercial affairs but in every other way, by the inattention to American obligations toward world thought. Now, in a few universities that are moderately well equipped with staffs for instruction in unusual as well as customary languages, new growth will come out of proper care. Financing of student aids and supply of teaching equipment in language laboratories are the next essentials to progress.

The experience of other nations must be drawn on. Great Britain, for example, passed through the same first stages as now face the United States. There the official concern over colonial possessions led to early though inadequate action, but at least sound domestic training programs were set up early in the century for India and Africa. They were slow to develop, however, by reason of scant technical support and incomplete analytical studies of the languages in question. It was not until 1933 that Great Britain, with France and Germany as probable participants, had ready a scheme for cooperative studies in Africa of native populations. They were to begin with analytic work on native dialects, leading to production of teaching materials suited to the use of European and African learners equally well. That fine and wise move toward peaceful change through education unhappily went the way of much else in wartime. Characteristically, however, British institutes have kept on with the tasks implied in that program and have won their way through to highly significant results.

In this effort Great Britain was applying certain ideas of statesmen and scholars who, at the opening of this century, set afoot an inquiry that should have had instant recognition from humanists in this country. Our scholars waited until the Second World War to start, under pressure, what might have been done thirty years earlier, in at least the preliminary stages, so that our nation might have entered two world conflicts with more power to understand others and to explain ourselves to them. At the same time, appreciation of cultural values on both sides in such two-way recognitions, through languages, might have aided peaceful change to limit or even to stop aggression.

IV

Among other nations, the United States is in a fortunate role because freedom of thought and expression exists here, and is known to exist. The demands for freedom of speech and for independence of institutions from government directives still prevail. The American belief in these fundamentals is as strong as in the other written law of democracy, separation of church and state. In effect, all are identical in origin and in purpose. Yet without enlightenment on means to maintaining these freedoms, this nation will not find its balance of power internally or externally.

Much can be learned by noting what has been the course of events in other countries to keep higher education free from outside controls. The issues of greatest significance appear wherever financing is critical. One is in medical education. This country is trying to solve that one, as must Great Britain and several other countries now judging how far to rely upon national taxation to maintain personnel and services. Another issue is raised by national necessities in languages. Slightly realized in many quarters, this one has been partly disposed of abroad, with government acceptance of responsibilities too heavy for universities to carry unaided and too intimately tied to operations of governments to be neglected. The entire matter of state aids is properly raised when, as in Great Britain, the subsidies to higher education reach as high levels as sixty per cent of total annual budgets. The discussions there, in part raised by Sir Walter Moberly's work, *The Crisis in the University,* have brought under review all the work of their University Grants Commission, and are producing a state of mind nationally that should be studied closely in this and other democratic countries.

The status of languages as academic subjects of study is directly of interest in this connection, and a review of British action is therefore of value to future decisions regarding need and supply in the United States.

As recently as 1940, both Great Britain and the United States relied on persons of foreign birth to maintain large parts of the work in universities and research institutes on the history of Far Eastern and Near Eastern civilizations. Though soundly done, the consequence was slight in terms of national outlook toward the events occurring during the past half century. Diplomacy and commerce proceeded with their own devices of communication, without much help from educational institutions. There was no source of ready supply of men and materials to produce results with less-used languages of the world. English was the usual medium of direct communication.

Continental Europe and Great Britain were much more aware of such shortages than this country. It is therefore advantageous to show by a few elementary examples how they met the needs of communication for international amity and national security.

It was in 1906 that Great Britain made its first comprehensive survey of national competence in the use of important languages for understanding of the contemporary world. The report of that inquiry gave full particulars on what by then had been done in other countries, particularly in Germany. It pointed out that specific languages and cultures had been allotted to the several universities, and that the teaching of German nationals was being maintained intensively under support of the government. By 1906 accumulation of books and assignment of persons to various centers of study had been going forward in Germany systematically over a long period. Advances in linguistic method had been steady, under programs for research in the universities and for field work abroad.

All the recommendations of this British report are valid today.

In its conclusion of voluminous testimony by witnesses from many sources and of the discussions in committee, the summary reads as follows:

The need for teaching not only classical, but also living Oriental languages has been recognized by the Governments of France, Germany, Russia, Austria-Hungary, Italy, and Holland, all of which countries possess schools of living Oriental languages supported by Government funds . . . We may mention here with regard to the two largest of the foreign Schools that the Berlin School has 42 teachers and a budget approaching 10,000£ per annum, and the Paris School has 26 teachers and a budget of 7,000£ per annum.[2]

Later surveys of the same sort show a growing intensity of effort throughout Europe and in Great Britain to master the thought of men in every influential quarter of the world. How much has been won of international understanding through the application of their recommendations is part of the history of modern Europe.

This British report of 1909 is an exemplar of the European approach to such problems at the beginning of the twentieth century. Among its consequences was the organization of the center that was to mature into the present London School of Oriental and African Studies. That center is today one of several available to Americans where they can learn how unusual languages are to be brought into effective use for international communication. It supplies a pattern deserving exhaustive study, not for purposes of duplication but for evidence on ways in which government and universities can cooperate toward necessary outcomes.

The American scholar will find in the four hundred and eighty folio pages of the 1909 British report considerable material for reflection. He will find in its testimony of specialists much that applies in part to circumstances within the universities and institutes of this country at present. For example, Professor Giles of Cambridge is reported to have ended his testimony with the sentence, "I think mere colloquial seems to be rather beneath the dignity of a university than otherwise."[3] In contrast, M. Boyer, director of the École des Langues Orientales in Paris, said that "old distinctions between the colloquial teaching, on the one hand, and the literary or academic teaching of languages, on the other, have been altogether broken down by the new methods of teaching, advocated by Viëtor, Widgery, Jespersen, and others. These new methods have been adopted almost universally, in one form or another; it is everywhere recognized that the first object of a student in learning a foreign language, European or Oriental, is not to be able to recite paradigms and lists of exceptions, but to be able to use the language in speech and writing, and to be able to understand when he hears it as well as when he reads it."[3] Very many other observations of the scores of persons giving highly valuable testimony to this Treasury Committee in 1909 demonstrate the strength of British experience in practical aspects of such matters and their subsequent deep concern over the improvement of all training services in which foreign languages are basic.

The report contains two striking statements with regard to German accomplishments to that time in comparison with those of Great Britain: "Despite the disproportion of the respective interests of the two Empires in the East, it is far smaller than the number of corresponding posts in Germany, where every one of the 21 universities has at least one or two chairs, in some cases many more, for Oriental subjects. While this is the case we [in Great Britain] can hardly expect a large increase in the number of students who from the first set out to devote their life-work to Oriental Studies."[4] The second note on German efficiency was that while British companies along the Persian Gulf and in Mesopotamia used only English or French in communicating with their clients, the Germans had discarded the use of any European language and were sending out all invoices and communications in Arabic, Hindustani, or whatever languages might be necessary.[5]

With this background from the record, recommendations of the committee had power to arrest attention. These brought proofs, instead of arguments of theoretical kind, to bear upon national plans for the future. Here the complete dependence of all planning upon languages was shown to be necessary. One section of the report contains a table that points out the countries and geographical areas with which closer contact should be brought about through intensive study of their languages. This was made the preliminary to any steps toward finding out what were the customs and present interests of these peoples. Direct contact of mind by the use of native speech by Englishmen was set down as the only way into the confidence of these foreign tribes and nations.

This table is in two parts. That to the left shows priority of importance, with the order of precedence further marked by the succession of the seven groups. The arrangement is suggestive of past British history and of what may be the course of future events.

The table is as follows:[6]

	Class A	Class B
Group I	NEAR AND MIDDLE EAST Turkish, Arabic, Persian	Armenian
Group II	NORTHERN AND EASTERN INDIA Hindi, Hindustani, Bengali	Assamese, Panjabi, Tibetan, Pashto
Group III	WESTERN INDIA Marathi, Gujarati	
Group IV	SOUTHERN INDIA Tamil, Telugu, Kanarese	Sinhalese
Group V	FURTHER INDIA; MALAY ARCHIPELAGO, ETC. Burmese, Malay	Melanesian languages, Polynesian languages
Group VI	FAR EAST Chinese, Japanese	Siamese
Group VII	AFRICA Swahili, Hausa	Amharic, Luganda, Somali, Yoruba, Zulu

This British pattern of 1909 has changed, due to shifts of emphasis and new demands from other directions. These are in the record of what has been done during forty-odd years to apply the theory as well as the fact in this and subsequent surveys. The searcher for ideas that may be useful in his own country will start with the tabulations of courses and names of teachers in the register of the University of London. He will turn to the sections on its School of Oriental and African Studies and its School of Slavonic and East European Studies. He next will proceed to every outlying university and institute whose candidates for special services have similar care given them. In the course of inquiry he will learn that the question of sovereignty in institutions is not overlooked, but that the sense of responsibility to perform is as lively in centers for higher education as in the offices of government.

Certainly, American onlookers will ask what all this has to do with the building here of similar resources. One answer is that the existence of such British centers may wholly obviate the creation of new ones, particularly as forty to fifty years may be involved in reaching equal levels of usefulness. We may begin to borrow learning as we do, internationally, in matters of science and invention. The larger answer is that out of studies of method and of aim, every such center with a life span of even ten years has a great deal to teach American administrators and scholars. The lines of demarcation between institutional independence and governmental interest can be drawn as proofs appear of what is needed and where are the resources to produce it, steadily, intelligently, and creatively to the benefit of others as well as ourselves.

V

During the first half of this century greater progress was made in the methodology of learning any language than in all previous time. This is so extreme a statement as to call for proof. The simplest, surest one is to be had in talk with any seasoned teacher of any language that is offered in colleges, or to examine textbooks produced before and after the dividing line. It also is true that since 1900 more dialects and languages of living peoples have been brought into form for universal study and use than in any comparable period.

If the list of languages wanted by the British Treasury in 1909 were to be revised today to accord with current demands, it would be a good deal longer. A parallel listing of accomplished work toward what then was asked for, would be a fine tribute to the scholars. Toward that increase the nationals of several countries contributed, and among them a large number of theoretical and practical specialists in the United States. National boundaries have not hindered scholars in search of evidence. Loyalty to particular schools of thought and method had no hampering consequences on the work of students of language during these fifty years; there has been the same universality that motivates the research worker in science or medicine. The technician in his laboratory and the theorist constructing new methods of linguistic analysis have developed the objective evidences of how languages can be taught with a simpler, surer, and more logical method year after year.

All this means a searching for the habits of words, individually and in groups, that can be reduced to practical descriptions. These are then codified as habitual, not as results of laws of language, to be brought to learners in formal grammars, rhetorics, and textbooks. It is possible at one end of the operation to reduce to print in logical style the facts of a dialect previously existing only in speech. It then can be learned without effort by either a native speaker or by one unfamiliar with that or any related dialect form. At the other end of this process is the making of dictionaries, a matter intricate and cumulative for highly developed languages. Like grammars and texts, dictionaries are primary tools of learners and users of any language. The labor and judgment demanded of a large staff in the preparation of an unabridged dictionary would seem incredible to casual inquirers. Ten years with an excellent force of aides were needed by Knott to prepare the 1935 Webster's International in its 3,210 pages, and without the cumulative work of hundreds of others over the centuries of modern English that outcome would have been impossible. So slow and yet so inevitable in final quality have been the century-long sequences of study by specialists in the uses of language.

Theory and application alike demand an intimate understanding of habits of thought among the users of any language. Their ways of life are thereby inevitably brought into question. Here is the point at which the anthropologist meets the linguistic specialist, to ask for help and to give useful data on the associations of words with actions or ideas. The blended records of all workers in primitive or dying cultures are among the finest proofs of modern scholarship. The novelty of some may give overemphasis to the unusual in linguistics since 1900, whereas the gains in techniques of analysis and of teaching are more consequential for greater numbers of people. It is well to make the studies in primitive societies and in dying cultures descriptive of what has happened or may happen in other cases, and to apply the lessons from all studies to the development of universal theories.

Here one enters a field of discussion that belongs to specialists. It is safe at least to say that the accumulation of data by anthropologists the world over has given to the twentieth century a body of fact unequalled in any other discipline for variety of possible applied uses as well as for its human interest. The explorers of primitive societies, passed away or still existing, have the same lure drawing them on as leads the archeologists to inert evidence buried under earth. The accumulated data of anthropologists are stored in the museums, universities, and institutes of every country. In the United States, the studies of Boas, Sapir, and Bloomfield exemplify the finest basic work in anthropology of men who made language a fundamental to all other evidences toward any conclusion. These demonstrate the ways of anthropologist and linguistic theorist in the assembly and use of evidence. They also lead on toward some of the principles underlying all modern methodology in learning.

The advances made in the teaching of languages are described in a great number of theses, articles, and books. For anyone, the "literature" would be matter of continuous study over many months on the four cardinal points of writing, hearing, speaking, and reading. Without that labor the general reader can gather conclusions from easily available descriptive summaries. How the specialists move forward, step by step, to leave their writings as guides for others who will learn and will follow—these are fascinating stories when told in relation to the persons who have done the work. Here the advances in teaching of one modern language, Russian, may be shown in briefest summary as illustration.

First familiarity with Russian thought came through the work of bilingual scholars who, as always in translating, tried to transfer ideas and emotional values from one language to another without great loss in thought and feeling. From these translations the backgrounds of history, customs, and institutions at successive periods in time were drawn by scholars whose specialties made them interpreters in such matters. Some generalized surveys followed. The number and value of these have steadily increased, to give readers of English finer insights. Two fairly recent works of particular interest to humanists are I. Deutscher's *Stalin, a Political Biography*,[7] and Richard Hare's *Pioneers of Russian Social Thought*.[8] These are from British scholars. A comparable work by an American is Ernest J. Simmons' *Leo Tolstoy*.[9] Many other comprehensive studies appearing since 1945 reflect maturity of Slavic studies in particular fields that would have been wholly impossible without excellent bilingual scholars as forerunners of the writers.

The array of implementation necessary to lead new and younger learners toward any such goals has been supplied partially by many persons who start with the two languages and proceed steadfastly toward production of the tools of teaching—translations, grammars, reading texts, bibliographies, dictionaries. Most important are the teachers to guide progress at every step of the intellectual journey.

The public fails to discern what the matured scholars of our time went through, here and abroad, to prepare themselves. Learning out of works in neither Russian nor English, possibly, and at times under circumstances completely foreign, they found their way toward their objectives. When George R. Noyes was in St. Petersburg over fifty years ago, as a Harvard fellow, to begin learning the Russian language, he was faced with all the difficulties of a pioneer in a forest wilderness. His state of mind, on one occasion, was close to discouragement. He tells of the circumstances, and of the turn toward fresh determination that came out of an incident in the city park. He was watching a keeper in the zoo who was feeding fish to a seal. The animal was reaching up for his food, while the keeper kept it just beyond his reach, calling out, "Higher, higher!" There, for Noyes, was the symbol of his own predicament and the way out of it. He surpassed all obstacles and became the first American humanist to have a deep and long influence upon all later students of Slavic literatures.

Great progress has been made in recent years to reduce these obstacles, but the novice will find many slow steps ahead before he can apply his understanding of Russian in a specialization. To help him, the scholar in this special province of the humanities first must see that the essential tools of learning are ready for use by other teachers who, in turn, will apply the methods of modern linguistic science to make Russian the second language of many persons capable of using it for thought transfer in both directions and on very closely defined topics—as historical, geographical, medical, military, literary, and political. We now own some of the tools that make the rudimentary phases of this operation practicable, given the students and the time to work with them. We still lack, outside a few centers, the specialists who can manage the vocabularies and ideas essential for fairly complete operations in the one-way transfer from Russian into English. The two-way ideal of all human communication for every purpose of understanding is somewhere ahead in the dim future. American scholars of native birth and educated here until maturity must hope to live in a marginal country for long periods of time if they are to express themselves in fine, contemporary Russian idioms. We have been slow in moving toward such goals in the humanities.

Yet the American story of cultural contact with Russia is long and inspiring. It was in 1870 that George Kennan published his *Tent Life in Siberia* and so prepared the minds of men for what later on he brought out from that country. When once asked where he had had his academic education, he replied, "Russia." The same answer to that question might be given now by a far more versatile and deeply informed student of Russian affairs, George Frost Kennan, whose service toward international understanding has been of highest distinction. Over the intervening seventy years many other persons have added to our stores of knowledge. Some have brought back to classrooms and seminars a personal awareness of Russian culture; as George R. Noyes in 1901 after his years in Russia started an American school in Slavic studies, so others at intervals, during this half century, have picked up the strengthening cultural strands. Only surmises can suggest the rate at which gains might have been won, even in advance of much important research into methods of teaching, had the United States through its institutions then fostered the study of all Slavic languages by younger Americans. It is almost equally tantalizing to wonder how far advanced, under such encouragement to learners, this country might be today in its relations at every turn of the road in its dealings with other nations.

VI

One comes down to the beginning of the Second World War to discover any general movement to extend linguistic services into areas beyond the customary boundaries of departments of modern languages in American universities. Some were following the example of the interested departments of government, sending a few to other countries occasionally to acquire a beginning in a language preparatory to residence abroad. Missionary societies were still sending out their workers to start on their labors in essential languages near the places of their future duty. Sometimes the preparation consumed years and was even then scantily done, but in a few countries solid programs were developed in institutions having designed plans of instruction.

By 1933 the great increase in demand was foreshadowed by events. By 1938 the movement to increase American resources of materials and men to teach those languages essential for war had begun in the universities. Within three years, under expert guidance of officers of the American Council of Learned Societies, eighteen universities were giving work in twenty-six unusual languages to over seven hundred selected students. As war progressed, this total was greatly increased annually, with a few centers carrying more than that number in a single year. Some of the students had the advantage of birth in the land of their second language, and others had been fortunate enough to get into the few intensive courses given in summer sessions to meet some anticipated demands. Many, therefore, were, upon entry into full-time study, at a slightly advanced stage of learning in Chinese, Russian, Portuguese, and Spanish. Among staff members guiding these earliest sessions under university sponsorship, the Council managed to find some who could fashion the first tools of teaching. Grammars, textbooks, dictionaries, sound recordings, and study guides came into production. Later, as the calls came for teachers of languages that had never been brought into working form by analysis and tool preparation, the linguistic theorists went to work. They broke down the raw materials and constructed formal descriptions of the habits of each language, and then with the aid of native speakers began to get good results with the recruits who were assigned to them by the armed services.

At every level of advance into more difficult materials and unfamiliar subjects, new guides to study were wanted and more competent teachers. It was then that scientific analysis of languages by the theoretical linguists came into full play, as did the technical skills of those who had tested thoroughly the uses of equipment for sound recording and sound production. The Bloch-Trager *Outline of Linguistic Analysis*[10] was useful, as were the aids in oral and aural training. The greatest help to students was from teachers who were uniquely qualified, through study and use of a given tongue, to display day after day the significance of its forms, idioms, and allusions.

Involvement of the United States in matters of world-wide importance had brought on, at last, a soundly conceived expansion of foreign-language study to which the Army and Navy programs contributed certain new methods and the incentive of necessity. The careful, steady research of American linguists had prepared the way. The existing resources were mobilized to do an adequate job. Minds of officials were opened to the need for constant concern with many unusual languages; they supported a program comparable to those started a half century earlier in Great Britain and still earlier in France and Germany. By 1942 the United States had, in many governmental departments, the point of view that was taken in the report of the British Treasury Committee in 1909. Then the following languages were being taught, in addition to those customarily offered by regular staffs of American colleges and universities: Hungarian, Icelandic, Iranian, Japanese, Korean, Kurdish, Malay, Mongol, Pashtu, Pidgin English, Portuguese, Panjabi, Russian, Thai, Turkish, Hindustani, Modern Greek, Chinese, Burmese, four of the major dialects of Arabic, and four non-Arabic languages of Africa. During the war and until 1946, the number of students working with each of these languages ranged between a very few and several hundred, in accord with known demand and the time required to attain useful proficiency. In some the term of intensive study was as high as fourteen months. Over fifty institutions cooperated in the program with various departments in the government and with all the armed services.

A person who is qualified to estimate the expenditures for all aspects of this national operation to help in bringing the Second World War to a successful close, says that the total was at least forty million dollars. Benefits then and since cannot be measured. Only dramatic incidents stand out from the slow, steady story of the devoted workers who served as interpreters and translators, as foreign participants in the teaching directed by American specialists, and as producers of materials. Scores of handbooks were written and fabricated in quantity; the soldier had his pocket guide for conversation in any one of fifty languages, a total number that has increased since 1945 to meet new demands. The more recent issues include conversation guides into English for citizens of strategic countries—for Koreans, Burmese, Vietnamese, Turks, and Iranians. Much larger works are now in print to expedite two-way communication of Americans and natives of Spanish-speaking countries, of Brazil, and of France and Germany. Finally, and of most interest to the general public, the Council has released its sequences of sound recordings to make them available through trade channels and has inspired makers of texts to produce many new and better books, dictionaries, and ingeniously organized manuals for classroom use.

In the five years after the end of the Second World War most of these training centers were discontinued. Fortunately, a few not only maintained their old strength but increased both research and teaching under the pledged support of their universities and in some cases from the government. Two of the strongest participants in the wartime program, Yale University and the University of California, started new linguistic ventures, while the University of Washington rounded out a formal center of Asiatic studies that brought into unison many different forces in the institution. Some merged their linguistic work in newly formed area-and-language programs, to the benefit of under-graduates as well as of persons in graduate studies. The two most important new developments were the Division of Modern Languages in Cornell University and the Army Language School at Monterey, California. Sporadically language laboratories are appearing now in all parts of the country.

The Cornell Division of Modern Languages has been fortunate in its support and its autonomy of operation. Financial and administrative aids, however, are second to the fact of expert direction from the time of its establishment. Professor J. M. Cowan had been one of the group that devised the comprehensive schemes of the Council, and as its chief linguistic officer had come to know every active worker in the language projects. Under university sponsorship he began after 1945 to fit his methods into the complicated timetables of the entire institution. He had too the task of recruiting native speakers who would give to students individually, essentials of speech and idiomatic usage that their formal work in classroom and laboratories did not give them. This recruitment is necessary for the fullest return on intensive instruction for all purposes of communication in any second language. It is a substitute for what a child learns at home and in play, and for the daily fashioning of speech given to adults by constant contact with others using their own language. A metropolitan center has clear advantages as a source of native speakers otherwise fitted to aid such programs, but the Cornell plan has had good fortune in its recruitments and is furthermore proving that fine sound-recordings can be a partial means to proper oral and aural training in less favored locations.

Like all major centers during wartime, the Cornell laboratory is supplied with equipment for registry and reproduction of sound. The leads from single instruments to classrooms and listening stations for individual workers, and the operative techniques for testing individuals and groups relieve instructors of much of the routine in elementary teaching. They also give students a limitless chance for self improvement, particularly in acquiring abilities of hearing and speaking with speed and naturalness in sound and rhythm.

The first requirement is that a student learn to read in his second language by the process of thinking in it "with speed and accuracy," and to that end a wide variety of material is brought into use. Acquiring the ability to understand the spoken word is set as "a valuable but secondary accomplishment." The important conclusion from these two points is that development of oral-aural skills and of ability in reading are not separable—in short, that the time given to oral work is not taken from reading time, to the detriment of progress in reading. Simultaneous emphasis on reading and speaking is right, apparently, for reasons that could be anticipated from the common experience of any learner of his mother tongue; the development of power to think in a language is easiest and most effective under normal conditions of contact. Also, the ability to move forward from elementary to specialized uses of any language is increased by the basic diverse benefits from reading, speaking, and hearing it in a compact period of intensive study. Writing is held to be of less importance. The testings of time will demonstrate how truly these and similar conclusions can be established.

The other center making advances on a broad front has been the

Army Language School. It is not typical of what can be developed on the Cornell pattern, for resources there are greater and selective processes more rigid than is possible in a university. For example, in a recent working period the staff was meeting with small class units in about the proportion of one teacher to seven students, and doing this in twenty-four modern languages. The technical equipment and the manuals prepared under the direction of the academic dean, D. Lee Hamilton, are scientifically and psychologically fitted to their applied uses, and many of the instructors are exceptional in ways not common in academic institutions. On the other hand, students selected for military reasons lack the motivations of those who enter college courses by personal choice.

These centers are demonstrating modern methods to help American citizens meet their external world with power to exchange ideas in many languages. A reverse order of research was necessary to assist the students coming to the United States from other countries without a working ability in English to handle advanced studies. They have had excellent general oversight in several universities and particular care in a few. Government funds have in some instances been provided for research and for training of selected students coming from abroad.

Each summer the Colorado School of Mines offers intensive courses in English for those students who will enter on regular work in the autumn. As many as thirty different languages may be represented in one entering group, and adaptations in teaching must be made accordingly. Obviously, the staff has learned a great deal about how language behaves under differing native conditions, and also how to meet the characteristic difficulties in each medium.

Another program of summer work for many years started off the entering classes of the School of Public Health at the Johns Hopkins University in a single-language transfer, from Latin-American Spanish to an American English that bore directly on the courses to be studied. There the success was marked, due to the use of a highly competent instructor on the same assignments year after year and also from the limited nature of the material to be studied. But a great deal was proved, as at the University of Michigan, about the comparable essentials of English and the Spanish of the American continents.

It is at the University of Michigan that the most carefully planned and longest research has been devoted to this problem—how to open to Latin-American minds the meanings and general characteristics of the English language. There the intent has been to reach the demands of learners in all vocabularies of higher studies and to make them facile in general usages. The published lessons and guides of the Michigan center will affect steadily the habit of learning in all parts of the country and wherever Latin-American Spanish is brought into contact with English as a medium of exchange.

From these sources and others any inquirer can gather the most recent facts on how teaching texts are being prepared, how teachers are being taught, how the usage and grammar of a particular language are to be mastered directly and indirectly, and broadly how the four essential ways of using any modern language can best be acquired.

The sort of analysis that was done before 1938 in the matter of usage, or more precisely of common use, yielded the knowledge of what vocabularies are to be incorporated in all early stages of teaching certain languages. Those most noteworthy because of successful application of results are English, French, German, and Spanish. Now the work of Josselson has added Russian to the list. In this analysis several refinements of evidence have been made touching grammatical and structural habit. All these analytic surveys, covering millions of words, have yielded new essentials for initial teaching.

These virtually endless investigations of language under a statistical schedule of occurrences and commonest forms, are about as near to ways of social science investigation as will be found among humanists. The results prove their merit. Statistics on word use, however, have no value in judging the higher levels of literary expression. Not quantity, but quality and variety, determine the values of highly trained and talented workers with words. Advisers on the teaching of English in foreign countries have not failed, despite a lack of such methodically devised plans to give them materials of work. In Japan, China, India, and in other large areas of the world English has been made generally familiar through skilled leadership from abroad. Processes that began under British or American direction are now maintained by native staffs of teachers.

Issues faced by universities in adopting intensive methods of instruction in foreign languages are the giving of added time in the initial stages, and unusual expenditures for staffing and equipment. The answers to both are to be made in terms of value. Only those who deserve the attention should be given intensive language instruction; and while the humanist will say that this brings in almost everyone at some stage of learning, if he is to be effective as a citizen if not as an expert in some form of international communication, the sorting of persons to have special care is first in order. The corollary is that college and university administrators can be more thoughtful of the consequences for American culture and for international understanding that can come from highly effective procedures to make second languages no longer secondary in the plans of American youth.

Languages are as essential for national existence as daily bread for an individual. This is known without recounting the cases of success or loss during wartime through the prompt use or total lack of power to communicate in a foreign tongue. American military power rose and fell in effectiveness often between 1941 and 1945 in accord with the strength of its linguistic services. Recent proof is at hand to show that such lacks still are deplorable. At highest levels of communication, this country is short in every foreign contact, remote or familiarly near.

At rudimentary levels, where disaster is as commonly met as in the more abstract realms of learning or diplomacy, American shortcomings in language power are dramatically proved by what happened in Korea in 1945. If the word of Louise Kim is to be taken, and no one would doubt it after reading her recent book,[11] she was told by an officer in American headquarters that the army moved in with only one man competent as an interpreter. The American and the Korean, individually, were reduced to sign language, while our high command apparently hoped for the best from enlistment of the United Nations in a righteous cause, but lacked one of the most needed aids to success.

Such instances are valid for emphasis. They solve no problems and set up no patterns of consistent support to the specialists on whom responsibilities fall. Yet with all that is to the credit of the scholars here and in Great Britain, far too little common sense is at work at administrative and financing levels for future security. The scholar is responsive to call but not responsible for neglect; in the essentials of language for all communication and for all cultural understanding, he has one of the keys to the future, and he should be enabled to use it.

VII

When Francis M. Rogers was writing out his conclusions on the uses of languages for war, he stated likewise their essential values for times of peace. His "Languages and the War Effort: A Challenge to the Teachers of Modern Foreign Languages"[12] was an outcome of his experiences that started with the American landing in French Morocco in May, 1941. It appeared in print during 1943, while Rogers was still on duty as an intelligence officer. His award of the Silver Star for gallantry in action was indirectly a consequence of his extraordinary service to the United States as a linguist. He had a mastery of French, German, Italian, Spanish, and Portuguese that enabled him to operate in and out of these languages and English with ease, and to do so in colloquial or military vocabularies. His personal fitness, however, only emphasized the lack of others with any share of his good fortune in preparation for that emergency. His urgent plea for sensible programs of instruction comes from grim experiences due to a lack of trained personnel. Even the slow routines of translation and interrogation of prisoners were almost impossible of accomplishment, and were managed only because untrained second-generation Americans were found to fill the gaps.

A paraphrase of the article with a few quotations will show what part teachers of foreign languages must have in producing greater national security and intellectual freedom throughout the world.

It is impossible to understand the inhabitants of any foreign country or to be accepted by them confidently without an intimate understanding of their language. To that end "the teaching of foreign languages in our country has been a failure." It is true that foreign language teachers introduce students moderately well to the culture of a given country at literary levels, but they fail to enable them "to think and feel as its citizens do." Even this literary introduction is lacking, for Americans, to Dutch, Russian, Japanese, and Chinese— all of which are as necessary in present time for future relationships as are all the languages of Europe, the Mediterranean Basin, and Latin America. One cannot appreciate the literary qualities of any foreign literature until his study has progressed far beyond the levels of the first two years of college instruction, in courses that present only the elements of grammar and the formal literary vocabularies of earlier periods in the histories of nations. Dictionaries, useful for preservation of variant meanings and therefore serviceable for decision on what meaning fits a specific passage, cannot give a free approach to the colloquial, contemporary significance of words and idioms. Even from the literary point of view,

it is impossible for the student with only a very elementary knowledge of the language to appreciate a literary monument. Reading the *Divina Commedia* or *Don Quijote* in one's first year of Italian or Spanish is pure bravado . . . In the selection of books for the beginning student to read, do not be preoccupied by literary value. Select only books with modern vocabularies. A fifteenth century architectural vocabulary or a late nineteenth century village-school vocabulary is of no use out in the world where the war is being fought. So reserve *Notre Dame de Paris* and *Le Grand Meaulnes* for courses in French literature or French general culture.

Such indications of method for practical, prompt use of a foreign language when in contact with native speakers are imperative for action during war. Instead of a vocabulary from its classical period, the necessity is for familiarity with ideas and customs on the level of today, and for a knowledge of the institutions and terminologies of special groups. The teacher of literature in the classroom has a point of view quite apart from the realities of daily life abroad, unless he has added greatly to his equipment by living in the country of his concern; he then has the ability to do something serviceable for peaceful change as well as for wartime.

In conclusion, looking toward the future, Rogers wrote:

As a final remark, in answer to those who might say that I could have found 200 American Ph.D.'s who had studied abroad and knew how to speak the languages desired perfectly and that I would not have had to take refugees, immigrants, and sons of immigrants, I should like to point out that our war effort is enormous, of indescribable proportions, and will grow more enormous still as we occupy an ever increasing number of countries and become more and more closely knit with our Allies. The linguistic demands of this effort are such, it seems to me, as to absorb *every* American who knows a foreign language thoroughly. The difficulty is that there are not enough Americans who have studied abroad, traveled extensively abroad, engaged in business abroad, or been brought up in a foreign atmosphere in this country while at the same time acquiring a bilingual education, to fill all the demands. We must teach foreign languages to still more Americans, but we must teach them realistically. The better we teach them, the stronger our war effort will be, and the sooner we can get back to teaching literature and general culture, and not the organization of armies and navies.

These statements were in print in the spring of 1943. They have even greater force today.

The same journal that carried the Rogers article had another[13] in which his colleague William Berrien applied its observations to practices of teaching, with a clear statement of the merits in American methods of linguistic analysis. He deplored the failure to give young people such materials to study that they might gain power of easy speech and quick understanding in a foreign tongue. Their training could be planned so that they would have these abilities. Methods of foreign language instruction before 1938 had shown the way to competences, at elementary levels, that can "in a short time be converted into a specialized knowledge by intensive application to the particular aspects of the language which are of importance to the concrete special assignment."

It is true, he further says, that we now are not talking of the abilities of specialists, of whom the United States has many of the first order in all phases of linguistic studies; we are discussing the imperative need for specialists in all the other professions who sorely need a second language. Even the specialists in smaller segments of the disciplines of the humanities freely admit their lack of such equipment. These persons know that most students in the present college generation, like themselves, lack the power to relate language studies to their life work or to general interests as citizens. Similarly, social scientists, repeatedly "accused of being inimical to the teaching of foreign languages in schools and colleges," state "frankly that their students have need of training in a foreign language in order profitably to carry forth their programs of study and research."

His recommendations are realistic. Stop the practice of teaching language solely as a preliminary to a major sequence in its literature. Offer an introductory course containing substance for intelligent thinking based on some nonfiction works of prose that present universal problems through writings of representative thinkers. Start immediately such discussions of contemporary ideas in the foreign country that is so represented, that habits of oral usage may be accurate in idiom and in colloquial terms. In such ways, make foreign peoples less strange and their intellectual interests a part of a total "community of interests among the peoples of the world." Furthermore, the future specialist will need access to the best and most representative thinking that exists in the language under study. His opportunities for reading in contemporary works must be wide, and also his awareness of the great works of earlier times; these he should assimilate in private reading. At least so much can be accomplished within the first two years of college, the years in which ninety per cent of all students taking foreign languages complete their formal training. That two-year period can be made far more fruitful; it can start a lifelong interest in advanced, nonliterary reading out of a foreign language among all who have participated in such courses of learning ideas and forms simultaneously.

Here may be the answers to many questions that perplex our teachers of both languages and literatures. The "quantity" concept of success has led them to judge too freely by size of enrollments, rather than by capacities of learners to read and to enjoy reading in later years. The criterion should be student interest as marked by progress, as well as numbers in courses and efficiency in formal tests.

The notion of applied uses of foreign languages is in itself made into an ideal as soon as recognition comes of the power that control of them gives. It is within the humanities that these universal means to understanding must be brought to full use, nationally and internationally, for the benefit of the individual who is to live in the world society of today. The issue is personal, not simply a matter of trade, international understanding, or national security. In order to understand others a person must first understand himself—a perverse way of saying in this context that he will not make fair progress in communicating with anyone, at home or abroad, until he has adequate control of his mother tongue. That fact raises all the questions of how the English language is taught in the American school and college, and of how deeply that teaching affects for good or ill what is done with other languages.

The past thirty years have brought remarkable contributions to the teaching of communication. These are not significant for learning until applied, and their application is still hindered by old practices and present novelties. It is necessary that schools shall remove the last traces of the traditional and hopelessly distorted presentation of grammar, and turn to work with meaning in phrase, sentence, paragraph, and page. As rules grew out of relationships, they are best learned from examples at their source. Equally important is the organization of training in school and college that gives appreciation of what we now know of general linguistics. The specialists have applied many principles of general linguistics in their programs of study in foreign languages, but have scarcely begun to influence fundamentally teaching in English itself. They still have also to show the uses of general linguistics in developing an understanding of meaning. Hindrances to the help of linguists and psychologists in these matters are from the treatment of communication as something identified with new devices of transmission, not as being based in an elaborate symbolic system of related words and sounds.

The challenging aspects of language study are clearly within the two areas of general linguistics and of the science of meanings. When what is known of these becomes familiar through teaching of our own language, many of the problems and opportunities presented by other languages will be met more effectively.

NOTES

1. The titles of the works are: E. L. Thorndike, *The Thorndike-Century Junior Dictionary* (x +970 pp.; Scott Foresman, New York, 1935); C. K. Ogden, *The General Basic English Dictionary* (x +441 pp.; Norton, New York, 1942); C. L. Barnhart, *The American College Dictionary* (xi +1,432 pp.; Random House, New York, 1947); V. H. Collins, *The Choice of Words* (222 pp.; Longmans, New York, 1952). This fourth item is a book of synonyms with explanations.

2. Treasury Committee on the Organisation of Oriental Studies in London, *Report and Minutes* (2 vols.; His Majesty's Stationery Office, London, 1909), I, 55.

3. *Op. cit., Minutes*, p. 143.

4. *Op. cit., Report*, p. 15.

5. *Ibid.*, p. 16.

6. *Ibid.*, p. 24.

7. I. Deutscher, *Stalin, a Political Biography* (xiv+600; Oxford University Press, Oxford, 1949).

8. Richard Hare, *Pioneers of Russian Social Thought: Studies in Non-Marxian Formation in Nineteenth-century Russia and of Its Partial Revival in the Soviet Union* (x+307; Oxford University Press, Oxford, 1951).

9. Ernest J. Simmons, *Leo Tolstoy* (790 pp.; Little, Brown, Boston, 1946).

10. Bernard Bloch and George L. Trager, *Outline of Linguistic Analysis* (36 pp.; Linguistic Society of America, 1942).

11. Louise Kim, *My Forty Years Fight for Korea* (292 pp.; Wyn, New York, 1951).

12. *Modern Language Journal*, XXVII, No. 5, 299–309.

13. *Op. cit.*, pp. 310–22. This and the preceding essay are urgent calls for more realistic teaching of foreign languages and a more constant use of them for other than literary pursuits. Answers are being provided to such demands. For example, Charles F. Hockett of Cornell University is showing how to apply the theories of wartime programs and still create appreciation of literary and historical materials. Others are achieving similar results.

THREE

Histories

I

Many adults still think of history as something dimly identified with books and teachers. They associate the word with a particular time in their lives when, at school and college, they "took" courses and were given grades in them. As these grades were called "final," they then had "had" history and could henceforth look back upon their accomplishments in that field of learning as excellent or poor according to the judgment of one or more teachers.

From then on history was displaced from the consciousness of many by current events in the world at large. These seemed to come along steadily but in unassorted order, much as did the incidents of personal existence outside those in work for a living. Both public and private happenings came to be estimated and valued as they affected intimately only one's self. Even major events of world-wide import were commonly judged by their implied promise of personal security and unchanged relationship with persons close to one.

If these seem to be unhappy estimates of human nature in general, that person who thinks so may congratulate himself; he proves by that reaction how much more progressive have been his own stages of growth in awareness of the vital meanings in history. Having made this adjustment in his view of others, whom he then sees to be unaffected by the implied historical consequences in major events, he is ready for two interesting conclusions. He can decide that something is at fault with educational processes that leave so many men and women without the keys to human progress through historical definitions. He also may decide, uneasily, that his own idea of history, at somewhat higher levels, has not led him to think, talk, and act on the enlightenment he has had.

Much fault in teaching the "subject" and "discipline" of history is due to its terminal nature. The work carries a student through an appointed round, by book and lecture. Toward the end of term or semester the pace may quicken in order that the designated distance may be covered. Then all seems over and finished. Yet all generalizations, such as this one, are imperfect. There is today less dependence upon textbooks in advanced courses and a compensating increase in elective reading. The student finds that there are movable margins to general ideas that were earlier taken as final. Total contradiction is often found for theories previously thought of as finally settled. Such correctives come from varying sources. Most important for development of the spirit of inquiry, are the informal discussions in small groups, replacing some of the set lectures, and the free reading in larger libraries. To imaginative and inquiring minds these are of great importance.

How far these experiences of formal study will carry into later life is determined chiefly by the nature of the individual. We say that American techniques in education are eminently fitted to create understanding and to guide without destroying initiative or individual development. Nevertheless, we have in the subject of history a true instance of possibilities not realized in adult life for the mastery of matters learned imperfectly in school or college. These are the particular truths of history, that its application as a method in every field of activity is important and that its formal study in school or college can turn the mind into channels of thought significant for an understanding of the present. Time has a basic value in every story of change in man as in nature, and nowhere is this demonstrated more constantly than in applied uses of knowledge about the past of man's practices and institutions toward prediction of future consequences.

This last point touches on the former question of how well history is taught in school and college. It should create a sense of continuity in human affairs, to be counted as a successful subject in school instruction and as a way toward world-wide understanding through the service of those who pursue its deeper meanings by research. In the popular sense, history is potentially fitted as a subject of study to establish a sense of continuity for life. At that point teaching apparently fails to a considerable degree. At least we have plentiful signs that the past and the present are not sufficiently related, one to the other, in the minds of millions of formally educated and reasonably intelligent persons. We can only assume that there is a cause for this in the way of teaching, and that many hold to the notions of history that developed five to forty years ago as an effect of their school and college experience. To these it is a closed book because the book is closed. If that youthful idea has stayed on in mind as more than a memory, its effect has been harmful. Its existence is unmistakable among those who today are whimsical with regard to all history, saying that it is delusive and dishonest.

Two different attitudes prevail among the nonthinking or vicious writers and speakers who are being read and heard in present time. One is the pose of those who, baldly assuming stupidity among the general public, affirm as facts of history what every intelligent person knows to be false. Or they operate boldly, forcing silent assent under compulsions of fear. That was a crime of Hitler's day that now mounts up to a monstrous pretense overriding the rights of millions of men to freedoms. The other attitude, less well recognized, is that fad of popularizing writers who discount scholarship because themselves ignorant of its processes and its accomplishments. The one is to be condemned openly, the other to be pitied and discredited decisively by thoughtful persons everywhere. Both are crimes against humanity.

Fortunately, in contrast, many persons today can point to the time when history first came alive for them. In early youth these men and women may have discovered on the shelves of family libraries one of the early nineteenth-century histories of the world. In four or twenty-five volumes, that compendium, with its graphic pictures interspersed through the text, made the whole seem to be verifiable truth. Even though it was not, it did open the mind to a new form of wonder. The scale of the plan, being most ambitious, had compelled a use of dramatic moments in historical time and a great deal of rapid narrative. Those imposing volumes, in half leather, the pictures, the finality of statements—all these marks of superiority gave them an authoritative place in youthful minds. Embodiment of that impression was there in the frontispiece, a portrait of the author, whose long beard and solemnity seemed to substantiate his claims to wisdom.

II

At home, or in the local public library, many American youths fifty years ago were establishing an attitude toward all history that was far removed from routines of school. Whatever their faults, those sets of volumes giving surveys of the known past, as of 1900, made histories something else than dates, names of places and persons, battles and discoveries, tests and grades.

By then the products of sound scholarship had not reached widely to the secondary schools, the point of contact with ideas of the past which is now being discussed. Even so, one might well mark down the year 1900 as abstractly significant for future growth in American historical studies, for the country had its specialists as well as exceptional generalists preparing the way toward sounder views in many types of writing. Alongside Ridpath, whose two major works have been noted as influential with younger readers, there were John Fiske and Henry Adams. Such writers were being read widely by persons of greater maturity than those who bought sets as library pieces. The names of Ridpath and Fiske, now rarely mentioned by historians or any but antiquarian book dealers, stand in contrast to that of Adams. His influence persists in several humanistic relationships, and among others in reference to the teaching of history in secondary schools and colleges.

It was soon after the opening of this century that both the old-style texts and general treatments of the past were changed. At least the preface of one representative work proves that there was a demand for inclusive treatment of a specific area of historic time and geographic centering in a single volume suited to the taste of literary and scholarly minds alike. It is symptomatic of maturity in our society that there was a demand then from a good part of the American public for something different from the compendium on the family shelf and the one-volume textbook in school.

In 1904 Henry William Elson prefaced his *History of the United States of America* with these paragraphs:

For many years I have contemplated writing a history of the United States in a single volume, that should fall between the elaborate works, which are beyond the reach of most busy people, and the condensed school histories, which are emasculated of all literary style through the necessity of crowding so many facts into small space.

In writing this history my aim has been to present an accurate narrative of the origin and growth of our country and its institutions in such a form as to interest the general reader. I have constantly borne in mind the great importance of combining the science of historical research with the art of historical composition. I have aimed also, especially when treating the national period, to balance the narrative and critical features in intelligent proportion. A mere recital of facts, without historic criticism, without reference to the undercurrents that move society, is no longer acceptable in this age of thinking readers.

I have endeavored to write, as stated, for the general reader, but not with a patronizing form of expression, as if addressed to the uneducated, or to children, nor with a burden of worthless incident and detail, nor yet with any effort to please those who delight only in the spectacular. At the same time, knowing that many intelligent people who wish to know something of their country are not fond of reading history, I have given careful attention to style, in the hope that the book might be easy and pleasurable to read, as well as instructive.[1]

These sentences seem to reflect fairly the state of mind in 1904 among our teachers of American history. Their writer shows a real concern for scholarly method and equally for the interest of students and general readers. This preface was written by Elson in the year when James Ford Rhodes brought out the fifth volume of his *History of the United States from the Compromise of 1850*. In it he carried his study of political history through the years from 1850 to 1867. Two later volumes added ten more years to the record. This survey demonstrates reader interest; it also proves the level of historiography to have been high despite moderate access to sources. The works of Elson and Rhodes are little more than landmarks today, in the view of professional historians, but they give signs of a changing interest toward public service socially and politically.

Changes in direction such as appear in these two works interest all humanists. They find their raw materials in many places, much of it in the works of professional historians. The teacher of literature has his mind on many kinds of "history," however, for the actual and the feigned in real, or imagined, regions and periods of time are all within his range of observation. He takes note of every human value in fact, fable, or combination of the two; of individual characteristics that are racially, traditionally, and otherwise representative of man and his ways; and of any incident or event that reveals human values.

Such are the materials that humanists draw from, in order to show how man reacts to monotony, to change, and to sudden stress. Their real or imagined characters may operate stamping presses, year after year, or in some other way personify the machine age. Out of that complexity of mechanism they will bring intensified images of human individuals. A single symbolic figure may so be enough to express life far more effectively than any amount of literal record.

The humanistic spirit can touch with art the work of any person. That treatment is given to materials by any creative worker from archeologist to journalist, by the maker of "feigned" history in Bacon's term, or by a professional critic of literatures. The span of time compassed by his studies may be many years, even centuries, or his perspective so shortened to contemporary life that the flash of response is by an almost photographic process.

Under the hand of a Gibbon or a Carlyle the unrolling of history is slow, the product monumental in its proportions. By contrast, the words of Lincoln, at Gettysburg, press the meanings of democracy into a few symbols that are sensed almost instantly and are kept permanently. Both are in the spirit of the humanities because in each the art of the maker is formative in style, thought, and emotional appeal. One man and a single mind speak to us through the complex patterns of Gibbon and in the almost artless symbols of Lincoln's rhythmic prose.

Histories for the humanist are fabricated by individuals, not by time. The stamp of the maker must be on them, else they are statistical statements and not significant to him otherwise than as sources of data out of which he may make something worth remembering for its own sake.

Selection of materials for artistic treatment may be by slow or swift process in the mind of the creator of humanistic history. He searches out his examples having universal significance. He turns to use the experiences of his own life. He familiarizes himself with the methods and potentialities of his chosen art form, in order to prepare for his task. He strives to become cosmopolitan in his knowledge of life and of all histories touching the part of man in life, that he may attain balance of wisdom and still keep his sensitivity to fresh impressions.

By now it should appear that histories which are in the spirit of the humanities include all that belongs to man in either past or present time, in actual or imagined form. It should appear that historical perspectives are as various as the persons who are involved in them, as doers or makers. One may re-create a story of the fifth century that is as fresh and vital as an account of personal incidents in his life during the few moments before these are recounted in writing. Time is incidental to creativeness, as to the relationships between details that are rearranged in new patterns by the imaginative mind at work within a form of artistic expression. The artist is led on by his personal aims, and yet he accepts the dictates of that art form in which he is to make his object.

Clearly there is still another force at work on him, and this is the environment that he is to serve. Imagine a Gibbon or a Lincoln addressing a society without long habituation to the printed word and to a body of values suiting it to appreciate the allusiveness of verbal images. Receptiveness of the public mind must be there as the work is concluded, in fact while it is in process, as inspiration to its maker. For he as creator or critic exists only if he has some sort of sustaining public. In this he is like the professional historian in his university, dependent upon favor of other men for his freedom in thought and action. There are some rebels and some ill-timed individuals who are recognized as being beyond or apart from their environments, but there are few of these in any single generation. The successful are received by their own times, to some degree, and the distinctive portrayers of man are kept as honorary citizens of other countries than their own for many years or centuries.

The original or critical work of a man can endure as an influence longer than during his own life, but only if he attains enough universality in values to arouse responses in successive generations, better still in varied cultural environments. To be translated into many languages and to be often reprinted in even one, are marks of natural distinction. Not the advertising vigor of a publisher of a first edition, but the receptiveness of the reading public brings these results to pass. Fortunate is the writer who is in himself so humanly fit that he unconsciously attains to these greater effects than personal gratification or the brief attention of a small segment of his contemporaries. The humanistic historian is in these matters exactly as are all others who deal in ideas and values. He must be bent on interpretation of man by art and on the cultivation of surrounding society. He does nothing that is sufficient to deserve praise until he satisfies himself, his medium, and his audience.

By these tests, histories are not simply products of events. They are expressed values of an individual who judges the human significance of incident, inner thought, and outward act; he then fashions the historical image in intellectual and emotional appeal to illuminate it. History is not story in time. It is meaning made out of reality that has been seized upon and reconstructed in the mold of a powerful imagination.

Without a body of reality, true or feigned, the fashioner of humanistic history would have no substance to work in, and without imagination there would be no heat to form the elements into artistic, logical unity. History is based on selective method. By its bare definition, the word implies nothing as to kind of data that is being brought into orderly structure. It can exist as surely in pageant or panorama as in oral and written presentations. Its substances may be drawn from any part of the mass of human records, written, spoken, or silently and inwardly experienced by the recorder. For our purposes histories are twice born, in some actual form of human life and again by some interpretive power in a human mind, heart, and spirit. Humanistic history, by its nature, is centered in man.

The varieties of understanding opened by this common term seem almost limitless. All of man and nature is within the historical process. All that the artist in any medium works on, imagined or actual, becomes historically valid to the humanist. Even a poor film may have its merits in fact, if not in taste, and even its bad taste gives to this and later times clear, if partial, images of the generation that produced it.

III

Attempts to divide the discipline of history are footless, but definitions of the function of all histories are of the greatest value. Under a discriminating description of histories all humanists gain. They are led to liberalize their own attitudes, and to make clear their peculiar competence in interpreting man and the past. They can demonstrate, if heeded by thoughtful minds, how heavily the affairs of daily life rest upon the strength of the humanities; in academic and public affairs alike, their function is to guide where no other guides are to be had—back to the sources of overt acts and hidden beliefs.

An extreme instance is in the bond between the humanistic scholar and the journalist. It would be oversimple to argue what the scholar does to produce new insights for all men. By building of cultural histories and by encouragement to creative minds and spirits, he has place in the affairs of today by his influence over writers working for daily readers. Journalism of the editorial page and special article could not hold to high levels of expository interpretation without scholarly production to sustain its views, making them well considered and convincing without wild search for evidence or speculative guessing.

Negatively, this fact is well proved by many incidents of recent years. The world has had enough and more than enough of scholarship perverted to maintain the false positions of despotic rulers. Nothing in recorded time outruns, for sheer audacity in the misuse of mind, some of the cultural hypocrisies of this last quarter of a century. It requires a cultural historian to dispose of them. As in comparable misstatements on science, only a fully informed scientist can convey the truth to the casual reader by an array of convincing proofs. When Leonardo da Vinci and Victor Hugo are grossly misrepresented and dowered with political-social views that are monstrously false, the historically trained humanist must be called on. Mere citation of statements in authoritative works is not enough for the layman, for he rarely turns to authorities outside his own field of experience. He must be led to think historically by a trained scholar speaking and writing in his own language.

The journalist has at hand in his own office a body of fact on the backgrounds of current events. When a man or an idea comes to the fore in the news of the day, he turns to this nearest source for facts of record. When necessary, he goes beyond to other stocks of print in general or special libraries. But these sources are often dry when issues of sudden emergence ask for definition against a clear background of fact and deduction. The point of departure in many interpretations of events may be in matter-of-knowledge not yet in the printed records of newspapers, weekly journals, and books. It is then that the journalist must rely wholly upon the scholar, and for our purposes the scholar is a humanist capable of giving correct answers on all histories involving people and incidents within his forms of research and teaching.

He is one who can stop the mouth of the demagogue before it is opened wide enough to release falsehoods that can never be overtaken everywhere by the truth. He can prevent the spread of propaganda that is based on errors and willful misinterpretation.

In his own college or university the professional historian sets the patterns of thought that are to persist in the minds of students for a lifetime. The one in a "department" of history may be more often called on, but is no more responsible than his colleagues in literature, in philosophy, or in any other form of humanistic study. Each is a specialist in his own way of search into sources, in analysis, and in interpretation. Knowing where to find the answers is his stock in trade. He must use them and point the way to them. He can tell his public how to view new issues that are raised in daily or weekly print, in broadcast and televised forms. Historians seem to have a double responsibility in these matters, to teach younger minds how to find facts and to supply correct information for immediate use by the journalist. If the scholar is held in high regard by his society, he will be asked for advice on difficult questions. In his writing and public speaking he will create such demands for his wisdom far beyond the closed circle of academic duties.

Recently the head of a great insurance company made a comparison that shows a shift in public opinion and particularly in that of journalists toward specialists in historical background. He remarked that thirty years ago every New York journalist would withhold his comment on an emerging issue in international law until he had an opinion on it from one of the recognized authorities in that field. In our time, he believes, men of equal acumen are at hand and available to newsmen, but are not thought of instinctively when some important issue appears that demands prompt, and wise, evaluation in the public interest.

Perhaps reasons for this change are easy to give. Certainly experts in international law are more numerous, inside and outside our institutions of learning than thirty years ago. And newsmen have many more sources of valid judgment today. But this is only a single example of potentialities; historians in every field of knowledge, in American colleges and universities, are responsible to the public for decisive opinions on facts and values. The American public has need of advice from scholars on semantics, on literary history, on contemporary philosophy. If new books of high quality have reviews in our newspapers and journals that are truly critical, the general reader will respond to this excitement of his curiosity. Many American dailies, weeklies, and monthly magazines prove this to be true. The American scholar deserves praise for his share in these enterprises of cultural reformation. His finer judgment in particulars is benefiting the general growth of understanding, appreciation, and self-expression. As one among deeply conscientious reviewers, the scholar can encourage the gathering of family libraries. The reader is so led to buy and to keep, because he is being helped toward his own desires; he is brought to reading for reflection, not solely for quick information on contemporary events. Such a change in perspective is well under way, as appears from sales of books of history and biography since 1940—a direct sign of a widening in individual interests and of our national horizons.

IV

It is an accepted fact that the history of this country should be studied in its schools. What is less commonly realized is that in many states the discussion of that belief has brought, under legal actions, a compulsory rating for American history. The order has gone out that "American history" must be taught, but as yet it is not said what kind or by whom.

Though these second and third steps may follow, with pressures as strong as laws, today we have little "thought control" of teachers in classrooms or of makers of textbooks. What has been common in competitive drives for adoption of texts—a sectional slanting of materials—is not a discarded trade practice, but at its worst is not significant by comparison with what overzealous laymen could do by laying down a line for teaching nationalism through courses in American history. These pared-down versions of history to serve regional prejudice are useful warnings of possible local, state, and national consequences from such practices. In no other phase of the American scheme of things have we a pattern so like that of Hollywood, with its maturation of films barely to the level of the lowest common denominator, or a little below that.

The active, serious hindrance to the uses of history is from a resistance to change. That dull resistance harms secondary education and limits the role of the scholar in society. It arises in organizations with special interests and in self-satisfied groups that dread any social change of possible effect upon their own constant survival as they are. When silent, these are useless socially; when active, baleful.

The right and the obligation to evaluate school texts are obvious ones for the specialists in education, and—to a sensible degree of inquiry— for all who live in a democracy. Constantly the requirement rests upon the scholar to meet, with sound reason, the issues raised in such inquiries. In the public schools it is as needful for learners to be free from distortions of truth as in any other association of free minds. Men and institutions moving through time, our historians point out, "must enter into the market place with their books, meet and learn to answer the interpretations of men who either derive the force of their arguments from an appeal to the past or else neglect it. If the sound historian fails to supply his contemporaries with readable history that is to the point, they will go elsewhere for it, to unsound historians. For history of some sort, by their nature, men must have."[2] The committee of historians making this statement might well have added something on the respect due the scholar from the public, as in every other relationship with specialists who serve it.

If asked to judge the merits of work in history in American schools, the professional historian would test by perspectives rather than piled up facts. He would stress principles underlying actions and turning points in the history of civilization. He would admit the use of current events as examples, to be tested by sources and possible consequences. He would have our national history fitted into a larger framework, without heavy emphasis upon war or economic influence to obscure human and humane factors. In short, he would ask of teachers and makers of textbooks a sufficiently universal outlook to bring this nation into the story of mankind and to counteract any spirit of sectionalism or false nationalism.

The forces to be faced in developing a historical sense in younger minds, are more complex than can be overcome by determining arbitrarily the content and amount of American history offered to them at the secondary school level. They are hidden in habits of free time, particularly during long vacations but also during the hours outside of studies and libraries and classrooms during years in school and college. Loyalties to principle grow less from formal studies than out of environment. The school or college is but one among many, and still stronger forces, that determine personal outlook. The church, the home, and companionship with persons, print, and pictures supply large stocks of impressions that qualify roughly as history.

In reckoning with all the elements of formal and informal education, the youth of today rely heavily upon teachers and from them learn something of the meaning of historical evidence. That lesson in use of evidence to yield a personal judgment is the most valuable—and most needed—benefit from school and college through courses formally classified as studies in history. Yet we have not had done, even so, with the heated criticism of the uninformed and the unscrupulous critics. First of all, we should separate the two types, in order to enlighten the one and to confute the other kind. Then we should examine into the methods of teaching, paying least attention to those who urge greater allowances of time as their sole solution of real or imagined shortcomings. What this subject, history, needs is very close to what is needed by the American mind generally—more reading that leads to discussion, more sense of responsibility to restock one's mind with facts and ideas worthy of personal attention, and more regard to the experience of reflection on what is read and heard. These are the honest means to understanding and belief.

Every parent has the same opportunity as a teacher to exercise influence quite apart from or beyond whatever is opened to thought by print. A good teacher can get on with a poor textbook, or none at all. He can make facts, through reflection, create an understanding of causes. He can establish that same freedom of discussion in the classroom as students create for themselves. He can train in what are the uses of fact and deduction, and how to arrive at understandings with others even without agreement. All this is within the powers of those who touch the lives of youth.

As parent or teacher the citizen depends on the wisdom of the scholar. Everyone goes back to the same source eventually, whether or not he knows it to be so. Channels to that source must be kept open, and not only open but free from the muddy criticism of the overzealous and bigoted. In that protection of the sources of wisdom through learning rests the future of all democratic living and freedom of thought. If but one fact could be impressed on the minds of university and college graduates in this country, it should be that they are responsible for the public esteem of learning. Higher education has freed them from narrowness of judgment. Scholars and scientists have shown them what is the true spirit of inquiry. Yet they have been slow to know and to defend the public school against false notions of history disguised as loyalty, or to demand evidence for random charges of indoctrination. Their duty has been made clear through the humanistic study of history.

V

By the time he enters an undergraduate college, a student has discovered that there are many histories—as of individuals, ideas, movements, nations, and all the arts and sciences. It is precisely at this point that higher education asks of him that he look on human progress as a whole, in order that he may become a citizen of the world, with some objective sense, before entering fully into its activities.

A description of liberal education is given him in the survey courses that are preliminary to all advanced studies. They open his understanding to those general values belonging in the lives of all persons, whether they end formal study in four years or carry on to meet the requirements of a profession or a "discipline" in graduate school. For a professional career or for a share in any business enterprise, the college must give a liberal education, that the citizen of tomorrow may begin a lifelong appreciation of matters outside his lines of duty toward a livelihood. A glance at the newer requirements for professional degrees shows that schools of business, law, engineering, and medicine are placing liberal studies as requirements alongside their subjects of specialization. Thus the entering student finds his college today ready to prepare him for early release into active affairs with a moderately clear outlook on life as a whole, or to carry him on into a special branch of studies with this equally necessary background of general values.

History has a special function to perform in the survey courses that lead students toward more specific studies in college. The courses in contemporary civilization at Columbia College have refined the method of approach to knowledge; by a planned use of history, in the broad meaning of the word, the directors of that program have made in thirty-five years a pattern deserving careful study. Other plans have similar merits, as those that make philosophical direction the most active force in survey programs. The contrast in method and in purpose is a strong one, however, between the survey that has historical time as its basis and the one that has relationship of events through time as its concept. In the same way, a philosophical approach that is historical, by schools of thought and by names of great thinkers, has in it the evil of exposition without demands for reflective thinking. At this point the reduction of values to terms in a definition blots out personal responsibility for choices, and philosophy like time-table history then becomes only a study of sequences. It is when philosophy or history elevates the mind to recognition of human values that the survey course is significant, and in our present state of philosophical grace in undergraduate education it would seem that history has surer outlook. Biography and all the implications of personality lie within its range; the variety of ideas on personality which history can draw to its purposes is extraordinary.

Those who are dubious about American survey courses for undergraduate students ask if they have not stopped "learning in depth" and substituted surface description for understanding. Perhaps the reply is that we are dealing with two different problems, the need to resist early specialization and the other need to bring order out of general education. The time when survey courses first appeared might be tested for conditions of cause comparable to the recent urge for area courses. It was in the nineteen twenties that the general courses in contemporary civilization, and in similar forms, were first widely discussed. War had gone and a temporary peace of mind had brought on a curiosity in the public that asked for overviews of man's past. The responses were natural to such works as van Loon's *Story of Mankind* from the first printing in 1921, and to Wells' *Outline of History*, which came out in the same year.

These two works are by men outside an academic environment. Their success calls to mind the remark of another historian, that all great works in history are by independent scholars. His friend in a university had two obvious comments on this generalization. He asked for a definition of "great" to narrow the discussion. Was it to be taken as descriptive of size, of comparative standing within its period of first appearance, or as a contribution to human knowledge? His more critical question was on the relationship of independent writers of history to scholars within institutions. Did they make full use of the monographs, bibliographies, and books on their subjects?

Conclusions of such discussions are that the successes of all are inter-dependent. The number of works having high significance for historical study is too large to be analyzed in any such manner, and their emergence in print for use in a particular generation does not limit the range of their influence. Solitary workers arrive at their goals without direct contact with resident scholars in universities, and those who investigate and "gladly teach" while doing so have advantages denied those lacking such incentives to production.

All that has followed in the train of events from 1920 to 1950 illustrates this general desire for comprehensive views of man's place in his universe. In every aspect of university organization the effects are discernible. Graduate schools modify their training procedures. Staffing for undergraduate programs of instruction is now with men of broadened intellectual interests, attained in some cases by a year or more of study following work for their higher degrees in specific disciplines. As when Robinson and others were establishing new ways of historical study among undergraduates, the anthologies of material are brought into form suited to new needs. Purchases for libraries and new types of examination also reflect generally the requirements of liberal studies as set by sponsors of the newer survey courses.

Effects within departments have been to free many from uninterested students formerly grooved into subjects by drafters of their programs of study with little regard to a student's interest. The elective system often was elective for the advisor. Modern languages and history have been possibly the ones most benefited, the former by sharper definition of practical and cultural aims and the latter by reduction of waste time and by an increase in variety of materials.

These changes, mainly due to better modes of historical treatment, naturally brought criticism on all survey courses and on such discursive works as those by van Loon, Wells, and others. High points in famous stories seemed strangely to be missing. Wars were played down, and the great figure in events was revealed as being only one among a number of farsighted men looking towards the same goal. Much of this criticism was caused by a familiar kind of unthinking sectional or national pride, or by a determined attachment to accepted views in prescribed textbooks.

Recovery from such resisting views has come about long since. Public interest now supports general and international treatment of ideas in textbooks and in newspapers, journals, and books. One cause of this is the growth into men of affairs of those undergraduates who twenty years ago began to see the world in larger proportions. These people see farther than their own fathers were able to see. Their descendants will outdistance in vision the members of all the generations in the first half of this century. The reasons are evident: Works in the first fifty years that have tried to show this century something of mankind on a universal scale have won general praise from literate individuals. That is proof of the presence in that kind of history of a true philosophy of values meeting the needs of these living societies. One can expect future histories again to show in proportion and in harmony the later evidences of man's advances and retreats in civilization.

When Wells was defending his *Outline* against meticulous critics, he ended his remarks about a few persons who were most irritating with a new statement of his purpose in writing it. He had not fancied himself, he said, as being the one who could produce a universal history. He had hoped to lead on others who could come closer to his ideal of the uses that history has to enlighten the public mind. His dream was of a story of man that would be without bias or prejudice, not rooted in political, national, or religious feeling. It would be the product of a generation far above his own time in its possession of persons of talent and of materials in full supply to serve their needs.

Because his statement in 1921 has as great or greater meaning today, its substance is given here in a brief quotation:

In a very little while, with incalculably great benefit to mankind, we could have the broad facts of human history taught, as chemistry is taught today, in practically the same terms throughout all Europe. And later, as the students went on to a closer study of their own nation and its literature, they would do so with a sound sense of historical perspective, and with their disposition towards national egotism and conceit at least corrected. On minds prepared in this fashion it would be possible to build the new conceptions of an organised world peace that struggle so hopelessly at present against the dark prejudices of today.[3]

He wrote this when his work, prepared with help from a few professional historians in the universities, had gone through two hundred thousand copies and was being translated widely. Wells may have found within himself the urge toward writing a book of such widespread usefulness, but he credited its conception to the aftermath of the First World War.

The same kind of appeal for more universal knowledge is coming today from the sessions of UNESCO to all scholars who will listen. So we have plans drawn for an ideal history of mankind, to be in three million words, bound in six volumes, to cost six hundred thousand dollars. A thousand scholars from around the world will participate, if these first drafts are final ones. Whether or not the end is won, the effort will be a magnificent proof of faith, and much beyond that; it will be the means of drawing minds to mutual understanding. The seventy-five scholars to form the first roster of workers have as their leader Ralph E. Turner, an American who has demonstrated his ability to find fact and to present it with clarity and vigor. Thus the meeting together of minds for idealistic purposes has begun, in UNESCO—another centering force for good that falls under suspicion of the zealot for Americanism.

On smaller scale by far, but now nearer to achieving the goal set by its distinguished author, is Toynbee's master work. His *Study of History* is answer, for several generations to come, to those who decry faith in values and even all belief in any study of man's past. This actual performance and the new one promised under international cooperation, mark the high levels of attainment and promise through historical studies thus far in the present century. For present purposes, they show the way in which all histories will be made more useful to all men in future time.

The parallelisms drawn by Toynbee prove the ways of rise and fall in human affairs, and the comparative likenesses in all cultural changes through time. The UNESCO story in more detail may give accounts of the rise, fall, and change in social structures; the fallibility or the vision of leaders; and the sources of strength or weakness in nations. All this interests the humanist by virtue of its reflection of personality and of the power in man or event to break through the slow, evolutionary processes of change.

What he looks for are those histories having in essence the universals of humanity, and in style the merits of an art. He is much interested in raw data, but only to see what he can make of it and not what it can make of him. He admires the mechanistic forces underlying science and the irregular manifestations of society. The humanist would be the last to say that social or scientific studies in historical form are less than great within their obvious purposes. He would only say that though he may use their data, they are not his kind but are at most sources of material to go into his own products.

Out of his belief in the value of all historical study and from a deeply rooted concern with liberal education, the humanist gives his full support to survey courses for undergraduates. He realizes their power to draw minds toward universals until at length some few learners rise to appreciation and to creative functioning through the arts. He sees too that, as a man's stock of usable information dies down, these courses give him for that time of need the resources of outlines and bibliographies to lead him to fresh materials. In brief, the college surveys give to the humanist his surest help toward a sense of unity in all studies of civilization that the undergraduate will pursue at college and independently.

These survey courses and the works of such men as Wells, Toynbee, and Turner can change "history" into histories. The general term never has satisfied the sense of histories used by the humanist; today, evolutionary and revolutionary forces make histories of everything in existence significant, in their own right and in relationships with other recorded and experienced meanings drawn from time. Invention and imaginative writing are as actual as what supposedly "actually happened." This broadened outlook is granted to students in the American college of this present time, and is a peculiarly useful gain for all who work in the humanities.

VI

Our professional historians, those persons in college and university faculties wholly devoted to research and teaching in departments of history, give an excellent account of their vocation. They have been and now are the most explicit of all humanists as to what they are trying to do. In individual articles and in books, and cooperatively at work in committees, they are producing clear accounts of changes in their discipline throughout the past century. Most surveys of this nature are dated within the past twenty-five years, a period in which departments and special research centers for historical studies have reached higher efficiency than before in their service to all other parts of universities and to many in government. Many publications of today reflect the results. In his ways of access to the public mind, the trained historian is active and effective.

These self-surveys of historians give credit to leaders in new directions, assess the merits of theories, outline major projects in social sciences and humanities, and propose fuller use internationally of historical studies through such agencies as the American Council of Learned Societies and UNESCO. The most penetrating discussions of recent years are over the kinds of textbooks to create international understanding and to eliminate false impressions of other peoples. In Japan, the occupation forces have had a substantial and wholesome effect through educational officers who worked cooperatively with Japanese administrators in all levels of education, to demonstrate objectively how that is to be done. There and in Germany, the historians of this country have learned something about improved interpretation while giving an international service that is of great value. That value will be lasting in the minds of another generation, whether or not freed governments maintain objective, informed staffs to develop teachers and materials. Results from the service of American historians abroad since 1945 should be well described in such survey studies as have been given us on academic affairs domestically. It is now a part of this "history of history" made by American historians and calls for inclusion in the record.

Two kinds of evidence, to be found in the articles and public addresses of American historians, are on foreign and domestic trends that have influenced historical studies over the years. One sort is on the break from European traditions; the other, on the more creative story of evolutionary and revolutionary changes in the practice of American scholars, teachers, and editors of critical journals.

It is a task for a social historian, to unravel the strands of evidence in the printed records since 1900. He would undoubtedly begin with the first issue of the *American Historical Review*, which appeared in 1895, noting the shift in substance and intensity of the reviews as new schools of thought came to the fore. The analyses of books so presented reflect the minds of authors, professional historians, and the American public in brilliant style—as do comparable bodies of material in new articles of all the learned journals issued during the same period of time. The story, to be sure, extends back to 1800, but for others than those in this profession the earliest elements are unessential to an appreciation of American progress in historical teaching and research.

One influence, however, has been so persistent that it affords a good example of intellectual vogues and imitative habits. Looking backward into the nineteenth century, a critic of any intellectual discipline can find in its development some marks of the Darwinian thesis. A querulous student some years ago complained that in all three of his courses of that year, the professors had spent approximately the first two weeks in analytical discourses on the influences of heredity. The parallelisms were drawn in such disparate matters as forms of literature, religious beliefs, and the course of European history. Talk of literary imitation or of use of sources in earlier writers was cast in terms set up under biological principles of hereditary growth. A like habit in analysis is to be found in the works of certain historians who were active when this definition of physical change was affecting all types of thought in Western Europe and this country.

Heredity and environment are convenient frameworks as aid to discourses on history, for its basic element is time. Yet as evident, and often more real in historical time, are the unexpected turns in events that defy all notions of evolutionary change. Events and also people can bring on revolutionary turns in scholarly interest, as when a brilliant, possibly erratic, scholar opens a new area of historical studies with unusual sorts of evidence to support his theory.

Observers who comment on the changes in direction given to historical scholarship make too much of the influence of Henry Adams, it seems, because they credit his writings with effects that had no distinct relationships with his suggestions. Disagreement among critics is a sign pointing to such a conclusion. On the other hand, there are many, such as J. B. McMaster, who are rightly credited with developing new sources of fruitful scholarship. Economic and social history have proved their importance, displacing the older schools of military and diplomatic histories from their dominance. The trend toward widened operations was helped by many others who established schools of historiography that still persist in the work of their followers—such as Cheyney, Beard, Turner, and Bolton among the older twentieth-century leaders. The list of such leaders is long and is steadily lengthening.

Before 1900 American scholars began the practice of writing cooperatively in a series of volumes. Several historians would set up a pattern within a prearranged plan and take individually their assigned parts. Generally these schemes had a chronological basis and left to each author considerable freedom in formulating his unifying thesis. Time breaks, which at best are artifices, had therefore the added factor of individual determinations, in outlining each section, as hindrance to a continuity in ideas. Of late the centering upon ideas has made such works more effective and more useful to all classes of readers. Ideas are treated as dominant, low in influence, or lacking in successive periods of time. Thus the flow of thought is kept unified, and the reader progresses under guidance of ideas instead of under a bondage to time. This change benefits the humanists by making history more and more an art form, less tied to the calendars of states and societies.

Against the objection that this lessens the accuracy in details, is the fact of a finer synthesis. On this difference the humanist and the social scientist separate one from another. To be sure, many scholars have characteristics of both, but it is the humanist who by nature delights in marks of personality and of individual judgment in producing patterns in history that are neither statistical nor impersonal.

In the Preface of his book *On the Writing of History*, Sir Charles Oman wrote on this important point as follows:

A book must bear the impress of the author's personality, and inevitably of his moral judgment of men and things. The attempt of certain worthy people to push selfrestraint so far that they merely record events without commenting on them, leads to the production of unreadable books. One feels sometimes that one might as well settle down to peruse Haydn's *Dictionary of Dates*. It is far more stimulating to the mind to come upon the effusions of a fanatic, or an acknowledged liar. Then, at least, one's attention will not falter . . . If I have any messages to deliver which are not mere glimpses of the obvious, they may be summed up in two phrases. The first is that the writing of history is a matter for individuals, and that joint-stock history is a mistake—despite of Lord Acton's pleading in its favour. The second is that in my conception history is a series of interesting happenings, often illogical and cataclysmic, not a logical and orderly development from causes to inevitable results. In short, history is full of "might-have-beens", and these sometimes deserve as much attention as the actual, but by no means necessary, course of events.[4]

If all this seems faint praise when applied to cooperative ventures in historiography within the United States, literally it is genuine in its appreciation of accuracy, wisdom, and personality in the individual who creates history as a humanist must. Particularly acceptable to him would be Oman's assertion on the unevenness of occurrences in time. Better than other reasons for the historian's personal selection, is this uncertainty over what is immediate cause in events. No one can assess all the intangibles of personality that existed alongside what is baldly reported in written records, for most of them must be guessed at. Lacking these personal elements in the total body of evidence, the humanist is unhappy. He may dissent from the demand for "objective" history and retort that such history cannot give any interpretation because it has no objective. He thinks and feels more nearly as does every individual who looks back on events in which he has participated personally, appreciating causes that no reporter can discover even out of prompt oral communication by observers on the scene.

What may therefore be counted as revolutionary in American historiography is but logical and reasonable. As the writer begins to interpret out of unexpected sources or by turns toward totally new bodies of thought, he is actually revolutionary only in the minds of his readers. The logic of what he does is entirely clear to him and is natural. If he has sound evidence for his assertions, he soon gains his followers. If he lacks proof, he will not for long inspire others or maintain his own line of inquiry. As a consequence, there is a good deal of misdirected effort, necessarily, but there need not be for very long the pursuit of impossible aims. Negative outcomes from partisan treatments of history are quickly recognized and drop from view.

Many writers on trends in American historiography point to the revolutionary influence of Bancroft's urging toward analytic work with American source materials to trace the "epic of liberty." They also note the losses of integrity in history caused by the outburst of nationalism after the Civil War. Next they point to the effects of the industrial revolution upon American life, bringing on social and economic changes that draw attention of historians to new growth amid the classic trees in the forest. These new shoots, under nurture, may develop to life of their own kinds.

So in manifold forms history touches all of the social sciences and is remaking some of them by giving structural organization to their substances. At the same time there appears to be prevalent a more personal and literary quality in interpretative exposition that supports what the humanities need and rightfully expect of historical scholarship so that its products may become more widely useful to the general reader.

There are many who profess "objectivism" under particular terms that hold back individual growth in judgment. The prevalent use of polls of opinion leads to reliance upon sampling as a way to generalizations in many fields. At best these are effectual in contemporary settings that are so well understood by devisers of procedure that individual judgment is applied at every step in the operation. The devisers of polls are always open to criticism on validity of methods and so of conclusions. Their analyses of final data sheets are based on secondary sources. Their end products therefore are questionable as to the reliability of reporters and witnesses. This doubt reaches to intent as well as to possible misunderstanding of intent or meaning. Since their concern is with forecasting on popular issues of the day, to a great degree, any opinion poll interests a historian very slightly and arouses his mistrust because of its ineffectiveness in matters of complex kind and its unreliability due to the use of intermediaries. The historian is as wary of secondary sources as a diagnosing physician of the data sheet on symptoms that is handed him by his aide. One asks to see the patient, the other goes to primary sources.

During the years immediately after the First World War, the obvious faults in sampling were less generally realized than today. A quick rise in use of this technique turned much so-called research into a "stop-thinking" activity. Having a formula, good or bad, an investigator could let it roll on toward its presumably inevitable conclusions. "Raw" data went into the hopper to be sorted and to reappear in receptive pockets gathering the several sorts of presumed proof. Realizing the limitations of the beginning and ending procedures, as well as of the field work, the Social Science Research Council has kept up a proper inquiry into inquiries—a review of the reviews and reviewers. This manifestation of self-examination is steady and fruitful, as is to be seen in the reports on American historiography and on particular disciplines that this organization and other national societies have sponsored.

Any review here of such reports and definitions is uncalled for. That is a matter for the social scientist as historian of his kind. To attempt plumbing the depths of such studies is not for the humanist, for his is not first and last a business of processes but of persons. His opposite colleague is the one to wonder about typical characteristics of groups, separate nations, and related countries lying within a major geographical area.

An excellent example of the achievements in valuation of this Council is its committee report of 1946 entitled *Theory and Practice in Historical Study*.[5] Perhaps no committee can reach such levels of incisive statement as are expected from individuals; there is too much cause to moderate individual views in order to mollify dissenters from those of the more venturesome minds. Here, incidentally, is a mark of difference that the humanist calls his own, for he seems far more distrustful of committee thinking than many of his colleagues. He prefers arriving at interpretation that rests upon a complex body of factual and emotional signs. To all these his nature has been sensitized through long exposure to very many, and varied, impressions.

This point may be overstressed and become a false generalization. There are philosophic minds at work in every intellectual discipline. The humanists have no monopoly of wisdom. Yet they may be counted humanists only if they maintain that inclusive approach to their work. They must go beyond most others in the range and variety of what is held in solution before any solid form is given to their patterns of thought and expression.

A satisfactory illustration of this difference in method and outcome of humane scholarship from those types using a more intensive limitation on material evidence from the beginning of inquiry, is in a comment made in 1950 by Henry Nash Smith. He had been discussing throughout his book the grounds upon which historians had made so extensive use of the idea of westward expansion. In their expositions of American solidarity, the thesis of an unceasing call of the land, over a century and a half, had been used with much justification to explain changes and developments. That has been, for many years of this century, one of the most invigorating ideas and perhaps the most simplified formula to capture the imagination of historical scholars. Yet after all the fitting together of evidence has been done, much is missing in the evidence, and some items are strained askew in order to be brought under the thesis.

He was questioning, therefore, this assumed dominance of "land-of-opportunity" in determination of American progress. Agreeing to the proclaimed significance of the westward movement, Smith nevertheless concluded, "In the restricted but important sphere of historical scholarship, for example, the agrarian emphasis of the frontier hypothesis has tended to divert attention from the problems created by industrialization for a half century during which the United States has become the most powerful industrial nation in the world."[6] In this tradition, as in all where even the most exhaustive research yields valid data on only one line of reasoning, one rightly looks for the error of falsely simple conclusions.

This doubt touches on another current consideration among the historians, namely, an apparently undue concentration of interest upon American themes. This criticism seems the more to be justified at a time when the greatest obvious need is for specialists on all foreign areas. To the degree that such needs are politically urgent today, they may get satisfaction through subsidy and other encouragement; yet the full duty of scholarship in historical studies now is to enrich the public mind with a decent minimum of understanding about the world around us. Almost as pressing is the obligation to transmute our own knowledge of American history into forms suited to ready appreciation abroad. Clear and honest representation of ourselves to foreign critics, friendly and hostile, must carry conviction by sincerity, breadth and soundness of scholarship, and a freedom from chauvinism. Many will say that this demand for export is as pressing now as for import to American minds of what foreign cultures possess that is to our advantage.

All informed judges of historical studies will praise the work done to increase the appreciation of all kinds of American history by foreign nations. The casually critical, with odd slants toward narrowly conceived ideas of what is the United States of America, traditionally and presently, must be enlightened or ignored according to the state of grace each is in at the time he expresses his negative observations. Such partial opinions would change into well-formed perspectives on American life through conscientious study of what has been done in half a century to produce a truer understanding of ourselves.

Any retrospective review of research in histories here will end in admiration for our scholars. They worked on the thirteen colonies, searching out likenesses and differences among them and of all in a national relationship with Great Britain. They gathered up source materials abroad and at home, adding new patterns of historiography in their work with European and American cultures. At the same time, they have been consistently self-critical. This is to be seen in the decision shortly after the close of World War II to make a survey of the done and the great undone in historical studies. In 1945 a representative group of scholars produced a comprehensive report that was at once a corrective or encouragement to their colleagues; it will become a guide to general and particular opportunities that await the next generation of American scholars.

This report for the Mississippi Valley Historical Association asks for a synoptic view of the several so-called "periods" in American history, with an intensive inquiry into the meanings of specific aspects of each and with a full perspective in the conclusions. There is wanted a progression from particulars, inside stated frames of reference, to a broad view and then to a comprehensive overview. The topics as stated included popular education, universal suffrage, assimilations of varied cultures, emphasis on truth and knowledge in contrast to absolutism, and recognition of subjects in need of intensive pioneer work. Agriculture and rural life generally were felt imperative aspects to be brought in alongside industrialism and urbanization. So, in detailed listings the committee dealt with the social organisms and intellectual concerns of American society.

Among other merits, this commentary notes the rise of American "intellectual history" after the end of the First World War. It also sets the time when American scholarship began to function freely in original patterns of research and interpretation. Earlier attempts to develop indigenous concepts of history had lost their way. Full resistance to scientific method, under European definitions, appeared in the twenties with the "new history" of James Harvey Robinson and his followers. This was to ask for, and to give, interpretations of change through a fine synthesis of contemporary meanings. Pursuit of a thesis and subjection to a routine of inquiry were to be deprecated; many sources of meaning were to be drawn upon and many common aspects of daily existence to be brought into focus. Europe dimmed and the frontier brightened in the eyes of men, even as some few still looked backward to foreign origins to explain facts of American growth.

Under any definition, this shift of attention marks the turn toward "intellectual history." Ideas became superior to periods of time. Causes of significant changes were sought for in native elements of American culture rather than in imitative uses of foreign ideas. This manifestation has not been unnoticed by the humanists, for the search of others for cultural symbols to typify their findings and to sustain their beliefs leads them to what the humanists have done.

Until recently, historians of literatures and languages have been looked on by many as being less in touch with active life than their colleagues in history. Philosophers too have been thought of as men apart, concerned with timeless and abstract matters. Now the trend toward intellectual and cultural histories is drawing several disciplines into natural relationships for a common purpose. So the anthropologist finds that he must pass beyond the primitive and undeveloped elements that engrossed the minds of his predecessors twenty-five years ago. Today he has on modern garb and takes to city streets in lieu of jungles and islands off the usual courses of trade and travel. All the social sciences and all the professions, sciences, and technologies are stimulating interest in their historical origins—chiefly to win greater spiritual momentum for today's work. Most distinctive of these signs, that history as method has a new function generally in higher education, appears in the appropriation of values from the arts to meet the needs of many historians. But possibly the most noteworthy of all signs in recent years is the term "cultural sciences," which the social sciences have as alternative and enlargement of their customary general referent. However weak may be the links of scientific method between their disciplines and however little culture in the sense of the arts penetrates into the social sciences through historical method, this is a fine signal of belief in symbols as well as in statistics. The histories of more recent times have aided these advances toward unity of meaning in higher studies. Perhaps nothing to promote that process of unification has been more actively useful than the earlier work of historians in literatures and languages and in the philosophies that underlie all action of mankind.

A typical instance is in the writing of Cochran,[7] who regards the turn toward "intellectual history" as "the profession's outstanding achievement of the last decade." In a more exhaustive treatment of his field, Higham[8] designates the stages of advance made by historians into all surrounding subjects and offers particulars of evidence on the relationships of their discipline with philosophy, literature, and all the other arts that bring direct and indirect pressures on the life of man. This second survey, a source of much in the following paragraphs, attempts a description of American life in terms that are above mere events as causes. It recognizes the composite nature of origins and effects. The thesis of Robinson and of his followers is thus carried onward with interesting implications for humanistic studies and, to a lesser degree, for the social sciences.

Tendencies in American thought were favorable to the new thesis of what history is in the life of a people as well as of the scholar. Events of the nineteen twenties made almost compulsory some recognition of the part of the arts in bringing on social changes, not simply in recording these in typical or atypical forms. The merging of arts and social studies after that decade is a separate subject asking of someone the attention it merits; here it is sufficient to point once more to the breakdown between paths of thought conventionally marked for workers in separate disciplines. That breakdown came out of the writings and teachings of historians who reached out for new substances to strengthen their expositions of the American scene.

Two observations of Higham are of special interest to humanists. One is to the effect that Parrington is to be judged as caring chiefly for literary art in relation to political and economic ideas—in short, that he saw only dimly what Turner saw and then drew his own formulation of literary history in narrowed proportions. Further, Higham sums up his praise for the school of Robinson by writing, "While historians hesitated on the periphery of intellectual history, a few literary and philosophical scholars plunged deeply into it. In doing so they capitalized on the potentialities latent in the 'new history' and inclined toward a similarly liberal, pragmatic outlook." He follows this statement with evidence from persons whose names are regarded highly by humanists for original and critically acute appraisals of American culture. There is a friendly, if remote, sound in his references to regional schools of writing, painting, and criticism, with concurrent acceptances of literature, music, philosophy, and painting as giving vital signs of delay or advance as we move toward the total consequence summed up in the term "intellectual history."

This fairly recent allegiance of professional historians to the more abstract concepts of humanities recalls the more familiar term "philosophy of history," detailing what these workers offer concerning the underlying principles of historiography. As the earliest, perhaps, Andrew White made mention of that term in his initial address before the American Historical Association, but it has remained until recent times a European rather than an American subject of devotion. Even so, the literature on this expression is large, making one wonder if the course of comment on intellectual history will prove to be as long. The allegiances which both terms imply between humanists and specialists in all forms of history, are gratifying, for they prove a unity of the arts to be as actual as among the sciences, at least by this much formative work on intellectual history and the historically symbolic values of the arts.

VII

One measure of value in a university is in the strength and balance of its disciplines. Those rated as fundamental should be kept at high levels of research and of teaching. They then must do more than function smoothly in the university scheme of things; they must contribute to the enlightenment of the people.

History is one discipline that should prove up well under these two tests, for it is amply supported and by nature is one of the most "practical" of disciplines. Its chain of effects from research, leading to better teaching, writing, and advising beyond academic limits, can be constant and effective. An excellent department of history can consequently make its influence felt widely, because its ideas mold the public mind in so many ways and because its asset of method, once understood, appeals to the individual as something applicable in all his personal decisions.

It is not enough that departments of history in colleges and universities can point to enrollments as large, or larger, than those of any other department; that, and the fact of relationships with all the social sciences and with most of the other disciplines in the humanities, might give historians a sense of professional security. Yet they fully realize that a control of historical method is not an exclusive possession of anyone. They recognize the fact that no ordering of historical data is worth a great deal, even in encyclopedias, until a philosophical mind has taken hold of them. Also, the continuing doubt of the American historian is whether he is driving into the most important areas of his subject. This uncertainty may extend to questions on the fundamental values in specific courses and seminars which his department is offering. He is aware in all this of that worst fate open to any scholar, an easy acceptance of things as they are, so that an unthinking formalism at length becomes some sort of fundamentalism, in the unfavorable sense, or unconscious dogmatism. His subject, by its very nature, makes him wisely critical.

The searching after new ways to service through investigation and interpretation brings limitless possibilities within the boundaries commonly marked by departments of history. In our own time, changes in institutions and in nations have created possibilities for historical treatment that are far beyond capabilities of men now facing the opportunities. At most, in the manner of UNESCO, historians may be aided toward greater usefulness on a world scale. Meanwhile, the historian as an individual has his two constant obligations before him at all times—to work in substances that are important to the life of his own time, and to maintain his share of historical backgrounds for recognition by persons relying upon interpreters to bring them the meanings of history. Both tasks are in contribution to the tradition of humanity.

Only recently have the citizens of these United States thought in terms of universal history. The people cannot manage the essential languages, nor in true sense can their scholars. For years all must rely on specialists of first rank to interpret events in many quarters of the world. At the moment, men know at least that in issues of international significance they no longer are satisfied with the glib statements of commentators on their daily duty, but must have the help of higher judgment of specialists in particular aspects of all histories. They require the critical acumen of wise interpreters of foreign cultures. In order to meet these unexpected and serious demands upon them, departments of history throughout the nation must have purposes and state them. They must know where one goes, or is sent, to find the answers to insistent questions.

In work with histories and literatures, our professors long foreshortened their vision by continuing to study and to teach within customary boundaries. They looked fixedly upon Europe and the borders of the Mediterranean Basin, but only scantly upon the rest of the world. Their concern with the American continents was late in coming; in spite of methodical restatement of cultural and political histories of the United States, the new fringes of understanding were slow to appear at home and much slower in matters of Latin-American

life. Before 1900 the American scholar was more imitative than creative, and certainly much too distrustful of himself in contrast to foreign
leaders of thought to praise or to appreciate well the qualities of his
own country. Since then, the archives of the United States have come
into free use. Curricula of universities and colleges have enlarged almost immoderately, and libraries have solidified their holdings by
systematic purchase. Simultaneously, horizons have been lifted for
all historical studies.

The way to discern these changes for the improvement of historical
work in the United States, is to examine thoroughly the rate of library
accessions within primary universities. Their accessions are a measure
of the discernment of librarians and of professors, and of the judgment
of administrative officers supplying the funds. One tragic fact out of
such inquiries is that there has been too little foresight. This truth
is a familiar one among those who have hoped to interpret from
beyond the customary limits of historical knowledge. Searchers into the
remote past have probably fared as well as any, by reason of the allure-
ment in archeology for men of affairs with financial resources to support their curiosity. Those who would make untouched areas of the
modern world their provinces have, until lately, been less fortunate.
The books and documents, travel to scenes of real life or to libraries
off the usual routes, and funds for publication have all been hard to
come by.

Some of the consequences are evident to everyone who wonders
about his own personal beliefs with respect to foreign cultures. These
are today, for adults, pretty largely beliefs formed in books and through
teaching practices of a departed generation. If a person would know
what is the general effect on American life in consequential terms, he
will appreciate the truth in the following dramatic statement, lately
made by George F. Kennan, on the state of the American mind in
world outlook and in judgment:

At the very worst, we can be sure that, had we understood better the
elements of our predicament during World War II, we would be calmer and
more united and less irritated with one another today in this country, for
we would have been better prepared for the things that have happened
since 1945 and less inclined to mistake them for the product of somebody
else's stupidity or bad faith. But actually it is my belief, which I cannot
prove, that the benefits would have gone much farther than this. The

possibilities which lie in human understanding, like those that lie in darkness and ignorance, are seldom hypothetically demonstrable; but sometimes they are surprising.[9]

Kennan then proves the other part of his understanding of history and the follies of ignorance of international affairs among the American people. In another passage from the same book, he demonstrates how we have injured others, as we have ourselves domestically, by a complacent dullness toward the life of the world:

Events have moved so fast that we have almost lost sight of this intensely interesting period in German history—the period before 1933, with its amazing cultural and intellectual flowering, so full of hope and yet so close to despair. In the decade of the twenties Berlin was the most alive of the capitals of Europe, and things were taking place there from which the Western democracies might have derived profit and instruction. It is true that the peace treaty we Americans concluded with Weimar Germany was nonpunitive. Americans cannot be justly charged with any political offensiveness toward the new Germany. We even financed her lavishly, though foolishly. But what I am thinking of pertained not just to us but to the Western democracies in general, and it was something more than political and financial: it was a general attitude of distaste and suspicion, intermingled with a sort of social snobbery so grotesque that as late as 1927 a German could still be prohibited from using the golf links at Geneva, the seat of the League of Nations. We did nothing to harm Weimar Germany, but we left it very much to its own devices. There are times when that is good policy toward another country. Here, in any case, were lost opportunities: and it is significant that they lay as much in the cultural and intellectual as in the political field.[10]

His words "as much in the cultural and intellectual as in the political field" are addressed to social scientists and humanists; they are always the ones responsible to open and fill the public mind in a democracy.

A few organic changes in the structure of higher studies since 1900 prove the positive side of this matter. It is obvious to all that, roughly dated, before 1900 this nation had little intellectual awareness of Asia, the Middle East, Africa, and Latin American countries. Scholars were following documentation, as is their custom, and likewise the traditions of their departments.

Latin America, for decades, had held attention of American scholars chiefly for its Colonial and diplomatic backgrounds of life on these continents. Even as late as 1941 a citizen of Argentina could say of the fall of France before German aggression, "You can't possibly understand in the United States what this means to us. It is as though we had lost half our contacts with the world, and more of our cultural life than that much." His statement is probably representative of the time and circumstance in the Argentine. This country was too long illiterate in regard to Latin-American life, dimly aware of Canadian affairs, and sublimely unconscious of Alaska as a potential bastion of the nation. It is mild satisfaction today to recall that the Hoover and Roosevelt administrations dramatized the "good neighbor" policy southwards, with very considerable sense and by a solid support of cultural relationships. The falling off in that direction and the inconclusiveness, so far, in scholarly ways of work with Canadian institutions illustrate the lags to which this country is subjected by an acceptance of customary fields for higher studies. For fifty years it would have been to our present benefit to have been developing an appreciation of the great good to be derived from both directions, south and north, for scholarship as well as for "good neighbor" traffic. Canada could have sustained classical studies, and Latin-American centers those philosophies and histories latent in the Latin mind but lacking in that of the American people.

This North-American ignorance of Latin-American cultures, before 1900, is forcefully underscored as one looks into the record of our relations intellectually and spiritually elsewhere around the globe. Like the nations below our southern border, many others had common origin with us in that cultural complex extending as far as the eastern Mediterranean—not only in religious thought, but in secular and political life. Again the Middle East of modern times, Africa, and even the friendly Scandinavian countries, remain in the American mind as scenes of pleasant travel or rugged adventure in queer or unfamiliar spaces rather than as parts of an inseparable unity.

Precisely in these areas the American scholar now is striving to make up the arrears of neglect. Today social scientists and humanists labor together on Latin-American backgrounds. The Near and Middle East, Eastern Europe, and the Soviet Union are being brought forward to attention, academically, as was the Far East necessarily under strains of World War II. UNESCO and the universities of the entire free world are making stronger international ties among nations through their peoples, not through abstraction of studies for the scholarly minorities. The American people are beginning to have international overviews to displace provincial opinions. Even so, the least and the greatest gains in wisdom vanish alike unless the sustaining information continues. The specialists and the informed public disappear at differing rates, but surely, wherever rising age groups that will form public opinion lack steady, sound teaching. To avoid future dangers of dim perception internationally, this nation needs greater stability, historically, than in the period between the two world wars; for wise influence, it requires that union of knowledge and interpretation amounting almost to prophecy.

Such overviews of others and of ourselves will come out of histories that are much more philosophical than the usual run of present work in this country. There must come in historical scholarship, such combines of resources as produce the discoveries of science. The solitary scholar, in his short life span, can add a point to a pyramid but could never lay its foundation. There must be a concert of work, in harmony, in order to bring about an understanding of peoples and potentialities within a land mass of the world. There must exist a balance of strength among men of learning in order to gain and to maintain living wisdom.

Such outcomes will be attained by decades of sustained attention within universities and by national societies of scholars. Rosters of workers must show the names of younger and older specialists in every pertinent discipline. The mass of materials must meet the demands of all and be fit to serve unanticipated needs. The men and the documents need not be in one or the same locations, nor even in the institutions of any particular region. They can be identified and correlated on a national scale, so that lags and omissions are prevented in the processes of production. Given time for interpretation, the scholar will make meanings clear to all his people.

The historical process will then occur in the minds of all, not in books of well-documented research. Then younger scholars will be supported fairly until they have overcome the first hardships of their profession, as costly travel and deferred advancement that compel them to work outside their profession in order to live. Then the scholar reaching out for international meanings will become so literate in other languages than English that he easily finds his evidence and also is accepted elsewhere as the intellectual equal of his professional peers. For introduction of American studies abroad, our scholars as teachers must have the necessary languages and a far more simple and philosophical account to offer to the minds of those who find in us such astonishing contradictions. We not only are unlike them but also are unlike the advance stories of us that have hardened the foreign concept of contemporary American life. The need universally is for cultural histories in the terms of thought common to each learner; he requires comparative cultural study, with his own as one of the two compared.

The ideal to strive for is a control of all fundamental kinds of historical knowledge within a stated time span or a philosophical interpretation of trends that reach through long periods touching lives of many peoples. There is a unity of studies in medievalism, internationally, and of Mohammedanism; one has closer boundaries in time, but both open avenues into every characteristic of human experience within time and under dominant ideas.

A sufficient illustration of integrity of purpose in historical studies is in this area of medievalism. In 1939 seven hundred American scholars were listed as medievalists. The roster included persons of many disciplines, among them being one hundred and forty historians. This twenty per cent of the total number had a direct reference to the specialized work of men in language, literature, economics, law, philosophy, theology, art, and music. Also, a review of the topics discussed in the 1940 meeting of the American Historical Association shows that sixty section meetings totaling attendance of over a thousand scholars had presentations of one hundred and eleven papers touching that period.[11]

Publication of medieval studies has been high, due to exceptional advantages of support. The centuries from 300 to 1600 A.D. are held in lively perspective of scholars. As to breadth of interest, the editor of the leading journal observed in 1941:

With rare exceptions, the articles published in the sixteenth volume of *Speculum* are studies of fairly detailed, not to say minute, problems and subjects . . . During such a period of change as that in which we live, it would seem that the need for reappraisal of the past in broad terms is even more acute than it would be in an epoch of peace with abundant leisure for the pursuit of detail . . . For in a period during which our very safety depends on technical achievement there is grave danger lest the values which are not spectacularly practical may be lost in the quest of mere security. The preservation of these values is a vital duty of every member of the Academy, but we may doubt whether they are best preserved by the chronic pursuit of minutiae.[12]

Such is the declaration of a single but substantial body of American scholars who view their obligations toward the "educational development of the whole man" as being those of "sworn foes of the single-track mind" and whose solid contribution to world society is by enlarging human appreciation of "the length and breadth of world civilization."

For the centuries after 1600, this country can show other processes to keep control of changing knowledge. Annual surveys are given us of new studies, as in Renaissance traditions, throughout the modern world; of work with individual authors or on formal periods of literary histories; and on specific schools in philosophy, criticism, and objective arts. In all such, history has as a discipline an eminent place. It is the tie, by method, of social sciences and humanities that helps all to control a culture area in space or time.

Some of these epitomes of progress in humanistic studies have very recent beginnings. Perhaps our greatest contrast of ignorance and understanding is in the annual *Latin-American Handbook*, giving a selective listing of publications for successive years since it was established in the year 1936, a date marking the turn from miscellaneous sources of reference to a considered, scholarly evaluation of what is the state of world scholarship on Latin America, apart from the sciences and industry.

One might name scores of less rounded schemes to advance our historical interchange within the areas of the social sciences and the humanities. The special bibliography is one form of record that has international circulation. A Renaissance scholar in history or literature turns to such a resource constantly, as do all whose interests are in older, matured disciplines. Overtaking these steady workers in well-cultivated fields are those persons who need the references to all that is being done currently on new areas of world-wide interest —on the Far East, the Near East, South Asia, and North Asia. Their needs are being realized, and fairly well recognized, by the practitioners in older fields. Scholars will rely on librarians, as well as on bibliographers, for their help to sources of learning. They will benefit more than the scientists from the great increases in stocks of microfilm and photostats that bring into easy reach the documents and rare books of the world. Beyond whatever is done for the social scientist, the scientist, and the humanist by way of supplying materials for the making of history, whatever its kind, is the spirit in which each serves as interpreter. That determines the range of his influence. It also proves whether or not the spirit of the humanities shall rapidly permeate all levels of education and lead the public mind toward finer, surer understanding of all peoples.

NOTES

1. Henry William Elson, *History of the United States of America* (xxxiv+911+xi; Macmillan, New York, 1908). In the tributes in the Preface to several writers of history, Elson shows his awareness of literary and artistic values. He regrets having written so little of American literature, and adds in a footnote (p. vi): "Wendell's *Literary History of America* is an excellent work; so also is Trent's *History of American Literature.*"

2. Report of a committee on "Projects in American History and Culture," *Mississippi Valley Historical Review*, XXXI (March, 1945), 499–522.

3. H. G. Wells, *The New Teaching of History, with a Reply to Some Recent Criticisms of the* "Outline of History" (35 pp.; Cassell, London, 1921), p. 35.

4. Sir Charles Oman, *On the Writing of History* (xi+307; Methuen, London, 1939), pp. vii–viii.

5. Committee on Historiography, *Theory and Practice in Historical Study* (177 pp.; New York, 1946).

6. Henry Nash Smith, *Virgin Land: The American West as Symbol and Myth* (xiv+306; Harvard University Press, Cambridge, 1950), p. 259.

7. Thomas C. Cochran, "A Decade of American Histories," *Pennsylvania Magazine of History and Biography*, LXXIII (April, 1949), 143–66.

8. John Higham, "The Rise of American Intellectual History," *American Historical Review*, LVI (April, 1951), 453–71.

9. George F. Kennan, *American Diplomacy, 1900–1950* (ix+154; University of Chicago Press, Chicago, 1951), p. 90.

10. *Ibid.*, pp. 80–81.

11. Loren MacKinney, "Medieval History and Historians during World War II," *Medievalia et Humanistica*, No. 5 (1948), pp. 24–35.

12. *Ibid.*, p. 34. Quoted from the annual report of the editor of *Speculum*, S. H. Cross, XVII (1942), 451.

FOUR

Philosophies

I

If histories of all kinds are of interest to the humanist, much more so are the philosophies that surround his life and thought. He knows their animating power. They lead him to reflect on the most intimate states of human consciousness and to find himself in the thoughts of others. Far beyond all histories, philosophies represent personality. The individual himself is in them. They can show us the full scale of being, spiritually, intellectually, and emotionally. Philosophies therefore open the mind and heart to what is near at hand in one-self and in others. The important systems of philosophical thought therefore seem timeless. Some have endured to serve humanity over many centuries. This is our warranty of value. They serve the common needs of man because they deal in universals.

This power over life and thought can come to us out of the reflective sayings of men who had no system, but wisdom. These sayings we translate into action as we cherish the names and emulate the lives of their makers. We also know the spirits of many who give us little or nothing in word symbols, but by their personality animate all who meet and know them. His "philosophy of life" gives to every person an identity in the minds of his fellow men, always recognizable and persisting to the end. It puts a mark on all that he says or does.

All this brings us close to a definition of what the products of the humanities are. They consist in representations of human spirit through emotional effect, with some beauty through art. They are recognized instantly as something known before, in the personality of some in-dividual whose philosophy of life exists in his every mood, word, and action; or they fix, as if known and felt, new impressions in our memories.

As we turn to the business of the philosopher in academic life, we find him at work trying to keep the public mind familiar with the reflective thought of man's past and to nurture its increase. He can give life and vision to every other intellectual discipline and to all who work with him. Or, by scholarly introversion he may lose all his interpretative power outside a narrowed field. This inward change, which may happen to any scholar or scientist, is wrongly blamed on research. Its cause is simply undue concentration on a single personal interest. A teacher can as easily lose his sense of perspective over bridge as by search after fine distinctions in literary criticism. What caused his loss is not so significant as its effect; he no longer cares deeply about the well-being of others.

That change can happen to any person, but it should never afflict one who teaches philosophy. His subject carries an absolute imperative to arouse in each student a sense of personal responsibility for handling himself well in crucial situations. If he is to perform this manifest duty of his profession, he must put himself in the other's place. The obligation is precisely that of any other teacher, with the added anticipation on the part of the student that the master of this particular subject speaks of what he knows out of experience. This man should ask for reflection after he himself has reflected. He should, without saying it in so many words, ask that his students discover values greater than self. So they through him can arrive at reverence, the religious element in individual existence, and be changed from what they were. That change follows unassuming and real personal influence. It comes through people more easily than from books. The teacher himself is the "text" studied day after day by his listeners. If, then, he is to transmit some of the higher values of experience, he will be one who has lived sufficiently to know reverence and to rely on values greater than self: to give that understanding, he must first have it within him.

Whenever an older teacher of philosophy gives over the introductory course to a junior member of the staff, that part of the teaching out of personal possession by having lived a reflective life, lessens. It may even disappear from the course entirely. The senior teacher has then thrown away both opportunity and obligation. As for the students, they have been cheated unawares of their right to guidance by a mature spirit along their way to self-discovery. Younger members of a staff in philosophy have their own special merits. They should be able to expose skillfully the skeletal forms of philosophical history; they may have the expository ability to handle even the most abstruse of theories. They undoubtedly excel in logic, for dialectics are natural to younger minds and fascinate untrained, but eagerly disputatious, students. They have some real knowledge of existence, so that each is, in limited degree, a textbook of personal history which can be studied by listeners. But the margins are still lightly annotated. Most of the teaching done by younger men is from books, with light commentary drawn from personal experience. They still lack that source of strength that maturity brings, a belief in values that are greater than those of self. That lack implies nothing of arrogance or even self-assurance above the usual; it is only a fact of limit put on experience and on reflection by time.

It is the unique function of philosophy to develop habits of thought on issues of the greatest importance. Since reflective thinking is best developed under mature teachers, it follows that these are to guide younger minds into ethics, metaphysics, and the varieties of human experience that are symbolized in religions. These men and women can present simultaneously a vital concept and a personal example of its application in living personality. So their students gather values for use in future years, when the experiences in a college class room, suddenly recalled, supply right answers to their problems.

Every subject of academic study has its laboratory method. Some rely on demonstrations in a lecture hall, with all eyes intent on an unfolding process. Others put the student into direct contact with materials. These are the methods of natural science. The laboratories of the social sciences are in the field. Urban and rural life, politics and industry yield their varied evidence to observers and inquirers. Philosophy too works by demonstration, as the teacher unites abstract theory with examples out of a life experience. He succeeds because he himself is disciplined in hard, reflective thinking and has a compelling desire to develop that same power in others. Since what determines the way of teaching in undergraduate colleges is the personal experience of the graduate school years, so there must be a likeness of method, in dealing with advanced students, to that they will use themselves. The laboratory method of demonstration through personality, day by day, is therefore actively applied in seminars that are patterns of the group meetings with undergraduates.

I was discussing this question of likeness in undergraduate method with that of the graduate seminar, and how far the teacher of philosophy was to go beyond the particular field of his own research. My companion was a widely experienced older professor, not a person to arrive hastily at generalizations. Our talk gravitated toward the common assertion that there were better teachers a generation or more ago. That he emphatically denied, without discussion or illustration. We soon crossed off the routine explanations for the supposed decline in stimulating teaching. Among others were inordinate concern with method, dominance of the research spirit, and the rigid requirements of graduate schools for their higher degrees. A more recent explanation is that a changing attitude toward religion has dampened the spirit of teachers of philosophy and of literature.

We agreed, and quickly, that these excuses represent one common human failing—to place the blame somewhere else than at home, unless trained to face facts with an objective spirit. I then led my friend to talk about himself. Throughout a long career he had been remarkably successful with both undergraduate and graduate students. Deprecatingly he disclaimed my praise of his success. He finally gave an explanation that has positive value. He said,

For one thing, my teaching in the college keeps me aware of the realities in living experience. I don't get enough of that from books and older persons. Every teacher knows how young people quicken the spirit, especially if the subject has some relation to their personal problems. That is one reason why we teach. At least that's the main reason with me for teaching undergraduates. But there's another one, and that's what it does for my graduate courses. In the college is where I find my recruits. Every year some of the best students in that introductory course go on to become philosophy majors. They are convinced that they have started on an unending interest, even though they know they will not follow it professionally. Some, though, do go ahead and turn up in my courses in graduate school. They go on into seminars, travel about in the department until they win degrees, and are teachers for the rest of their lives. I've had those teachers send their own students back to college and graduate school— not always for philosophy, but always for some part of it.

Another professor, not in philosophy, often relates the account of his discovery of an exceptional teacher. All of his own activities were within the graduate school, but like the specialist in philosophical studies he had kept on with the basic course required of entering students. By introducing newcomers to their life in graduate school through a course in methods, he became familiar with each individual and learned something incidentally of the colleges from which they had come. One year he had two young men from the same small institution. He recalled their unusual ability the following year when two more came from the same college. They likewise proved to be excellent students. The third time in succession that he found two more equally good workers from that same college in his basic course, he began asking questions. The answer was simple and final; all six had been students under a teacher with a sense of responsibility toward those working with him. Their college professor in chemistry had made these young men eager for more learning. His method was elementary, yet inspiring. Each year he had asked two men in the graduating class to stay on in his laboratory, with the injunction that they were to do what they liked for twelve full months. They worked with him, not for him, at the pace they set for themselves. Stipends were at subsistence level, but their experience much more valuable than in all their four years of college. They then went on into graduate study, matured by their steady emulation of a sound and inspiring scientist.

These illustrations are from the two critical times in personal development, at the shift from preparatory school into college and again from college into graduate studies.

A teacher of philosophy and his student have an exceptional sense of responsibility to others. By its nature, philosophy engenders a concern for human values. No other study can so profoundly affect one's attitude toward life, and so toward all people. Nothing so distinguishes the mature, reflective thinker as his frankness and sincerity, without sign of timidity or any sense of superiority. When this person is a professional philosopher, by teaching and example he will prove why every rational being is wise in following some distance, or far, on the same road.

II

Every noteworthy philosopher must often have feelings of hostility toward his ill-favoring critics; if so, he does not show it. His profession fortifies against neglect, abuse, and misunderstanding. He is perhaps most grateful when most heavily attacked, for then he knows that his message is reaching to the inner parts of personality. There are philosophers so buried in recondite studies that only like specialists in analysis can ferret out their meanings. Such persons are not now under discussion, but only those who consider the issues of life with wide perspectives. Professionally, they have taken on themselves a lifelong obligation to make assault upon human complacencies. They may not leave their brother man alone. He it is for whom they think and speak.

The spirit underlying Christ's adjurations of the Pharisees is typical of what a true philosopher offers to his generation. He is one apart, yet close in understanding, ready to reach into the life about him when examples in action can demonstrate beliefs. It is his duty to press down on tender places in hardened consciences and to shake into self-criticism the complacent ones. And if all this seems at a moralizing level, unnatural for serious talk on an intellectual discipline, the reason is clear: philosophy, in all its parts, deals with man's strivings after excellence. It is source of all in creative and critical work that touches the individual. Every informed judgment of an artistic product or performance is, in its own kind, as sincere and uncompromising as on any ethical or moral issue. Both are from the same sources, in experiences that establish standards of belief, conduct, and action.

True teachers never fall into the error of intellectual isolationism. Least of all should this happen to professional philosophers. They are to give themselves wholeheartedly to teaching and doing, so that significant systems of reflective thinking may be known everywhere and be always related to contemporary living. They must interpret new beliefs and old ones in a language suited to general understanding. Academic work with philosophies must have that outlet into life; if not, the discipline itself cannot long exist—or the form of society that was raised up by its cumulative thought and experience. It is wrong to think that philosophy, or religion, is productive only in the fields of conduct and belief. There is some philosophy behind every open, human expression through science, social practice, or form of art. The sceptic who scans the records can easily convince himself that every creative work had its origin in some sort of reflective thought. He will see, too, that expression of self, in creative work or in discovery of new truth, depends upon inspiration and knowledge out of man's past. Anyone who examines the contributions from philosophy soon finds the names of great reflective thinkers reappearing, generation after generation, as other men restate old beliefs and add something out of their own experiences. No discipline, he must conclude, is more deeply in debt to tradition and none more nearly self-regenerating through its contacts with living parts of its own society.

Not all thinkers and doers have learned out of the philosopher's book. Some have developed their outlooks on life in spiritual solitude and have transmitted their beliefs to others almost spontaneously. A Bunyan or a Thoreau can give new color to thoughts of man, God, and nature without a systematic statement suited to embodiment in philosophical tradition. The truth was in them. They needed no interpreters, but gave their messages directly to the minds of readers.

These two demonstrated that living and thinking can make a personal philosophy that irradiates every spirit touched by it. They proved that truth of being and of becoming can be communicated by words, with precision and lasting power. Both men had unusual experiences that gave them substances for thought. Their concepts and ways of expression are products of intensive reflection. Thoreau arrived at his fine simplification in English style after wide reading. Bunyan found another kind of simplicity in diction and phrasing, having read little outside the Bible in English. The swaying, rhythmic prose of Thoreau is out of his own person, and the strong, uplifting sentences of Bunyan have something of him in all of them. The works of these men are never marred by imitation. Someone has said of Bunyan that he was the last British author to write without an eye on the literary critic. Certain it is that he wrote without fear or concern about temporal things. Like Bunyan, Thoreau looked steadily into himself, so that what he wrote is a reflection of what he saw there. For these reasons, both have kept their places as expositors of man and his world. They professed no systematic schemes of thought. Their philosophical positions were personal. Though origins of their writings are known in part, they are close themselves to being originals in fact as in form, and so meet the two elemental tests of humanistic arts.

This leads to an accepted generalization about the humanities, that all depend upon the same man-made resources. The writer is typical of all who work in the arts. He requires languages, histories, and philosophies before he can begin to lift his pen or voice. Even those whose reliance on words is for acquisition, and not for expression, cannot move into any humanistic purpose until they have help from these three elements of production. To raise an enduring building of stone without mortar and a design, would be no more difficult than to function in any other expressive art without these three forces at work in harmony. Every humanistic effect is from words, ideas, and beliefs.

One somehow comes to believe that this fundamental relationship of languages, histories, and philosophies has gone unrecognized, at least for the forming of processes to make the humanities as productive as they might be in American higher education. There is a kind of strength that comes from a sense of true interdependence—from the kind of relationship that the basic sciences have to their specializations. It would appear that much more could be made of language-learning and of historical background in all its manifestations. The humanist is busily engaged with the needs of his own primary discipline, and yet he has time to direct students into essential preparatory work for their particular kinds of future activity. He must see that they have their studies in balance.

Once this fundamental relationship of languages, histories, and philosophies is recognized and put into action, study and production in the humanities will take on better form and be of finer quality. All who teach, do research, and create through the arts will have a new sense of mutual benefit. It is true that American institutions for higher education are today making room for workers in all three of these processes. They have also a tolerance toward the world of arts outside academic operations that is advantageous to everyone. But the humanities have still to draw together their existing resources for an orderly development of the humanists for tomorrow. These are to be persons whose abilities in special subjects have not displaced their concern over liberal studies or their determination to guide younger minds into appreciation of the values in a developed humanistic spirit. "Value" with the humanists is not defined in the terms of men on the street. It is of a sort that can enlarge the range of public interests, increase mental powers of concept as well as for content, and make curiosity about meanings of life as commonly counted a reality as is the bare fact of existence in space and in time.

Philosophers can be as meticulous as linguists in their objective analyses of evidence. They can be as pedestrian as the lamest historian in cataloging his names and dates. In actual fact, none of these three disciplines is timid, slow-moving, or unimaginative. Yet it is philosophy, of the three, that most fully animates existence. For one thing, philosophies accept no conclusions as ultimate, and so teach humanity with hope. Out of that single cause comes the most probable explanation of the nature of an active philosopher. He is the most agreeable of companions, always searching for what lies beyond the thing said and always proving himself incapable of dogmatic statement. In this quality of temperament he is representative of all the humanities, having tolerance but determination and an infinite variety of interest in all that pertains to man.

III

Two close allies of philosophy are education and religion. The academic terms "philosophy of education" and "philosophy of religion" mark their close relationship. A simple question that needs answering is whether or not our academic discourses concerning their "philosophies" are helping education and religion to serve the common needs of humanity. The question needs two answers. One is from adult life, the other for childhood and adolescence.

Religious education of youth has had intent interest for so many centuries that certain patterns might be expected now to be fairly fixed in American society. But the opposite is fortunately the case; education in religion has changed through the years precisely as has every other kind of education, in methods and in design. A striking instance is in the granting of free time during school hours for religious instruction. Today many city systems provide this permissive release of children for instruction, outside of school buildings, by teachers not employed by their boards. The studies and the teachers are determined variously, as is to be expected, but, unless by indirection, staff men from colleges and universities are not in charge; only in parochial schools would one find that this responsibility rests on scholars with particular training in philosophy and religion. A new kind of specialist is being developed to meet assignments that are significant for the future of American character and for the future specifically of the discipline of philosophy.

This issue is one for American academicians to consider, at least to the point of decision on what formula can be devised for acceptance within the schools themselves. Jewish, Catholic, and Protestant families have a deep and common concern in what may be done to make the elements of philosophical idealism available to youth on a common basis. This would seem to be a matter not of Constitutional valuation by a negative prescription, but for common cause among men in higher education toward a solution. Here the personnel of divinity schools cannot make progress, in mutual discussion, as simply as could professors of psychology, religion, and philosophy from the arts faculties.

National interest in this dilemma of the school men is shown by news in the public press. Much of the talk starts from an informal attitude of mind that carries only a little into the practical phases of developing change. The custom seems to be, as in the report of the President's Commission on Higher Education,[1] to put a burden on consciences instead of on curricula, with hopes that colleges and universities will rouse to duty. That is precisely the purpose of such a report—to give direction for action, not substance on content of studies. It asks such clear hypothetical questions as, Are spiritual and democratic values synonymous? and, What are the relationships between higher education and the public mind in America? These lead, or at least point, in useful directions. But for our proof of admonition instead of guidance, as an example from this context, one sentence suffices. It reads:

If our colleges and universities are to graduate individuals who have learned to be free, they will have to concern themselves with the development of self-discipline and self-reliance, of ethical principles as a guide for conduct, of sensitivity to injustice and inequality, of insight into human motives and aspirations, of discriminations of a wide range of human values.[2]

The full application of that credo would resolve most of the problems met by graduates of colleges and by teachers and other professional men and women. One logical enlargement that could be made in thought would be to advise deep study, rather than general mention, of teachers' colleges, surely as great a common denominator of public education as all other types of institution counted together. Of these, and of one in particular, President Eisenhower spoke emphatically soon after joining the ranks of educational administration. He observed that the most important citizens are those from seven to thirteen years of age; therefore, he said, "any institution that reaches so many of that age group has my full support, and I shall keep on encouraging the work of teachers' colleges." This direct, purposeful statement of intent is a great deal more heartening and realistic than a passage in the Commission report that tells of "duties" for teachers: to point out the holy quality in heroism, love, fortitude, endurance, and to make life reverent.

It is easy to stray into discursive commentary on religion and its place in an educational experience. Not long since an American scholar and cleric, Anson Phelps Stokes, published three volumes with the title, *Church and State in the United States, 1787–1947.*[3] In print three years after the end of that period, it leads through an amazing variety of instances to show how action has violated and changed the Constitutional provision for legal separation. The record is good in respect to useful change, and the conclusion encouraging. Certainly this country never again will have its private colleges identified generally by their sectarianism or display the intolerances of fifty years ago toward the objective teaching of religion in schools, colleges, and state universities. Today over five hundred nondenominational colleges have general courses in religion, and a far greater number maintain partial equivalents under philosophy. Several universities maintain schools of theology unsurpassed by the foundations of any church. Future social and intellectual leaders, whose services will be given in every community, are coming out of these training centers and from the genuinely liberal colleges that make religion a humane study.

Having said all this, one returns to a fact of separation as definite as the legally established one under the American Constitution designed to keep church and state in independent freedom. That formal separation is durable and right, but its very existence places a special obligation on those who train and appoint teachers. The student is to learn from examples, in living people, what is the nature of the good. Two avenues, always open, are by personal contact with the teachers in public schools themselves and by practices in teaching that will make graduate and undergraduate education a fit preparation for work with American youth.

A personal incident will illustrate how advantage is to be taken of opportunities in a public school for teaching ethics under the name of literature. Fifty years ago a midwestern town of thirteen thousand citizens had four hundred young people in its four-year high school. Along with other cultural benefits from informal work in art and music, there were excellent courses in English and in foreign languages—four years each of English and Latin, two of German and French, and one or two of Greek. The school successfully maintained both classical and vocational programs, and so served the two familiar needs of an American community without bickering over the "essentials" and their presumed opposites.

So much is useful background for an example to show how philosophy, if not given its formidable name, can reach youthful minds and spirits, and do so without benefit of clergy or any consequences disfavored by legal restraints under American democracy. The principal of the high school was an "educator," in the language of university men fifty years ago; he also was a philosopher in ways that they commonly were not. He taught, or better, reflected on Emerson. This he did daily for a year in the company of nearly all in the senior class; there were seventy-eight marked "present" every morning in 1901. They made a critical study of "The American Scholar" and had discursive discussions of "Self-Reliance" and "Compensation." An illustrated talk on Emerson's life was the one visual aid, and that unneeded though enlivening. Sentence after sentence, Emerson's essays were read aloud, to be brought down into consciousness by slow exposition and then into permanent possession by discussion. Any one of the learners probably would have been amused if asked how many pages were assigned and read during the year: he would not have known, because the teaching was not done in that way, nor by prescribed paper work with firmly criticized answers to questions in examination, nor by reports on supplementary reading. None, perhaps, learned literally anything of religious creeds or philosophical systems: none, surely, ever lost the meanings of that experience.

Some teaching of literature in secondary schools arrives at such personal benefits; yet sampling of works in prose and poetry cannot create so deep an impression by ideas as can a continuing discussion of the values revealed in the writings of a single author.

Also, there is sometimes a lack of inclination or ability in the teacher to go beyond the conventional patterns of instruction. College requirements for admission and the ease of following routines by pages and by weeks perfunctorily, are hindrances working against the student. The prized exceptions are wherever secondary school teachers, in private and in public institutions, arouse American youth to think and to believe in ethical-philosophical values. The students who pass through the classes of such men and women understand that individual growth is out of matured reflection and experience quite as much as out of books.

The example of influence from Emerson in preparatory school calls to mind another that shows his value for the mature scholar. Thirty years later, several university men were en route by train to a week-end conference. One of them was to open the discussion, which was to be on regional characteristics of the northern Great Plains. The aims of that meeting were to derive ideas for formal education and particularly to encourage interpretative work for print, broadcast, and film. Writers from Canada and the Mississippi Valley were to participate. The first speaker was one of those composite personalities disguised as an anthropologist. Before his breakfast in the dining car, he was found intently reading, as he said, "what I like best to read before informal public addresses," something from Emerson's *Essays*. When and where Redfield got the incentive that created that habit, no one inquired. The fact itself was so important, and reasonable, that every one of us accepted it as a sign of wisdom. How we might possibly make habitual among students such reliance on great minds, no one considered at the time. Yet every one of us knew the cause, as of a similar habit of Tom Peete Cross, who once confided that before sitting down to write he was wont to read his favorite passages from Sir Thomas Browne. Both men were in search of such effects as the seventeenth-century philosopher, physician, and stylist denoted in that sentence, "I love to lose myself in a mystery, to pursue my Reason to an *O Altitudo!*"

The habit of free reading in such authors follows a conditioning of some sort, most commonly by the influence of people and of books read during the years of secondary education. If one were to devise a plan for developing this habit, he would incline toward progressive reading from Emerson, Whitman, Royce, James, and Whitehead. These and other writers counted as favored idealists will meet the needs of youth, particularly if experienced teachers are in their company as guides. This is not new counsel for the improvement of education in secondary schools. The difficulty has been, and is, to have it taken seriously. Such advice toward enlarging the uses of philosophy—by whatever name—is almost a commonplace, and like many other commonplaces honored more by neglect than by observance.

Yet it is well to listen again to an excellent spokesman for ethical and religious education of youth. A recent survey of the place of philosophy in American life has in it all that need be said on the subject. Among others to contribute to *Philosophy in American Education: Its Tasks and Opportunities*,[4] was E. C. Lindeman. His professional experiences amply qualified him to speak and to write, as in this instance, on the need in American schools for something new. He wrote:

The way to learn philosophy is to put it to work in the realm of action. "I cannot praise a fugitive and cloistered virtue," wrote Milton, a virtue "which never sallies forth and seeks its adversary, but shrinks out of the race where that immortal garland is to be run for, not without dust and heat."

My first proposal is that philosophic instruction should be introduced at an early age, certainly in secondary education. I doubt whether individuals ever think as clearly or as logically as they do in early adolescence. Nor do I believe that individuals ever again raise more important questions about life and its meaning than they do at this age. I do not mean to imply that formal instruction in philosophy should be introduced at this period. On the contrary, I merely ask that teachers be so prepared as to be able to discuss, with students, the philosophic phases of all issues which rise to importance in the minds of youth. Certainly, the basic principles of logic, ethics and esthetics will have direct application to the entire secondary school curriculum.

My second proposal leaps beyond the classroom completely. Unless we find some way of teaching adults, there is no likelihood that our society can be kept steadily progressive. It is adults, not children or youth, who manage our world. I said above that the true philosophic age is youth, but I should add that in old age there may be a return to a more disinterested form of reflection. The irony of this situation is that these are the periods of minimum function and control. During the middle period when life is at its highest energy peak, when our decisions affect life and society directly, then philosophy is at its lowest ebb. It is at this stage of life when one so frequently hears the successful ones say: "Yes, it's theoretically sound but not practical." Or, "That's a beautiful ideal but I live in the world of reality." In short, this is the age of compromise and lowered sense of value. How to keep philosophy at work in the lives of persons between the ages of twenty-five and fifty, that is the important task. . . .

What American philosophy must say to this generation and with unequivocal clarity is that *action without direction leads to catastrophe.* The American people are confused. They scarcely dare think about the future. How do they resolve their confusion? By more activity, or by listening to their favorite radio commentator, or reading their chosen news columnist; in short, by becoming more dependent. What they want is a sense of direction and this they cannot achieve unless they know how to choose among assorted values. Nobody can do this for them, not in a democracy. But philosophers can teach them how it is done. Philosophy is the liberating discipline. Unless we are free in our minds, how can any other form of freedom have meaning?[5]

In Lindeman's phrase, the "true philosophical age" is youth. Then is the time of first introspective asking about self. The answers that should be supplied young minds that may not know how to phrase the questions formally, are identical with those to be given later on for philosophy and for religion. But at that age, neither word, "philosophy" or "religion," can be brought down to common terms of childhood. These are then strange, adult words. Young people are as inept in defining them, usually, as in discussing ethics, logic, or aesthetics. Yet all five words have bearing on what youth is considering constantly—the satisfactions and the inner meanings of existence. Education has baffled youth. It has given too few answers on values that are sought after, but unrevealed, during this period of philosophical awakening to life. There must be a point of beginning and a way for learning the unknown. The essentials for growth appear when time and impulse are in conjunction. That point and the way will be found by teachers who have awareness and freedom from artificial restraints. Psychology and philosophy ought again to be brought into relationship, as before they separated under research descriptions. The related forces of human understanding should surround them. Then the present wonder why philosophy comes to men late and religion often not at all in its personal values, will disappear.

IV

So far I have been discussing philosophy in a personal way. Professional philosophers will bear a little longer with such observations as these on the place of philosophy in the scheme of the humanities. I shall return to what in my limited learning appears as the contemporary formation of philosophical studies in the United States. But first I wish to deal with the methods for enlarging the scope of belief in reflective thinking. Next, I shall present an interlude depicting the true scholar whose detachment is for the ultimate good of all men. That is as preface to a contrasting statement on the tyranny of ignorance, showing our need above all else for enlightenment from philosophical minds and hearts. These three passages, of which the present is one, are intended to show our present academic need, the inspiration to be found in recognizing the nobility of true scholarship, and the tyranny of ignorance over the public mind. Finally, I have recorded what are, in my reading, the marked ideas on what philosophy is doing in our time. We begin, as always, with the teacher.

By placing the processes of philosophy near the center of all work with the humanities in college and university, one runs the risk of being thought a moralizer or reformer. That error cannot occur, if only because any who know college youth realize how little chance either would have for success among them. Talk of character development is an artificial and self-conscious act: so is the fear of using the terminology of philosophy or religion in discussions of the arts. That cannot be avoided, nor should it be, when exposition or self-expression is of human personality. No, the sole purpose in heightening the influences of philosophy is to initiate the learner into the world of the humanities under fullest favor.

The point may be labored that philosophy is the best possible guide for young people at their entry into college. Under fine or even indifferent teaching, the subject brings the learner to identify himself with values to be won through study. The effect of early emphasis upon values reaches to the instructors in other subjects, all of whom are prone to judge new students in terms of things known. The college teacher is disposed to estimate them in percentages, rather than as personalities. It is far more fruitful to make a cautious study of himself, in order to bring some aura of enthusiasm and of individuality to whatever he hopes to accomplish.

The teaching of literature or of history gives a college instructor the chance to capitalize on the familiarity with the materials that he finds in students lately out of preparatory school. He, as teacher, should be pleased, rather than disturbed, to learn that these young people have "had a course" in his subject matter before their first experience under his guidance. Then is when he proves himself to be a mechanistic operator or a philosophical interpreter in the arts. The immediate effect upon himself, and upon his classes, is what he instinctively feels. Let him recall how he became interested in sounds and meanings of words, or where and when he unexpectedly found fresh meanings in a piece of literature. That should be enough to bring back something from his own childhood that is in every aspect of the humanities—the power of association and the artistic effects of repetition. He will discover that he has not changed. He still appreciates repetition of sound and of imagery. At length, in this self-examination the teacher may find why religion and the surrounding forms of philosophy must mean very much to young minds, once their suggestions are understood. No one, it must by then be clear, enters at all into the world of the arts until he loves symbols and myths, until power of suggestion is to him more satisfying than that flat clarity of fact as fact.

All experience proves that nothing finally is more pleasing than recognition, under new circumstances, of something already known and liked. Everyone remembers this to have been true in his childhood, when stories repeated *ad infinitum* constantly increased in delight-giving properties. This is equally true of music among adults. Literature is much less understood in this fashion by older people, outside the circles of attentive readers, and for a deplorable reason; all habits of re-reading, reading aloud, and memorizing have been broken down by present-day customs. If poetry is read aloud, it quickly wins that echo quality of music, always recurring in silent memory. Thus the obvious deduction for the instructor in literature is that he can give greatly enlarged values to familiar texts of days in preparatory school. That background of experience will help, instead of hindering.

All such talk on philosophy and religion, as related to other work in the humanities, and on the uses of association for enjoyment of literature, has its proof in example. The reader can find his own, but a familiar one brings all three into conjunction and so gives conclusion to general observations. Though "a lernèd man, a clerk," Chaucer's "poure persoun" of a town was not hampered by his learning. He established fine human relationships with all sorts of people. The characterization given him by Chaucer is also that of a true teacher:

> This noble ensample to his sheepe he yaf
> That first he wroghte and afterward he taughte.
> Out of the gospel he the wordés caughte
> And this figure he added eek thereto,
> That if gold rusté what shall iren doo?

This passage seems to belong precisely here as a summation.

The conflict of religion and science is no longer alive, as was true twenty to fifty years ago according to the level of local enlightenment. The Scopes trial of 1925 was a belated phenomenon, proving only that higher education had yet much to do in a dimly dark world. The processes of change must be slow because inborn, not borrowed. It has been said that philosophy has a missionary duty to perform, as alternate for traditional religions, in the upholding of "standard" beliefs. That would be disastrous, to philosophy and to all that it touched as antagonist. Philosophers are like scientists, in being constrained from turning objective disciplines into purposeful programs. The sciences and the humanities develop the truths of fact and of belief. The word "applied" contradicts the spirit of both, as they exist in universities. Science is not there to bring profit directly to industries, and philosophy is not there to distribute partisan aid to favored beliefs.

The great truth to hold is that philosophers individually can maintain—as may all other scholars and scientists—their widely divergent positions. Every one of them must be secretly possessed by an ideal of his own: else he is nothing. But that passionate attachment does not change his tolerance. Out of the variants rise man's most creative strains of ideas and concepts; these are essential to the life of the humanities. As a discipline, to enlarge the boundaries of learning and to diminish error, philosophy has this other mission—to present all views with penetrating accuracy. Dispassionate exposition gives sure protection for the individual against either religious or political domination and prepares the way for new and stronger faiths. The searching scholar remains his own man.

That natural characteristic of the philosopher to follow his thought wherever it leads has produced in this country men of originality and wide influence. A change in the administration of many church colleges within the past half century enlarged that individual freedom. By lessening formal allegiances to their Protestant denominations they brought their faculties within the requirements of certain national pension systems and ostensibly at least broadened their outlook in studies of religion. Though many of the private colleges maintained their strong religious spirit, they no longer dealt with religion apart from philosophy as a subject of instruction. In form and in effect they met the legal requirement of benevolent foundations financing such plans, that as public servants they remain free from action in religious or political matters. The purpose of that provision is to liberalize education for the benefit of all citizens, and incidentally and happily, for that of the teacher. In consequence the American college became more genuinely liberal in religious education and in its teaching of philosophy. The results appear in the attitude of faculty and students. They have widened perceptions, more varied patterns of thought, and a tolerant curiosity toward novelty of belief—and all to a single purpose, that the learner may come to think, to believe, and to act for himself.

It is proper to ask whether or not departments of philosophy have realized fully on this opportunity. They show no great increase in concern over the meaning for our time of current political, social, and ethical theories; by comparison with the concentration of interest in other aspects of philosophy, those touching on moral philosophy have had slight attention generally. Yet the outstanding examples of work in that particular province, under this or other names, attract increasing notice. There is at least no tendency to ask for silence on unfriendly and destructive ideologies, as though ignorance were protective in matters of the mind but not of the body. The conclusion must be taken that philosophy in higher education today has freedom of action but less than full exercise of its opportunities in the opened areas of ethics, morals, and religion.

The place of philosophy in undergraduate education and the kind of teaching needed in an arts program are matters of longstanding discussion. Ten years ago a committee of the American Council on Education debated with little disagreement what were the obstacles to satisfactory development of work in the field. They were marked down as traditional practice in graduate school along the lines of personal interest, and concern with theory rather than with personality. One view offered as a premise for action was that the colleges should declare their desires and set out to realize them. It was proposed that philosophy departments in the colleges should designate annually at least one graduating student for distinction in the subject and urge that he go on to advanced studies at a university of their choosing. There he would follow a program designed by the staff in his own college, regardless of any requirements for a graduate degree at the moment but with intent to stress those aspects of philosophy most within the concerns of undergraduate students. These persons then would return to their own colleges as teachers. In the one year to follow, they would be advised and guided in their reading and elementary teaching by their former professors while achieving at least a minor distinction from actual status in the faculty. Two valuable results were to be anticipated; incentive toward teaching as a career would come at precisely the time of greatest good to the individual, and at the end of two years he would know how to prepare adequately for an established post in some other college.

Indirectly, as choices of place for graduate training brought to light those universities ready and willing to give advanced training for their degrees under partial guidance from college departments, useful changes would come in graduate instruction. Gains for the colleges would be almost immediate. As these developing scholars brought new ideas back into their departments of philosophy, the incentives given older staff members would lead to similar desires among undergraduate students. They would become more conversant with new ideas in the field. The young teachers would be drawn toward mature ways of instruction, and the older staff would inevitably be given clearer insights into the minds of all youth coming under their care.

This might be a fruitful means to improvement of undergraduate studies in philosophy, if diligently followed by a number of colleges. As with all else in education, the process is less than the persons involved in it. Much has come about to change the teaching of philosophy and to enlarge interest in its values since these discussions ten years ago. Groups have been organized increasingly by labor unions, rural organizations, and by churches, in which philosophy is brought to adult learners. The studies of "great books" and of our national "heritage" are consistently in philosophical terms with a definite religious direction. The impetus toward such interests among adults derives in part from action taken at the close of the Second World War, when temporary universities were created to match in time of existence the months of demobilization; the students so gathered in did not thereafter demobilize their interests, but went on into college under further government aids. These men, matured, are now making progress in their mental as well as physical means to living, and planning for adult education is responsive to their demands for guidance.

To turn back to conditions in the colleges, where philosophy must live and grow if it is to be related to all formal and informal uses, one finds most encouraging evidences of change. One is in the placing of philosophy as the controlling center of survey studies covering the first two years. Another is in the return to diversity in matter, so that logic, ethics, and metaphysics are presented with less allegiance to the routines of strictly historical procedures in dealing with the various schools of thought over long expanses of time, and with less seeking after novelties in learned expositions of modern schools of philosophy. Most realistic and creative are the seminars that deal honestly and directly with ideologies and dicta of contemporary times.

Also, there is much benefit to philosophy in American colleges from the recent changes in texts and from new works giving historical and interpretative aids to learners. The temporary universities of the recent demobilization period started a trend in all college instruction, by the form given to teaching of philosophy in these centers abroad. The texts to appear since 1946 apparently have been affected by the one devised for those Army centers, under the title *Preface to Philosophy: Textbook*.[6] Reprintings in the past five years are to satisfy a constant demand for philosophical treatment under the terms satisfying to veterans newly freed from military duties. Another work, of different kind, is Schneider's *History of American Philosophy*,[7] appearing in the same year and noted as the first work to make possible an orderly account of changes and increase in philosophical discourse throughout the life of this country. A third valid source of new realism in academic practice is the series of volumes edited by Schilpp, under the general title of "The Library of Living Philosophers," during the period since 1939.[8] These three references may be taken as instances of what can be found in the reviews and bibliographies covering teaching materials of the past ten years, a decade in which philosophy has enlarged its zone of influence and increased its impact upon American life by a simplified manner of expository approach.

Teaching as well as texts obviously must be scanned in order to assess the changing order. Yet as this is beyond even the practitioners, in any national sense, one is brought to informal and yet informed critics of the place of philosophy in American life generally. One observation in the first pages of the *Preface to Philosophy* points to the critical importance of ethical issues that have risen out of the present crisis in civilization. To make this a matter of note so prominently is to create responses in public opinion. What is talked about, creates still more talk, and in many new circles economically, intellectually, and socially different from those of the past. Thus, the news and magazine press of today carry many columns of comment on the need of our times for finer ideals. This extends into literary criticism, with deprecation of tendencies that have remained in fiction over a decade or more to play up the sordid as a way to easy sales. Today, happily, a critical assessment of book production and of reading habits shows a steady change toward more natural and significant portrayals of humanity.

As an instance of response to the call in 1946 for stress on ethical issues, by reason of the present crisis in civilization, a foreign critic five years later offered a dispassionate survey of contemporary conditions. The 1951 "Survey of Cultural Trends of the Year,"[9] by Isaiah Berlin, singled out the rise of interest in religion in this nation, as evidenced by the success of many new American publications having large numbers of readers. His supplementary comments on the vogues in history, poetry, and criticism prove again this current serious and hopeful outlook. Of philosophy and theology, his commentary deals with writers abroad as well as here in less hopeful tone, for he charges against certain rising concepts a "relative exclusion of older liberal and humanistic writing." Some response to this estimate is to be found in facts concerning new scholarly journals, of which more will be said later on. It is evident enough that Berlin was rightly impressed with the rise in continental Europe of a philosophic mood suited to the vagueness and hopelessness of people generally with regard to the future until some political stability appeared to be certain. It is not his claim that American thinkers are responsible for this tendency.

The need in colleges for counteracting force against aimless or evil tendencies in discussion groups, is heightened in this decade by the rise in curiosity regarding communism, and by a resultant increase in adventurous speculation without guidance or experience in judging values. This is comparable to the lesser furore among undergraduates back in the twenties over the milder excitement aroused by the writings of Mencken, a kind of seer to the undergraduate as much by his boldness as through substance of his comments. Then, as today, the faculties in American universities had their opportunity—to deal directly through a theme of student interest, not to ignore it, and to reclaim students from the clubs and corner talk-fests leading aimlessly to doubts even of the wisdom of the changing speculations of the participants.

The conclusion, on philosophies to be formally treated in college education, lies in the simple fact of a great increase in student interest. Enlistments in idealistic causes are matched by enrollments in classes. There cannot be satisfaction of these claims from youth on the attention of teachers in every field of learning and science, without a comprehending plan for philosophies in higher education. Part of this fresh planning is due in the graduate schools, and a part must come out of understanding the public mind more fully, in order that the teacher and his followers can consider other aims than the confined ones of institutional thought and living.

Two quotations from a recent survey, through conferences, are pertinent to the issue of planned development of ideals and ideas in American life, as a task of the American undergraduate colleges through departments of philosophy. If the task is not assumed there, or at least defined, it will be taken over by less considerate, less objectively altruistic minds. The two comments, to be found in a work entitled *Creating an Industrial Civilization*, relate philosophy and religion to the necessities of men in two utterly different cultural environments. The first, from India, expresses an abiding sense of well-being spiritually, through contemplation; the second, from this country, shows what are the prospects in an industrial civilization, such as that of the United States, for a rediscovery of moral and religious faith.

Miss Rama Rau, the Indian delegate, stated the universality of philosophy in the culture of her country, saying,

In Asia, and in my country in particular, the philosopher—and by that I do not mean the man who studies various other systems of philosophy; I mean the man who quite simply sits in his chair and thinks—is a respected man and a necessary member of society. It is considered a perfectly good, sensible occupation for any human being. It is considered more than that. It is considered a rather necessary part of anybody's activity, regardless of what else he does. And I think that concern with and respect for philosophy is something rather serious that is lost in the West.[10]

The counterpart, from an American, Robert L. Calhoun, is self-critical and uneasy, ending in the familiar mood of asking that "something be done about this." It is no less valid than the other as a point of departure for thinking on what formal work with philosophies must do toward a better and surer future. The longer passage, here quoted, seems to be justified by its texture of hope mixed with doubt. It reads,

There is need, lastly, for rediscovery of a basis for the most ultimate sorts of moral and religious faith. One requisite for such rediscovery is refusal to be stampeded by the familiar fact that during the past century and a half the hold of traditional religious forms upon men of the West has greatly diminished. There is need to remember that throughout the history of Judaism and Christianity in the West there has been recurrent ebb and flow of religious conviction and moral devotion. There is need to recognize the familiar character of this repeated rhythm and to reject, on the one hand, the paralysis of despair and, on the other hand, the appallingly destructive alternative of idolatry. Idolatry is a word that seems peculiarly out of place in the modern world, but its primary meaning is relevant now if it ever was. When men turn away from a God worthy of their worship, it is likely to be not long before they transfer their unanchored cravings to gods unworthy of their worship—to deified emperors, political systems, races, or economic class organizations.

To aid in maintaining the stability and balance of outlook that is urgently needed, it is necessary that we seek more adequate appreciation of the real character and implications of the sciences and technology, that we get them into a suitable perspective in which their benefits may be frankly and gratefully accepted and their aberrations may be as resolutely put aside. But there is need that we seek more adequate understanding and practice of the moral and religious convictions that actually exist and their closer integration into everyday living. The quest of security through the discovery or establishment of some new religion or new morality is likely to be disappointing. Religions, like languages, grow in their own way. They cannot be constructed to order. But the religions deep-rooted in the life of the West need and deserve to be understood as most men do not now understand them. Their rediscovery and reinterpretation is an urgent task for churches, schools, and all men of intelligence and goodwill.

Needless to say, this is not meant as a defense of uncritical conformity. New knowledge, new insights, new demands call for continual rethinking of both moral and religious convictions. There is every reason to explore unbeaten paths and to attempt fresh formulations of what seems to oneself in one's own situation true and basic for life. At the same time, what each of us can know and actively believe now is largely determined by the heritage in which we have grown and which lives more or less consciously in us. To rediscover and reclaim it, and to make its resources more fully understood and accessible for hard-pressed people is a major part of our job.[11]

This is a long quotation, justified by its signs of good intent and of self-examination. It would seem, however, to be directed to adults and in a spirit of reclamation, of regeneration, rather than of giving to youth a new heritage out of our own life and times; if we begin where we are, the way back to old values will be opened to younger minds. The professional teacher knows this to be true. He practices what he knows. His subject may not be philosophy, but his approach is that of philosophy as he guides other minds from their own present toward the sources of human thought and belief.

V

History has its examples of the benefits of philosophy when it works beyond academic environment. Grotius and Milton were two who talked to the people. Though neither was an academician, in modern terms of definition, they had their allegiances to particular groups in their contemporary societies and to types of intellectualism that separated some individuals from persons in other social groups. Yet both broke through into the life of their time. They carried their messages of spiritual and political survival to the minds of the people.

Philosophy has this power to demonstrate what scholarship must mean to a nation that sustains it, and to the times surrounding those who profess it. The immediate and the remote ends of all scholarship are here involved and must be accepted as real by scholars themselves. Partisanship of Milton and Grotius for important ideas demonstrated to contemporaries what the mind of the scholar can mean to his nation, and so to the world. Men then were led to esteem learning for its true worth; they could not think of it as a devised ornament to enhance personal dignity. It was made clear that scholars are the mediators who bring the lessons of man from his past into his present. To the scholars, it was made equally clear that they were due to maintain high standards of public service.

The role in life of the "pure scholar" was stated most articulately for our century by Eduard Schwartz. He did this in the following sentences, set down to be read at his own funeral as his profession of faith:

In the prime of life I addressed these words to a learned gathering, "The world cannot endure without compromises, but scholarship [Wissenschaft] goes to ruin if it does not work out problems sharply and if it consents to bargain away somewhat of their antitheses. Scholarship does not, like the preacher, bring peace, nor does it unfetter hearts, as the poets do; but the few who take upon themselves the yoke of enquiry are concerned that life and movement may remain in the spirit of humanity, and that the endless striving and endless yearning after knowledge may not fall asleep. That is not everything, but yet it is so much that those few must not complain if they give for it a life full of doubt and restlessness, full of abnegation and loneliness." I used the same words in writing to the Theological Faculty of Strassburg when they gave me an honorary doctorate in 1917 on the occasion of their Luther celebration. Now too, at the close of my life, I take back nothing of them, but only add, My soul belongs to Almighty God; His will be done.

All who have heard or read this translation by Arthur D. Nock, used in his address before the Harvard Divinity School in 1949, remember it as a kind of testament of all scholars, more durable than stone and more animate than any words untouched with the light of scholarly insights. I had so full an impression on hearing him repeat them years ago, at a Princeton conference, that they became the summation of an exceptional meeting. They are proof of greatness in translation, so much so that the sentences were fixed in memory at first hearing.

In this address, Nock stated the case for religious teaching and study in a passage that concluded with the sentence: "The serious study of religion is a part of humanistic study in general, and for its well-being needs to be conducted in a community where history, language, and philosophy receive the full service of scholars who have integrity, competence, and zeal." This is the description of scholarship that gives practical requirements for its successful outcomes, as necessary as were the motives guiding the life of Eduard Schwartz. Religion would not be subject to intensive, comparative inquiry without these three helps of history, language, and philosophy. It is as dependent as are all parts of the humanities upon the "integrity, competence, and zeal" of scholars giving full service in a community of scholars.

Those who accept their religion, as their politics, by inheritance, are not aware that it is something else than theology. For these persons, the philosophers have a revelation; to realize that the theme of religion is greater than the theologies partly expressive of its spirit, is to know what is one important mission of philosophy.

The Schwartz translation is in itself a revealing example of what the humanist experiences before he expresses; his words are symbols of himself and of all that he has read and thought. To bring out the very nature of this difference of one humanistically matured from one who is not, I gave the Schwartz original to an able student of German, and asked for his version. These are his words, as he chose and arranged them:

The world cannot exist without some degree of levelling off, but science perishes unless it clearly dissects all its problems without obscuring any of the sharp contrasts. Science does not bring the peace of the preacher, nor does it like the poet relax the human heart, but those who take upon themselves the task of scientific observation must see to it that the human spirit remains alive and active and that the desire for endless striving and the longing for knowledge does not succumb. This is not everything, but it is at least enough to forestall complaints on the part of those who in pursuing the quest of science lead a life full of doubt, anxiety, renunciation and loneliness.

The original text, to match this second translation of the first three sentences, reads thus:

Die Welt kann nicht stehen ohne Ausgleichungen; aber die Wissenschaft vergeht, wenn sie die Probleme nicht scharf herausarbeitet und von ihren Antithesen sich etwas abdingen lässt. Sie bringt nicht den Frieden der Prediger und löst die Herzen nicht wie die Poeten, aber die wenigen, die das Joch des θεωρετν auf sich nehmen, sorgen dafür, dass Leben und

Bewegung bleibt im Geiste der Menschheit und das unendliche Streben und die unendliche Sehnsucht nach Erkenntnis nicht einschläft. Das ist nicht alles, aber es ist immerhin so viel, dass jene wenigen nicht klagen dürfen, wenn sie ein Leben voll Zweifel und Unrast, voll Entsagung und Einsamkeit dafür einsetzen.[12]

Each passage is a biography and, rightly read, each reading is a biographical note on the person who has these three passages brought to him for the first time simultaneously. A long and interesting history lies back of every response to words, sentences, and total effects of passages—by readers as by writers. Translators and readers must bring understanding in order to find it.

VI

A general application of this evidence is useful. It bears upon the uses of philosophy, and on the ways in which people look at life about them. Unless they are steadied by an inner strength, their perspectives are distorted. Most obvious is the influence of propaganda, then perhaps trade advertising, and so on through the disorderly appeals of American print to all who have not learned to select.

We commonly think of propaganda as something coming from without, and as being cunningly devised to be a determining influence over our personal actions and decisions. It is more than that. It can also be administered by concealment, as in a denatured translation or by incomplete transmission of what has been said or written. There is an old saying, credited to the French, to the effect that nothing else matters much except having the reporter of a conference favorable to one's interests in matters under discussion. A wiser and truer description of the idea held in that cryptic observation is in the brilliant, convincing article by Elmer Davis, "News and the Whole Truth," printed in August, 1952.[13] He teaches as much about the variants in propaganda, by words packed into seven pages of a magazine, as humanly is possible, and for two reasons: he has depth of experience in manner of writing, and he has that naked projection of an idea that comes by using your mind hard over a very long time.

But what does this mean to philosophy, to scholarship generally, and lastly to the American scene with its backdrop of higher education? The short and useless answer is, "Everything." The long and productive one is made as well by the reader himself, out of reflection on a few common ways to develop opinions (one's own, not "public opinion" this time) into convictions, faith, belief, judgment, taste, creative work on paper or with any other medium. In brief, every person has his own answer to all the issues of life through the humanities of higher education, or otherwise, within his own personal philosophy. Now, he may not like the answers he gets there. He may be led to ask elsewhere for parts of the wanted answer. He may find that he cannot rise above the level of his personal philosophy until some cause gives considerable urging from within. He will not, for example, succeed if he does not instantly see the point in an observation by Davis, to the effect that a particular United States senator wrestled with his conscience—and won. But our hypothetical seeker will discover at least what are the existing boundaries of his own philosophy, in case he exposes it to a private inquiry.

The point to be remembered by all is that enlargement of a personal philosophy had best be begun at those times of ready adaptation and of quick learning. The latest of such periods for many comes during the years of college education. The earlier ones, during the years of school and family experience up to years of adolescence, may have been used inadequately, and those of adult life may turn out to be quietly ignored. A full use of all such opportunities would be excellent for the individual, for the family and environment that will know him best, and for all parts of this total world that he is able to reach with hand, heart, and mind. He then will be acting the part of the philosopher unawares.

There can be a tyranny of ignorance as well as of learning. Either sort may be from within or from without, imposed by self or by some external force. At the end, either inner or outward compulsion of ignorance can reduce life to a state of helplessness. That finality of failure will never come to people in a democracy of living and learning, provided only that adults are kept free and youths have before them demonstrations of high standards in thought and action. Those results come in a society that speaks its mind and reads in order to think.

A sidewalk news dealer faced the homeward rush at a New York ferry, with the fingers of one hand spread into the half-folded papers that were held in the hand of that extended arm. His eyes were on the crowd as, without a break, his voice incessantly intoned the question, "Whadda ya read? Whadda ya read?" At a signal or word, instantly out came the right paper, slapped into a double fold and held out as the coin fell into his cupped hand beneath it. This operation was repeated time after time until the push ended. One wondered how much the news dealer or his customers reflected on the implications of that question.

A business man in the Middle West, discussing with another the news of the day, was aroused to affirm that their self-styled "World's Greatest Newspaper" was for him the best in the United States. One must wonder what he had read and what would be his comment on one sentence in the article by Elmer Davis that was noted earlier. The sentence, without its context, reads, "There are no more honest newspapers in the country than the New York *Times* and *Herald Tribune* and the Washington *Post*; perhaps no better newspapers either."[14] Here the contrast is between a well-meaning but limited opinion and the thought of an expert mind, between confident error and liberal wisdom.

Not caution, but practical wisdom is in the observation that the presentation of a difficult truth to another person is best made in the form of a question. That avoids, at least temporarily, a forcing of an issue. It also calls upon the reader or listener to think. This, therefore, would appear to be good counsel, and for these two reasons. Others may be in the proof of open-mindedness in the questioner, in his sign of tolerance, and in an evident readiness to wait for agreement. There is no doubt that the question, "What do you think?" is better in strategy than the single imperative word posted on the walls of some business offices. It would seem that the person who conceived the notion to use this obtrusive verb as a prod, was lacking in psychological sense, and that his imitators are no better than he. A much larger doubt, deeper down, is of the personal philosophy that controls the individual who uses this categorical imperative on himself and on others day after day in a lifetime of action.

One known path to better levels in judgment than appear in these examples, is through higher education. It would be folly to suppose there is no other way. The minds of some who never have thought of formal studies beyond years of childhood prove that to be in error. These persons arrived at habits of reflection without many books or many teachers as their guides. The fact to remember is simply that the processes of higher education create the habit of inquiry. The spirit of inquiry, given by habit, leads to the habit of reflection. They work together. Both are learned out of philosophies, formally taught. They are then most easily developed, simultaneously, for a lifetime of use. It is because philosophies are summations of humanistic values that they prepare the way toward those limitless varieties of human experience which the humanities keep, give out, and create in the formal arts and in individual lives.

VII

Surveys of specialists give a record of changes in American philosophical studies during the past half century. Though a layman can follow these discourses only at a distance, he reads them with an increasing confidence in the future effectiveness of the American scholar within this important field.

Two landmarks were set up in reviews of the first twenty-five years of the American Philosophical Association. It was in 1925 that H. N. Gardiner made the retrospective survey for his colleagues. In the same session, Wilbur M. Urban, as president, made personal observations on successive gains in concepts and aims.[15] Twenty-five years later, in preparation for the 1951 meeting, three other members produced studies in review of progress under the topics "Speculative Philosophy," "Two Dogmas of Empiricism," and "Moral Philosophy at Mid-Century."[16] The third of these papers had the conclusion that in 1950 "more able philosophers were working in ethics, at least part of the time, than ever before in history." Other commentaries over the years have stressed the ever increasing stream of American books and articles in journals, the rise and disappearance of certain transitory ideas, the effects from the theory of evolutionary change, the merits of pragmatism, and the return of many to metaphysics paralleling the intense objectivity of the few in the study of symbols. The second quarter of the century has brought noteworthy discussions, such as that of James Collins,[17] of theories that have American hallmarks and also able criticism of older systems of philosophical discourse.

A new recurrent recognition of individual contributions has come through the formal election, by his fellows, of the member who is to deliver the Carus lectures, each series being devoted to the values of a particular school of philosophy. Another sign of cooperative action is the appearance, by 1950, of several works that were planned and written by specialists to achieve particular purposes. Such is the 1930 work by Adams and Montague as editors,[18] giving a clear summation of contemporary American philosophy. A closer index to trends in research and in speculative thinking is in the papers read before separate sections of the Association and as the annual presidential addresses. Books by individuals have appeared that provide teaching materials of the first order. Near the end of this fifty-year period a series was started which joins individual and group commentary in a symposium on the work of a living philosopher. Each volume, dealing with a representative figure, has contributions from persons on separate aspects of his work, and every volume has a critique of the critics made in its concluding pages by the philosopher under review. The plan of the editor for the series, Paul Arthur Schilpp, achieves its purposes—to deal with ideas exhaustively by participation of their originator in a formal review, and to present the discussion in a way suited to the powers of the general reader.

Through these manifestations of personal and group concern the course of American philosophy has been marked during the half century by signs of originality and by successful interpretations of what the field is giving to the public mind. The rise and lessening of various interests within the circle of professional workers are shown by the titles of articles that have been accepted for publication by the editors of philosophical journals. Even more indicative of change are those new journals that were established with defined attachment to particular kinds of investigation. Such are the *Philosophical Review*, that since 1930 has centered on idealism; the *Journal of Philosophy*, primarily concerned with pragmatism; and the *Personalist*, which exemplifies the traditions begun and maintained by Bowne, Maritain, Gilson, and others. A more recently founded journal than these, the *Review of Metaphysics*, gives a new centering point for papers on that ever enduring aspect of philosophical thought.

In addition to our national advantage out of the coming of foreign scholars, the United States has been benefited by direct contacts abroad. New sectors of Europe, all of the Eastern world, and particularly Latin America have come into closer relationships. A new international trade has begun, in ideas and in men. As a result, the storehouses of philosophy are being enriched and opened to all, as never in previous decades.

In part our new alliances with Latin-American institutions is due to a new association. This brings together many scholars of both continents, and also induces exchanges of men and materials. This new philosophical association is but one of several new transmission lines laid down by Krusé. Others, projected on a world-wide scale by UNESCO, may likewise become steadily useful. What thus far has been accomplished by its committees is shown in a report on its third International Council of Philosophy and Humanistic Studies.[19] The sessions in Paris during February, 1952, brought together some sixty scholars from representative cultural strongholds, to merge their plans in new forms of intellectual union. A journal named *Diogenes* is to be the organ of international exchange and of planning for philosophers.

A particular gain for this country is in the extension of its contacts beyond areas of free use of English in speech and in print. The next generation of American scholars will have, in consequence, world-wide opportunity and possibly world views. One fondly hopes, for them, such swift and close communication through their familiar use and control of languages, that the American scholar abroad may not, as now, often be held incommunicado in tongues other than his own. Two wars have given to the United States a great increase in possibilities to learn other languages than English. Varied and intensive experience with languages at advanced levels of study would give the American scholar immense advantages. He would win "free speech" abroad. He would also add precision to his own thinking, by having at command the idioms and other intricacies in usage within the languages containing his materials for comparative study.

The summary of signs from 1900 to 1951 concerning the state of philosophy in this country shows a constant increase in kinds of interest that now has its effect upon the work in colleges and universities. The more rapid increase has come during the second quarter of the century, partly because wartime contacts and thoughts have brought people toward new concentrations of attention. The transfers of advanced students, in and out of the country, have been beneficial to American thinking. Stimulation has increased as persons came from India under the fellowships of the Watumull Foundation, and under similar special grants from private and public treasuries. History and philosophy have been benefited by these interchanges of people, as have all the other areas of knowledge and of the arts.

Though this country has not done exceedingly well in its export of books until more recent years, it has today an increased competence for exchanges of materials as of men and women. As Collins indicates,[20] we are well prepared, apart from lacks in foreign languages, to present abroad the ideas of the American tradition. He notes such works on philosophical and cultural history as those of Mead, Schneider, Perry Miller, Sears, and R. B. Perry. Of Perry's two-volume work on William James, he remarks, "If there is any such thing as 'the representative American mind,' it is found at its best and most elusive in these pages." This critic goes on to note two other titles as significant aids to foreign understanding of American accomplishments in his field, namely Blanshard's *The Nature of Thought*[21] and Brightman's *A Philosophy of Religion.*[22]

In 1930 only four professional journals were appearing regularly. Thereafter, in order of time came *Philosophy of Science* (1934), *Journal of Symbolic Logic* (1936), *Journal of the History of Ideas* (1940), *Philosophy and Phenomenological Research* (1940), *Journal of Aesthetics and Art Criticism* (1941), *Review of Metaphysics* (1947), and *Philosophical Studies* (1950). To this listing by Collins is to be added the title of a new quarterly on Oriental and comparative thought generally, *Philosophy East and West.* The first issue, in April, 1951, carried on the results of an international congress that was held at the University of Hawaii in the summer of 1949. The report on the conference, that continued for six weeks, is in a summary volume entitled *Essays in East-West Philosophy: An Attempt at World Synthesis.*[23] The summary volume and issues of the journal are directed toward closer understanding of philosophical likenesses and differences throughout the continent of North America and in all countries from Japan to Iran and the Near East.

One essential and important addition to results from journal publication and congresses on philosophy since 1926, came with the issue in 1938 of two volumes in the *International Encyclopedia of Unified Science*, a comprehensive work planned and begun by the late Otto Neurath and carried forward by his associate editors Morris and Carnap. These two volumes, titled as *Foundations of the Unity of Science*,[24] are signs of the international program to create appreciation of the "unity of science by demonstrating that all scientific terms are reducible to the language of physics."

In more general terms the progress of philosophy is indicated as notable in symbolic logic, in phenomenology, in aesthetics, and in the production of histories here and abroad. Discussions are various on how programs of mutual interest will develop into agreements on fundamentals. There can be no doubt of the long-range importance of American and Oriental exchanges of ideas in every field of knowledge, as our scholars become competent in the essential languages for research and translation, and as cooperative projects are made realistic through mutual efforts of Eastern and Western specialists in history, literature, and philosophy.

Specialists coming to the United States for temporary duty on cooperative projects have often remained. Many have come out of Europe in the decade from 1940 to 1950, and philosophical studies have benefited greatly through the work of certain among these enforced migrants. Philosophical studies as related to religion have had national and international benefit from the teaching and writing of Tillich, and from the work of other scholars trained in the Greek and Hebraic traditions. Out of the Far and Near East and from Latin America, have come others to take up permanent residence. In consequence, the rosters of our learned societies and the bibliographies of research productivity show many new names. Most noteworthy in philosophy is that of Whitehead. The far reaching benefits from his writing and teaching continue and multiply. Surely no other force equals his toward a unifying of knowledge without loss of idealistic values. All of the humanities are in his debt for his wise words on art, education, literature, history, and above all else on matters within his own fields, mathematics and philosophy.

VIII

Report is made variously and often in contradictory terms of the changing status of various philosophical traditions in Great Britain and in our own country. We are advised that the dominance of logical positivism continues; that in general positivistic philosophy shows signs of greater moderation; that Thomism is increasing its following, and is declining in influence; that the opposition to metaphysics persists, despite many new and effective partisans; that our most flourishing science is symbolic or mathematical logic; and that the logicians and empiricists are still encamped over against the metaphysicians and quasi-religious thinkers of German and Latin-American origins. Nothing could be better as sure proof of the significance that philosophical ideas have in American life.

A special variant that grew out of our seminars to bring great benefit has been social philosophy, a term that today has its deepest implications in the objective studies of Marxism made first in political science and then in economics. On this particular theme, contributions of great general value are being made by American philosophers, as exemplified in the writings of Perry and of Cohen and in the field studies with attendant writing by Brownell on the practices of American democracy versus theories of Marxism. Perry's work on democratic theory and Cohen's discourses on the meaning of history support from the humanistic side what the political scientists and economists effectually accomplish realistically. By his union of democratic theory and proof through action, Brownell demonstrates the fallacies of communism without discussing them.[25] He shows that true social theories arise inductively in the minds of the people, and that the surest signs of their validity are in actual doing and being. His purpose, successfully shown, has been to help people to practice before they preach, and so to bear conviction within themselves. Another who has worked into philosophical valuations of present and future times is Lewis Mumford, as his major work, entitled *The Conduct of Life*,[26] demonstrates. Completed in 1951, it calls for a social philosophy of individual regeneration making each ready for acceptance of a personal responsibility that is lost or destroyed under dialectical materialism, existentialism, and the various mechanistic theories of being.

A fresh exposition of existentialism in English is from the French writers contributing to the volume edited in 1950 by Farber, with the title *Philosophical Thought in France and the United States*.[27] The first half of this collection of papers greatly advanced American appreciation and understanding of contemporary thought in France. That part of the survey gives to us who are least competent as critics a balanced summary.

The second half of this symposium deals with the changing conditions and kinds of philosophical discourse in the United States. The introduction to these eighteen essays is by A. C. Benjamin; he also contributed an essay to the sequence, under the title "Philosophy in America Between Two Wars," pointing out the signs of healthy growth in societies and in universities. He lists the usual journals, noting the discontinuance of the *Monist* and the addition of *New Scholasticism* and *Philosophical Abstracts*. New societies to be reported are the Association for Symbolic Logic, the Philosophy of Science Association, the International Phenomenological Society, the Charles S. Peirce Society, the American Society for Aesthetics, and the American Catholic Philosophical Society.

As a side effect of newly devised programs in "general education," the teacher of philosophy has been cast in the role of generalist in the group of lectures. This directive power came by a kind of logical force of gravity. Subjects within the curriculum of the first two years passed out of departmental control and into the hands of a fairly independent faculty. That shift was possible in the larger universities. It became clear that philosophy has a relevance to all three major categories of study, to make unifying possible under it: sciences, social sciences, and the humanities found a common meeting ground there, a point of exchange. Therefore general concepts common to all discourse on God, Man, and Nature may be best presented in the introductory survey courses by a philosopher.

Interesting administrative consequences have followed. Today these new faculties are taking on the role that their predecessors tried almost violently to keep from the control of schools of education thirty years ago. In that contest, neither won. Today, in philosophy the traditional departments may have their protagonist. To give philosophy the central function, these faculties redesigning college education of the first two years have weighted their staffs accordingly. Some unpredictable effects will follow. Work in the senior college, and particularly in the graduate school, will bend to meet the demands for generalists with a philosophical disposition of mind. In days to come the graduate schools in humanities will make philosophy a general requirement, of necessity, but at the moment the involvement touches students, teachers, and training centers disturbingly. It also calls for new materials or, at the least, soundly planned courses of reading that tally with the successive stages of lectures and group discussions.

Everyone knows what the benefits will be. They have been had, through the trial flights of survey courses running back to the beginning of simplified introductory requirements for all junior college students. They result in better reflective thinking and in more intensive reading. The lecture has lessened in status. Younger staff members have lost what students have won by these changes, deferring for the present their chances of steady promotion for work in special subjects. No one doubts that a broader outlook will be beneficial to all, once the modes of administrative organization are reformed so as to develop faculties for new duties without destruction of old and essential talents, and also to train younger men for general studies without hindering their departmental advancement. As Tatlock once remarked in a discussion of the many experiments in education during his time, the student must not be allowed to suffer under them. Nor today, he would add, should the staff.

Two universities, California and Columbia, are collaborating in principle on ways to extend the power of philosophical discourse. They have asked that doctoral candidates complete an additional year of study in some related field. Less formal measures are being taken elsewhere to give persons already in service an added year for what someone has dubbed a "period of cross-fertilization," implying that a mind once trained by subject thereafter is never able to think of anything else without external suggestion.

Two essentials are wanted if any national consequence is to come out of broadening the duties of philosophers educationally and administratively, and their lines of inquiry into related fields. There must be national recognition of validity in the ideas, and a sure protection of that sense of adventure motivating individuals to research. After scholars and masters, or students and teachers, the third essential of higher education is materials for study. Again our surveyor gives assurances of progress. Benjamin lists, as evidence of American originality and distinction, the names of the Carus lecturers whose addresses are in print. For the years 1925 through 1947, he lists seven volumes, by the following men: Dewey, Lovejoy, Mead, Montague, McGilvary, Cohen, and Lewis. One might well add the eight titles in "The Library of Living Philosophers," on the work of Dewey, Santayana, Whitehead, Moore, Russell, Cassirer, Einstein, and Radhakrishnan. Also, of fairly recent beginning is a symposium held annually in New York City under the inclusive title of science, philosophy, and religion. Participants prepare papers for study in advance of the formal sessions. The published volumes have had influence on public opinion, as on academic thinking. They have shown how science and religion turn to philosophy and in turn benefit it. Such materials contribute greatly to the breadth of view sought for in survey courses, and are prized by those faculty members who conduct them for their philosophic values.

By their demonstration of concern over the blending of forces to sustain the American people in a critical period, the universities have given a present example of moral philosophy; for our grandfathers that term included, in the definition of Hendel, "all that is the subject-matter of psychology, aesthetics and criticism, ethics, political and economic science, and the rudiments of sociology, and it made a consummate moral knowledge available for action aiming at the general welfare and happiness of mankind."[28] Today philosophy is shorn of much of the responsibility that these and other terms have in the newer disciplines of the American university. But philosophers are not freed, because the term "moral philosophy" itself seems outworn, from the onus of creating a spirit of morality among the peoples of the world, beginning at home.

Any reviewer of the American scholarly scene would say that the rise of new philosophical schools has been immensely beneficial, but that some of these have blanked out the individual. Their purposes are with other ends than personal or social aims within the contemporary scene. They are building new scientific structures toward another goal that, when attained, will doubtless have meanings of morality in its fullest sense. The humanist looks ahead for the fulfillment of Whitehead's words: ". . . I suggest that Symbolic Logic, that is to say, the symbolic examination of pattern with the use of real variables, will become the foundation of aesthetics. From that stage it will proceed to conquer ethics and theology. The circle will then have made its full turn, and we shall be back to the logical attitude of the epoch of St. Thomas Aquinas. It was from St. Thomas that the seventeenth century revolted by the production of its mathematical method, which is the re-birth of logic."[29] But, for these times, the humanist looks to other men than the logical positivists and the historians who consummately depict civilizations as sequences of confrontations in the rise and fall of nations. We shall scarcely wait on time to bring in the proofs. We ask now for more usable answers.

Let the uneasy humanist look to philosophy for ideas to help him in these times. He will find something in Morris's *Signs, Language, and Behavior,* and also in this author's earlier work called *Paths of*

Life: *Preface to a World Religion*.[30] Even without full understanding of either book he will derive benefit. This is certain, even without agreement with the thesis of the second one; he may be ready to turn philosophy toward religious conclusions. This study of human values proves that a philosopher who is at home in the remoteness of symbolism and semiotics still thinks on the individual and on the society of his own generation. Morris concludes his argument saying, "Life is lived in the present, and the future issues only out of a present. One lives now in the light of ideals held for the future, otherwise future and present alike are betrayed."[31]

With the same anticipation of finding stimulating ideas and possibly some answers to problems of today, the humanist who is no philosopher looks into the writings of Northrop, beginning with the much discussed early one, *The Meeting of East and West*. Next came *Logic of the Sciences and Humanities*, then *Ideological Differences and World Order*, and finally in 1952 *The Taming of the Nations: A Study of the Cultural Bases of International Policy*.[32] Another humanist, though disguised as a political scientist, is equally effective in arousing thought and quick to give his message. Paul H. Douglas takes his philosophical and moral conclusions to the people by speech as well as through print. The person who reads his two works, *Economy in the National Government* and *Ethics in Government*[33] will declare him a true exponent of moral philosophy.

The positive statements of belief found in such American books illustrate the interplay of religious, cultural, and political values; through the philosophic spirit that is typical of the total impulse of the humanities, these writers speak to the people. They do not praise "a fugitive and cloistered virtue," themselves unwilling to enter "the race where that immortal garland is to be run for, not without dust or heat." Fame does not interest such men: human values do. Their counsels are to be studied, used if fitting, and bettered if possible by ourselves.

Yet the teaching of our time is that no ultimate answers are hoped for, and that the pursuit of ideals is itself a discovery of values. So the militant dissenters with those who make teaching a review of fact are justified when the subject is philosophy. Religion has a diffuse and deep influence on the life of our times. By comparison with its place in individual lives five years ago, it is a new power in

American life. Men and women returning to college from war duties brought with them a sense of concern for personal values. They were committed to their faith in religion by experience, not necessarily or in actual truth by any attachment to a formal body of doctrine. This we know from the teachers of philosophy in our universities and colleges. If this be true, as by all signs it appears still to be, then the direction of philosophical instruction—or guidance—should be toward expressed desires of such young people. When teaching is related to the student, its progress is clear and its value is made certain.

NOTES

1. President's Commission on Higher Education, *Higher Education for American Democracy* (6 vols.; Harper, New York, 1948).

2. *Op. cit.*, I, 10.

3. Anson Phelps Stokes, *Church and State in the United States* (3 vols.; Harper, New York, 1950).

4. B. Blanshard, *et al.*, *Philosophy in American Education: Its Tasks and Opportunities* (xii+306; Harper, New York, 1945), pp. 284-85. Citations from this direct examination of public opinions on philosophical concerns in American society would make intelligible the views in this chapter. The variety of new evidence in the composite study merits full reading of this text.

5. *Ibid.*, pp. 285-86. The reading of Milton as given in this quoted passage illustrates our need to rely on scholars. The true text, in modern printing style, is as follows: "I cannot praise a fugitive and cloistered virtue, unexercised and unbreathed, that never sallies out and sees her adversary, but slinks out of the race where that immortal garland is to be run for, not without dust and heat." Those editors who take "seeks" for "sees" and "shrinks" for "slinks" fall into the old error of assuming that the easier reading is what an author wrote or intended to write.

6. W. E. Hocking, *et al.*, *Preface to Philosophy: Textbook* (x+508; Macmillan, New York, 1947).

7. Herbert W. Schneider, *A History of American Philosophy* (xiv+646; Columbia University Press, New York, 1946).

8. Between 1939 and 1951 The Library of Living Philosophers, Inc., Evanston, Illinois, issued volumes on the work of Dewey, Santayana, Whitehead, Moore, Russell, Cassirer, Einstein, and Radhakrishnan. Each concludes with a review of his critics by the subject.

9. Walter Yust, ed., *Britannica Book of the Year* 1952 (xxx+768; Encyclopedia Britannica, Chicago, 1952), pp. xxii-xxxii.

10. Eugene Staley, ed., *Creating an Industrial Civilization*. A Report on the Corning Conference held under the auspices of the American Council of Learned Societies and the Corning Glass Works, May 17–19, Corning, New York. (xvi+368; Harper, New York, 1952), pp. 103-4.

11. *Ibid.*, pp. 351–52.

12. Quoted by A. Rehm, *Sitzungsber. Bayer. Acad. Phil. hist. Abt.*, 1942. iv, 65ff.

13. Elmer Davis, "News and the Whole Truth," *The Atlantic*, Vol. 190, No. 2 (August, 1952), pp. 32–38.

14. *Ibid.*, p. 37.

15. H. N. Gardiner, "The First Twenty-five years of the Philosophical Association," *Philosophical Review*, XXXV, No. 2 (March, 1926), 145–58. Wilbur M. Urban, "Progress in Philosophy in the Last Quarter Century," *op. cit.*, pp. 93–123.
The first paper before the newly formed society was R. B. Perry's "Poetry and Philosophy," in title and in content a mark of independence from the parent organization, the Psychological Association.

16. *Ibid.*, LX, No. 1 (January, 1951). Papers by Grace A. De Laguna (pp. 3–19), W. V. Quine (pp. 20–43), and W. K. Frankena (pp. 44–55).

17. James Collins, "A Quarter Century of American Philosophy," *The New Scholasticism* XXV (January, 1951), 46–80. Much of the following comment is based on this article. It is followed in the next thirty pages of the issue by Mortimer J. Adler's paper on "The Next Twenty-five Years in Philosophy," a retrospective review of positivism in Great Britain and the United States, with comment on the dominance of the past in philosophical study and on the distinctive structures of philosophy and science.

18. G. P. Adams and W. P. Montague, eds., *Contemporary American Philosophy* (2 vols.; Macmillan, New York, 1930).

19. *ACLS Newsletter*, III, No. 2 (Spring, 1952), 33–36.

20. *Ibid.*, p. 67.

21. B. Blanshard, *The Nature of Thought* (2 vols.; Allen & Unwin, London, 1939).

22. E. S. Brightman, *A Philosophy of Religion* (xvii+539; Prentice-Hall, New York, 1940).

23. C. A. Moore, ed., *Essays in East-West Philosophy: An Attempt at World Synthesis* (xii+467; University of Hawaii Press, Honolulu, 1951).

24. The two volumes noted were published at the University of Chicago Press in 1938.

25. Baker Brownell, *The Human Community: Its Philosophy and Practice for a Time of Crisis* (vi+305; Harper, New York, 1950).

26. Lewis Mumford, *The Conduct of Life* (ix+342; Harcourt, Brace, New York, 1951).

27. Marvin Farber, ed., *Philosophical Thought in France and the United States: Essays Representing Major Trends in Contemporary French and American Philosophy* (x+775; University of Buffalo, Buffalo, 1950).

28. C. W. Hendel, "The Character of Philosophy in Canada," *University of Toronto Quarterly*, XX, No. 2 (January, 1951), 133.

29. Alfred North Whitehead, *Essays in Science and Philosophy* (255 pp; Philosophical Library, New York, 1948), p. 99.

30. Charles Morris, *Signs, Language, and Behavior* (xii+365; Prentice-Hall, New York, 1946); *Paths of Life: Preface to a World Religion* (vii+258; Harper, New York, 1942).

31. Morris, *Paths of Life*, p. 213.

32. F. S. C. Northrop, *The Taming of the Nations: A Study of the Cultural Bases of International Policy*. (362 pp.; Macmillan, New York, 1952).

33. Paul H. Douglas, *Economy in the National Government* (viii+277; University of Chicago Press, Chicago, 1952); *Ethics in Government* (114 pp.; Harvard University Press, Cambridge, 1952).

FIVE

Literatures

I

The study of any literature has its sources of meaning in language, history, religion, and philosophy. These have much that the worker with literatures must possess, whether he be writer, critic, teacher, research scholar—or any combination of these. Fortunately all such kinds of literary interest are recognized today by faculties of American colleges and universities. Unfortunately, at times, the bearing of the three basic disciplines on literary studies is passed by unnoticed. More commonly, the relationship is clearly realized, but the flow of students and the pressures of immediacy lead the teacher of literature to accept conditions that he alone cannot easily alter. He knows that literary studies are dependent on firm grounding in language, history, religion, and philosophy. He knows that his own subject is at the heart of liberal and humanistic studies; yet he cannot, by desire and knowledge, make it central to the entire enterprise of higher education.

That rank literatures should have, in the judgment of humanists, and should hold it by exceptional merit in literary production as well as in literary criticism. To that end, every institution of importance should have adequate supplies of material in its libraries and constantly replenished staffs in its departments of language, history, philosophy, and literature. That need is as real in graduate schools as in undergraduate colleges. Nothing grows or even lives without nurture. This is as true in the intellectual and spiritual realms of the humanities as in the barest physical forms of existence. For the faculties, that means a sense of well-being and a willingness to cooperate toward the general good of their institution and of society. For their administrative officers, it means full moral and financial support, and protection against the vagaries of individuals who have no understanding of freedom in thought for discovery and interpretation of unknown and unrecognized values.

If literature is to rise to its place of first rank among the humanities, plans for its growth must run from the first impression on an undergraduate up through the levels of advanced study and out into the duties of humanistic faculties. A balance of studies must be attained, so that languages, histories, and philosophies may be literally the roots, trunk, and branches for these final flowers of civilization known as literatures.

Fifty years ago relationships among these four disciplines were less close than they are today. Then the conduct of affairs in departments was simple. One or two professors determined what should be the routines of a small staff in each subject. Little thought was given to interaction toward defined and stated ends. The number of students was small, and decisions on what and how to teach them were made by individuals. Committees to decide on policies for the humanities were rare. Consequently, a general practice was to retain a student fairly closely within departmental boundaries; that practice, happily, has been discredited and forgotten. Now the interplay of interest among these four disciplines is constant and increasing. Languages are effectual instruments of research as well as of interpretation and of expression. Literature, philosophy, law, and religion show this, as do discourses on aesthetics, logic, and literary criticism. The twentieth-century concern with the history of ideas was based on tracings of word signifiers. A similar widening of influence out of history and philosophy into studies in literature is constant. Because the academic idea of literature now contains all the implied interests of research, criticism, and expressive writing and speech it forms a bridgehead for the movement of ideas and the arts out into contemporary life.

Internally, changes in the status of literary studies have come by the action of faculties. Most important are those that brought critical writing and all other forms of expression through the arts into departments of literature. English, Spanish, French faculties have made drama more than a subject to be studied in books. The experience of using the arts has had parallel in the induction of students into methods of advanced study by which faculty members became specialists in their profession. Undergraduates and graduate students are being shown the means to analysis, synthesis, and expressive action in literary studies. Fifty years ago a few selected graduate students were in seminars, a few in undergraduate courses of writing. Tutorials, honors courses, free discussion in common rooms and study groups, and comprehensive examinations have changed those tiny patterns of individual development. Large lecture halls still are needed for the full effect of finished interpretations, but less so than even ten years ago. Out of the perspectives given there came the individual views of students who now form their own opinions and ask for answers to their spontaneous questions. These are among signs of progress overlooked by those who deplore the "mass" education of youth. The American college has kept its tradition of intimate relationships, and even the largest of state universities demonstrates refinements in teaching methods that bring students from lecture halls into group discussions. Free reading and direct interchange of ideas in talk are the accompaniments of formal training by a use of literary examples and of sources. So the learner of ways in the humanities is led toward a familiarity in the field that is like that of the experienced scholar.

A second relationship of literature is to the other expressive arts. The American college has for many years had its experimental courses in writing, for undergraduates of evident talent. They have been significant in proportion to the intensity of student effort and the directing abilities of the staff man, who usually is himself a successful writer. Graduate schools have fewer examples of this encouragement to original composition, apart from term papers and thesis; yet a few are accepting performance in literary arts as their final tests for higher degrees, and intend these liberalizations of routine as signs of a new philosophy in graduate studies—that all shall be encouraged toward their highest promise within the scope of the subject.

It is, however, in undergraduate colleges that literature is now joined with the other expressive arts most effectually. Music, drama, painting, sculpture, and design are being brought to literal meaning through experience. In a few colleges, the student is required to experiment in order that he may realize the elements of creative design, conceivably to discover an aptitude; the soundness of the idea is proved by what is produced and by the altered attitude toward every humanistic study in consequence. Certain graduate schools have gone a great deal further in one or two of the associated arts that give professional insight into creative writing and critical judgment in prose, poetry, and forms of drama. Every aspect of theatrical presentation, from the rudiments of staging to full production, is now being taught in laboratory theatres of American universities. There, in full relationship, the arts of the humanities are brought to harmony in experience as an aid and even as an alternative of objective learning.

All of these changes in conduct of studies have effect upon the place of literatures in colleges, graduate schools, and in active life. All, or nearly all of these excellent gains, would have been impossible without the protection of institutions. There no compulsory demands for quick results compel to vague and slanted conclusions, nor is the spirit of individual freedom translated into one of irresponsibility to professional and artistic standards.

That sense of responsibility appears in the concern shown today by teachers of literature with ideas and values of this present time. Their critical writing relates to change and growth in the cultures of many more peoples of the earth than a generation ago. Translators, trained artists in handling of meaning, lend increasing aid. The total number of men and women dealing in literary values, within and outside our institutions, has its direct influence as never before on public taste and on all workers in the other expressive arts.

II

Trends in literary production and criticism are watched so closely that the mass of printed comments over this past half century is almost measureless. Some of the more significant are in the learned journals, in magazines, and in newspapers. The long statements that have appeared in book form have merit as retrospective reviews of older literatures and of individual authors more commonly than as ways of insight into contemporary letters; yet it is surprising to find how many exceptional analyses of present and recent writing have appeared within these past twenty years. The amount of such evidence is too great for survey, and since sampling is not a practice of humanists the opinions of a few representative persons must stand as landmarks of our progress in literary productivity and appreciation.

These are dated by the contemporary outlook of their authors so well that the professional man of letters and the scholar will need no other clues. Each statement is in itself a criticism of the times for which it was written and of the writers themselves. From the recorded statements of any earlier decade our critics and our writers on literary history can draw an image of the society being served, for the written page is accessible. What was written to be printed and what was passed over silently are equally significant. Other proof of how the American scholar today spends his time is in the sign of a merging or a separateness of his views from those of the nonacademic critical reviewer. When students of trends in literature have much in common, whatever they say or write proves it. Subject to corrections for personal equations, as our scholar-teachers speak of their profession and of literary works produced in current print, so is the rating of their profession for social relevance. It is not needed to approve, or to judge, contemporaries by any absolute standards whatever; the true critic works in relative values, but draws his evidence from the text under study rather than from presumed absolutes. He too should be judged in close reference to the time when he lived and wrote.

One insecure generalization is that the literary scholar in America in the formative period after 1900 had his mind mainly on philology. A common deduction from that statement has been that he in consequence left to others outside colleges and universities the critical evaluation of current writing. That notion is disproved by what we know of men in classics; E. K. Rand was one whose teaching led students down through the centuries of literature in many languages to the present, and each reader of this sentence may recall one or many such classicists who taught many literatures through one. We must believe that the scholars of the early nineteenth century had their minds on many matters apart from philology. They possessed a diversity of interests.

Only by their professional constancy were they bound to the formal bodies of classical literature and to the successive growths in Romance, Germanic, and British environments. From them all, the American scholar was drawing ideas on style, substance, and origin for his critical interpretations. Only American letters seemed to be neglected. A considerable span of time was to pass before students reflected on the original elements in their own literature. It seemed necessary before doing this to judge the American writer as a product of foreign inheritances slightly tinged with native values and therefore more interesting by reason of his relationship to somewhere or something overseas. The American scholar himself began to produce writings that now rank as literature before he looked about him closely at the works of his countrymen.

On such grounds one must look beyond the university of the first decade for signs of a rising interest in American literature. The scholars were intent on the lines of descent from the classics to the foreign models nearer in time, and on the master works of Western Europe. American readers were like them, to a considerable degree, being dependent on books and journals brought out of Britain and on lectures by foreign visitors unfamiliar with the life and thought of this country. Though scholarly lectures were given on a national scale in larger centers of population, in 1900 only the Eastern seaboard had the two advantages bringing critical attention to contemporary writers—a society with a solidarity of intellectual and cultural interests and publishing houses that responded to the taste of constituents. In that area, therefore, came the first important opinions on the state of American letters. Most were from men having no active connection with university life. The editors of magazines and the publishers of books gave the first significant evidences on contemporary taste by their choices of manuscripts. During the first decade the public critic rather than the academic student was influential; he advanced public appreciation of what American writers and publishers were bringing into print. Then, while the scholars attended to their tasks of developing our first scholarly journals, the writers for monthly and weekly journals were finding a third outlet through the metropolitan newspapers. The era of popular reading at many levels had begun.

These surface changes denoted real originality and self-reliance. By 1900 Lowell's essay "On a Certain Condescension in Foreigners" was thirty years old, its implications out-dated. A spirit less creditable, in some ways, was displacing that sense of dependence; nationalism and a self-conscious pride in American writing did not produce critical judgments. Of such tendencies editors and publishers were natural allies, but by opening the channels of production they started the habit of critical reading. The popular printing press, with its mixed output, became an active power in American culture, displacing in this the speaker on the lecture platform, the minister, and the journal or book with a limited circulation. Popular demand made the press a benefactor of all readers, releasing them from that sense of subservience deplored by Lowell and preparing the way for the new scholar.

At that time one favorite spokesman for American writers and their works was William Dean Howells. His opinions still stand as valid in many respects; though he was not in the tradition of higher education, what he fails to say reflects the spirit of his times. Howells is to be judged today by his own standards of value, and on his estimates of American letters as native works. For he turned his eyes directly toward what was then being written in his own country, where, and by whom. Apart from fiction, he was not deeply interested in literary forms, and critical rules were for him unimportant compared with the signs of public interest and a knowledge of the creditable craftsmen to satisfy it.

Howells issued his *Literature and Life* in 1902. One of its essays is on "American Literary Centers." This is a noteworthy contribution to the study of our literary history, for it rests on new evidence collected under a clearly felt interest of its author. Howells made his forecasts of growth in American literature by looking to the locations of publishing houses and the leadership of favored writers. Such persons, he believed, would inevitably set the tone of production and draw to them younger writers to serve the public within schools, or coteries, that had the approval of publishers on grounds of past successes.

Some of his prophecies have come true, as on the effects of sectionalism after 1865, in bringing eminence to certain cities as literary centers and in adding new themes to American fiction, poetry, and history. Howells saw Philadelphia as having reached its highest level with Franklin and Charles Brockden Brown. It then yielded place to New York, on account of the prestige of Poe, Irving, Bryant, and other men. Thereafter, he noted that Boston took the leadership and held it firmly for forty years, under the favoring hands of Longfellow, Lowell, Whittier, Hawthorne, Emerson, Holmes, Prescott, and Parkman.

So far, in the minds of his readers, Howells was on familiar and friendly ground. They were in the habit of looking to Boston and New York City for their current journals and new books, and also for their critical guidance.

Nevertheless, the devotees of these two familiar places and of their accepted writers must have doubted his forecasts of change. They could scarcely accept the views of Howells on the rising significance of other cities and of authors living then in other parts of the country. Nor would they readily agree, in consequence, that some of his newly chosen favorites could draw others to them. More natural, in their view, would be the customary faith that all outlanders would be drawn to the publishing centers and there submit themselves to an urbanizing process toward existing standards. For the South, Howells named Joel Chandler Harris as the forerunner of a new school; for the Middle West, John Hay; for the Western Plains, Owen Wister; and for a "new" New England, Sarah Orne Jewett. He fixed on the Middle West as the most promising of all potential new centers, and for his usual reason—faith in the influence of significant persons. He judged Hamlin Garland and Henry B. Fuller to be then so notable nationally that they would create a representative school of American letters and start a westward movement of writers and publishers.

The judgment of Howells has been cared for by that of time. Even so, his long views that now seem illusory were refreshing then and still are. Particularly appealing is his concluding remark, "It would be hard to match among our critical journals the *Dial* of Chicago."[1] That estimate, for its time, was amply justified. Also, the later career of Fuller would have made Howells pleased to have written that sentence, could he have lived on to see how Fuller helped in every noteworthy movement in American literature, particularly by the encouragement of new writers. He was influential in bringing the magazine *Poetry* to international recognition. His large share in that wholly new demonstration of how growth in a literary center is to be fostered and of ways by which young writers are to be aided, make Fuller a historic figure in American cultural history. That fact is accepted. His direct and indirect helps to the Midwestern school of writers and to new poets everywhere, pointing toward the advances of the nineteen twenties, are proof of possibilities under wholehearted support from such personalities inside and outside universities, in publishing houses and editorial offices.

One of his few concessions to academic men was indirect, as he praised the fiction of Brander Matthews alongside that of Stephen Crane and Henry James. He turned back quickly from this to his expansive view of American writing, in the observation that ". . . more authors come here from the West and South than go elsewhere; but they often stay at home, and I fancy very wisely."[2] He held until the end his most speculative guesses on future centers of American writing, under his formula of person-plus–printing press. In 1902 Howells pointed to Northampton as one of two, by reason of the residence there of George Washington Cable. The other, Riverdale-on-Hudson, was the home of Mark Twain.

Fifty years ago the American literary scholar surely read and discussed the ideas of Howells, but in a detached spirit. The literatures of Western Europe and the Mediterranean Basin held his attention. He and his philological brother were engaged properly, for their day, in self-appointed tasks, nor do we find either urging on younger men systematically the opportunities in other literatures than the ones traditional to higher study.

When Ashley H. Thorndike in 1925 brought out his *Literature in a Changing Age*, the university had a spokesman of cosmopolitan interests. His criterion was, that as scholars our interest is in "the emotional effect on the reader, and our search is for the cause of this effect." He was looking at the document, at the public, and at the critic in his own present time. A logical effect was in his high praise of newspapers, "for the time being far more alive in literature than many of the essays in Addison's *Spectator* or than long passages in *Paradise Lost*." He also jarred his contemporaries gently by asking for a reconsideration of Wells, who was being rated enthusiastically as more "valuable" than Sir Walter Scott or Shakespeare, with his remark that "one does not have to share their opinion to see that it indicates that Mr. Wells has made some impression on the imaginations and sympathies of current readers."[3] The postulates of all his criticism were democratic, in his own terms of definition. Living in a machine age, and feeling its impact on American culture, he asked for a literature with social and religious import and an ennobling spirit comparable to what he found in British writing after the Battle of Waterloo. An attractive phase of his mind is displayed by this reference to his own favored field of study, the Victorian period, in praise of originality and imaginative writing in terms that custom had established as belonging to the Age of Elizabeth.

An educational turn is in the praise from Thorndike for the textbooks that were coming into use at the time of his commentary.

He held the American product to be exceptional for number, variety, and quality. His gratification over the improvement in resources for the study of literature would be far greater could he now examine the materials in print. Present-day scholars can make such a comparison easily, by running through the pages of advertisements in the 1925 issues of the *Publications of the Modern Language Association* and then doing the same with those of 1952. They would wonder at the methods that must have been in effect when anthologies of literature were few and formal, critical works of book length infrequent, and bibliographical guides decidedly scanty. The intervening period has brought into daily use an excellent variety of works touching on every literary form in the traditional fields. Also a fine beginning has been made with the apparatus of scholarship, and for teaching, within areas uncultivated carefully until recently.

While Thorndike was writing, his ideas were being brought to trial. Those were the first golden days of bookmaking, with royalties made large by rapidly increasing enrollments. In graduate schools another kind of increase was coming through adoption of the Turner theory of a westward movement underlying the changing structure of American life. As Parrington applied in literary studies the thesis of general historical change, there began a slow rise in scholarly concern with all growth out of native ground. Increasingly, too, colleges and universities gained in influence through reviews and articles of their professors in public print, until by the nineteen twenties the literary scholars began to invigorate the criticism in newspapers and the quality magazines and to arouse discussion of literature among the readers of the weeklies of opinion.

Those were the days when Greenlaw, Hanford, Foerster, and Sherman were starting new movements that changed formal studies and enlarged the interest of scholars in critical appreciation of all forms of literature. The year 1908 found Sherman starting his attacks on graduate study. By 1917 he was exemplifying his ideas as the leader of his own school of letters in a university and as a writer for the public print. In his own manner, he assailed the existing standards of criticism and taught by demonstration. By the time Thorndike's book was in circulation, Sherman had done many of the things that it recommended. His career was briefer in time than that of any of the others, and the results were to be felt over a shorter period than those from

Spingarn's call to a new criticism; yet the power of his personality broke down the aloofness of scholars and made them aware of the interests of the people.

The slower moving but insistent reforms that came out of the work of Greenlaw and Hanford were to modify the ways of thinking on the "great tradition" and to substitute humane for historical concepts without destroying standards of critical judgment. Schools, colleges, and graduate schools were changed by influences of which these men are symbols, not the full innovators. Secondary schools had shortly better texts and more competent teachers. Graduate schools in the Southern states took on a new authority, as in other sections of the country. As the state universities developed in maturity of interests, the chance came to Foerster, working in a new center, to make his outright protests in print against old methods of graduate teaching in English, even while setting afoot a demonstration of his own principles. Each of the four, in his own way, was a symbol of change.

Meanwhile, in the closer studies of the graduate schools, such leaders as Kittredge, Babbitt, Lounsbury, Manly, Neilson, and Lowes were giving new directions to investigation and teaching. All were exceptional in their own kinds of research, and equally so in their ability to encourage younger men to enter fresh fields of study and to apply there entirely new methods, if need be, in the uses of evidence. These are again typical of a growing movement to make literary scholarship serve the widening interests of American society, through its service to colleges and universities and so by all the avenues into which the graduates of these institutions carry their views on the nature of literary art.

The two iconoclasts of the twenties are so dissimilar that their names are not commonly associated; neither are they thought of as responsible for two fundamental shifts in academic practice that are as noteworthy as what the others were accomplishing within the universities. Spingarn left a new concept of criticism. Mencken, who strove with Sherman over ideas slightly off center for either of them, by 1920 may be said to have reduced the outworks of philological conservatism. He was not so much right and the others wrong, as he was successful in demanding that words be considered as living things. By 1924, five years after the issue of the first form of his *American Language*, the name of Mencken was heard everywhere in American colleges and universities. That was also the year when, as editor for himself and eight other writers, Spingarn partially removed the name of theorist from himself by bringing out *Criticism in America: Its Functions and Status*. The successes that now may be attributed to these men, as iconoclasts in theory of critical and linguistic studies, in no way alter the limitation of their approaches to discourse; destructive attack may end in vital reform, but it will not perpetuate its ideas in the work of followers. Both men would have had advantages from an academic environment. They would have enjoyed and endured critical give and take with colleagues, and they would have had the chance to be heard daily by younger persons likely to make lasting the positive values in their work with ideas. Though Spingarn had had the background of an early experience in university living, his full career, like that of Mencken, was in open territory where criticism is more at random and less precise. Both missed the advantages that academic surroundings give during the evolution of an idea and the addition of its positive values to the tradition of literary studies. It is sufficient in praise to affirm the benefits that such critics of the established order bring to the work of scholars, hastening the processes of benefit to the public which slowly and perhaps too late the scholars themselves would bring to bear.

III

Acceptance of literature as an academic subject equal in rank with science, medicine, and theology came late. By comparison with the status of most others in the present curricula of higher studies, in 1900 the literatures of Western Europe had still to make their way in both teaching and research. Men of comprehensive interests that commanded recognition outside of their own institutions were few. Those few were excellent, by any standards of judging, but philological disciplines and languages of Biblical or classical interpretation initially outdistanced general literary studies in American universities. In the colleges a hindrance that was less recognized came from moralistic, even doctrinal, tendencies of teachers who were overburdened by a direct or indirect attachment to the faiths of denominational institutions. At some colleges, if the stories told are true, a search after the lesson in each literary example was almost standard practice; however, in a few universities and stronger colleges the teaching of modern literatures was held at the high levels set by the classicists. Lane Cooper, for one, bridged the gap, to the honor of both ancients and moderns. The comparative study of types descendant from Greece and Rome, country by country, stressed in each author the evidences of imitation and originality. Epic, lyric, drama, and eventually prose fiction came under such scrutiny. Even so, a review of critical writing on modern literatures at the beginning of this century shows American scholars to have been unready for penetrating analysis and interpretation. The contrast with originality in more firmly established disciplines is clear and definite.

As all literatures came to better recognition among higher studies, American ways of work with them quickly appeared. Foreign influences were strong and constant, but so too were the operational plans of leaders to train younger men and to produce new materials. Every practice in teaching, research, production, and criticism had its testing or actual development on native soil. The originality of American scholars had created a national pattern of higher studies by the nineteen twenties, when production of trained men and women by graduate schools had become significant in quality, kinds, and numbers.

Several causes created this quick increase. One was the appearance of leaders with the variety and depth of knowledge to direct higher studies effectively. They opened new fields of study and improved on methods and theories of work in all. An invigorating change began with the trend toward a use of native materials. Others of great importance were started by American scholars who opened to intensive research the British and continental literatures of the seventeenth, eighteenth, and nineteenth centuries. Then the range and variety of advanced studies in all the humanities rose rapidly. As research in all modern literatures brought new critical standards into college teaching during the second quarter of this century, financial support for higher education rose with enrollments that demanded larger staffs, better libraries, and solid backing of research activities. All these advantages came at a time when scholarship in modern literatures was ready to share in their benefits and to give new prestige to the humanities.

By 1925 the American scholar had, at his best, that maturity in other literatures previously recognized as being common among the classicists. That is to say, patterns of investigation were well formed, resources were good, and teaching in undergraduate and graduate schools was being done with distinction. Many examples prove these points, but only one must suffice here. It is useful as proof of what Thorndike had asserted, hopefully, at the beginning of the century, and interesting because he himself is brought in to illustrate his own argument. Joseph E. Baker's recent study, *The Reinterpretation of Victorian Literature*, has in one sentence a comparison that may or may not be justified; its value lies in his undoubted certainty of merit in American teaching of literature, as shown in the assertion that "no British university has done so much in the social interpretation of Victorian literature as Robert Morss Lovett and his followers at Chicago or Ashley Thorndike and his followers at Columbia . . ."[4] This critic could have named many other persons, here and in Great Britain, who were breaking the old patterns of literary studies twenty to thirty years ago. He was held, by the subject of his investigation, to make his point from the period of British literature in which familiarity had delayed serious inquiry, but out of which could come immediate benefit to younger scholars.

The lasting impressions from a reading of this citation in Baker's book are only of the originality shown by two scholars at work in an undeveloped field and of their skill in interpretation to the public mind. A stronger case might be made for the influence of Trevelyan on ideas of social history, in the Victorian Age as elsewhere, but in the end such flat comparisons fade away into differences in personal belief. The example is, in its own terms, one evidence among many to prove that by 1950 the American scholar in any field of literature can rest his case on the prestige of his accomplishments. By comparison with law, medicine, and theology—the oldest claimants to recognition—and in parallel with attainments of specialists in older disciplines of the social sciences, the literatures of higher education are being served admirably in American institutions. Also, beyond academic distinction, they are brought to the general public in ways to increase appreciation and original expressiveness through all the arts.

In 1932 I brought away from Cambridge a personal impression with respect to their honors work in English which was different from any others gathered at home or abroad. I. A. Richards had shown, with comments, the papers set for undergraduate honors. They put upon students the requirement of much reading and of careful preparation on the ideas dominant during successive periods of British literature. They compelled, too, a good grounding in social, political, and religious history, in classical ideas, and in theories of literary criticism. Most impressive was the requirement of a knowledge of representative writers so intimate as to assure the beginnings of a critical sense in matters of prose and poetic styles. Twenty years ago, therefore, I could believe that, so far as British standards were to be judged by an outside observer, the slow development of literary studies beyond the classics had come to full returns when judged by the expectation of faculties and accomplishment of the better students.

A quick comparison with British practice strengthens appreciation of what this country has finally accomplished by its secure establishment of modern literature in its universities. In neither country has it been easy to bring in work on literatures lying outside the conventional patterns or on periods in time since 1600. There, as here, these newer disciplines met hindrances such as never were encountered by the classics. Resistance in both countries was on identical pleas—that doubt existed on the substance worthy of treatment, and that popular appeal of what substance lay in them would disturb the balance of serious study. At both Cambridge and Oxford, consequently, modern literatures were late in coming into recognition: the Scotch and provincial universities had different points of view, but maintained late some of the same restraining ideas. It was held, by the more vigorous minded, that a study of political and social institutions gave the only valid fact on cultural change and that literatures, as such, were not fitted for work in the higher schools of university discipline. History, as an honors subject, was defended by its partisans against contamination anticipated from a subject lacking definition and so compelling someone to examine candidates on matters of taste, rather than on elemental and universal laws of political or social history.

Hostility lessened slowly, but by 1893 Oxford had its honors work in literatures; successively, decade by decade, the field has had further development at advanced levels in every institution of Great Britain and Eire. An interesting sign of change in university standards, is in the present opinion of Saintsbury's contention that a library was sufficient professor, tutor, and guide to all who would have careers in either critical or original work. This country has not had a like protagonist of the informal approach to literature, but even now it has a few who can gravely agree with Stubbs that doubts exist on the reliability or necessity of formal instruction where history is eminently represented.

These impressions of the rise of literary studies to their present place in higher education, against fairly heavy odds, are sufficient to reveal how inexpertly the universities of both countries examined the means of humane living that are responsible for its continued expression at the higher levels of individual consciousness. They showed a faith in the power of knowledge as something objectively true, and useful, but a neglect of the ways by which an individual could come to control knowledge and to maintain intellectual, spiritual, and aesthetic values in his culture. The lessons of formative change, from this establishment of literary studies as disciplines in American universities, are that fundamentally every literature is product of the deepest and oldest values in human experience. Unless languages, histories, and philosophies prevail, no culture can win through to lasting life in a literature; and, without embodiment in a literature, its signs of nature-in-man will disappear.

IV

The student of literatures will advance his own thinking most surely by placing in proper order and relationship the essential elements of what should be in his earliest learning. He will bring himself to develop judgment and taste inductively, for his approaches to the more difficult exercises of appreciation must be by the ways of normal advance—through language, well assimilated, and through histories and philosophies to understanding by the medium of words what are the guiding ideas and ideals contained in any literature. In effect, then, "criticism" is a result of personal evaluations, not of rules made by others. This personal sense must dominate the initiative of individuals as literatures are created, and therefore as they are studied.

It is a futile pursuit for the younger student to search after reasons to support a particular method in the study of literature. The chase may be profitable as mental exercise, but not from any hope of triumph over other views regarding practical procedure. "History versus criticism" would be a poor subject for debate, except as a forensic exercise, undertaken in a spirit of intellectual play. These two words are so variously understood that the debate would be delayed until an agreement was reached on distinctive definitions to bring them into direct opposition. Historical and critical methods are constantly employed by the writer and by the scholar, with every degree of variation. Either would fail without the other.

There is profit, however, in stating the aims of literary studies in institutions of higher education. These are individual, social, and universal in character according to the purpose and the capabilities of each individual. If such studies lead toward nationalism or toward partisanship for a particular literary school, they can defeat the hopes of men. The consolidating purpose in all scholarship is to display true values, humanly expressed through the arts, and so to break down the walls of ignorance separating people from one another. The student learns to find himself by learning out of literature how others think, feel, and believe. It is the duty and purpose of the scholar-teacher to reveal such meanings. He is expected to know intimately the physical and abstract environments surrounding the body and mind of each author, and then to interpret what he understands to men of his own times. If the scholar becomes, by intense study, so much a part of the past that he is removed emotionally and intellectually from life about him, he becomes an antiquarian, in the unfavorable sense, and is lost to literary studies. His return to effective usefulness will be when historical and critical perspectives bring him back to discover himself and those about him. He then will be ready to guide students out of limited opinion into comparative judgments of lasting value.

It is the role of the scholar as teacher to teach as the artist creates, with a new approach each day to his subject in the light as he sees it. He is not manufacturing a standard product to distribute under guarantees of quality and kind. He is an individualist, and every interpretation is an original. Yet the scholar and the teacher agree on their need for public appreciation, not for themselves but for their aims and for the materials that they work in. They know what part students and teachers have in forming the taste and ideals of oncoming generations. For all in humanities, therefore, it is by devoted attention to literary studies that such services to the present and to future time can be performed most satisfactorily, but only after the essentials of work with literatures are known and used by the investigator, interpreter, and reader.

Whatever the language and period of time in which a literary work took its form, three circumstances were present—a matured form of language, a body of meanings that could be appreciatively heard or read in that language with some beauty of effect, and a person capable of giving life to words and ideas by the transforming power of personality working through a familiar art medium. These are the essentials of literature in the making: they are accepted as needed for critical appreciation. The scholar knows that he must begin at the beginning, with word symbols and intricacies of structure and changing of meaning. He proceeds toward something like mastery of the ideas, facts, and concepts that were in the mind of the maker. In short, he retraces the movements of another mind and spirit as well as he can. Efforts of many scholars may be necessary for satisfying elucidation; we have not done with Scriptural sources and we lack definitive texts of most primary authors. Yet each new time has the benefits of what was done before.

V

Repetition of these common sayings on scholarly and critical practices is to remind the student that all work with literature succeeds by realizing the three forces producing them. Like the scholar, the student will remember that languages and histories are the taproots of the humanities, and that he must know them. They are out of the soils of centuries. Should either be cut off, new growth in literature would stop, and the living forms would soon become meaningless. Without the nurture from language and incidents of human experience, literary production is as impossible as any physical change in nature. As languages and histories are growths out of civilization, so the literatures which they yield are the final flowers of human culture.

A fairly mature language is the first necessity for a literary mind and for the society which it is to serve. These are as essential for growth of folk literature—sometimes called "folklore," which it is not—as for the production of sophisticated writings by a contemporary poet or essayist. The unnamed creators of oral literature, in song or legend, had their relationships to their own times through living languages and historical-traditional substances of many kinds. It was purely coincidental that over long periods the thoughts and feelings dominant in their societies were given out only in oral forms. Eventually, these were saved from death in silence. Parchment, paper, and recordings on other materials brought them to a fairly secure state of being. Ballads, epics, chronicles, and simpler tales came to a kind of permanence, enabling them to travel far beyond the range of the voices of their narrators and to live on in immeasurably greater spaces and in unlimited time.

In its origins, folk literature illustrates the natural ways by which every "literature" attains that level of recognition. It has qualities of thought and of expression to be counted lasting in art and in meanings to men. Any body of material, or a single product, qualifies under the restricted meaning of the term if it portrays representative characteristics of individuals, or of peoples, with a peculiar strength and beauty. There will be a kind of reality that is familiar to readers or listeners, made by a union of thought, feeling, and imagination in the writer's treatment of his theme. He may live in a society incompetent to appreciate his work, or periodically his merits may fail to attract; yet having attained to a universality of expression and of artistic communication, he may count on satisfying many others, as himself, in the reading of his writings.

Folk literatures are also illustrative of the uses that all histories have in literary productivity. The materials of legend and myth are as valid with the artist as the most completely verifiable facts. It is in this sense that the interpreters of human meaning, and their critics, consider histories of every conceivable kind, and out of all the sources of the imagination as well as from reality. The humanist and the creative worker in the arts make histories from such minute elements as the experience of a moment and such sweeping stories as that of the lost nations of antiquity. An incident or an imagined experience qualifies as history in that both happened. Like other products of the humanities, history is more than literal recording of what may be thought to be all the details. It is the work of an informed and active mind that possesses some power of imaginative reconstruction.

The end of a literary vogue or the death of a great writer starts two sorts of appraisal—by readers and by the critics. Their tests may be made at the same time, or one may be deferred until some special cause raises the materials of that period or the work of that particular writer again to public notice. We have had both literary and scholarly vogues of long-departed writers—of Piers Plowman with the scholars, of Donne and Melville with both scholars and general readers. Any such revival creates new and enduring estimates, provided that the minds of the critics are informed and judicious. The inclinations of criticism are for such reasons useful. They show the depth of intelligence and the sensitiveness of spirit in the society that produced it. A scanning of the critical works of several generations will therefore show something true on causes of success in the arts.

Another reason for such reviews of critical writing may be to seek for an answer to the tantalizing question, What *is* literature? Each critic is to be judged useful if he answers only from the work in hand. There is no total definition of individual differences. When a critic is satisfied to write against a backdrop of critical theories, he is engaged in "high-level" controversy with a real or imagined opponent. To aid the public mind, he should confine the scholasticisms of critical schools within himself. He stands or falls by the same tests as the author he is to judge for his public. When he aids his own generation to discriminate among the writings of their own time, he raises the level of public taste precisely to the degree of his personal intelligence and sensitiveness. When he works in the literatures of earlier periods, he benefits those discriminating students who from then on will place his work in two perspectives—that of his own period and that of his subject as treated in the history of literatures. There is place in scholarship for the refinements of critical disquisition; yet it seems true that a critic is wise to write with clarity for the general reader as well as for the specialist in criticism. He too must be read in order to have influence.

As a literary vogue comes to its close, the writings of its creators are brought under the test of later generations. Then begins the same selective process that has winnowed out what is read from the writings of earlier times. Even those so carried forward in time fall into widely different class divisions among men, according to their special or universal appeals and their artistic merits. To survive at all, a literary work must be read. It can die as easily on shelves as in the fading memories of unlettered folk societies. To continue in the minds of men with a good share of its original values intact, literature needs also the aid of the humanist as interpreter, the reminder of each successive generation to look at life through the writings of great, representative men.

A command of languages, living and "dead," is essential for a full understanding of the literatures embodied in them. At best, translations are poor substitutes, prized most when they give us our only possible insights into societies now vanished and completely dependent upon exceptional scholarship for discovery and reconstruction. As such specialists in rarer languages pass on, they must leave trained successors, lest once again the old symbols become unintelligible and the works themselves incomprehensible. Then the literatures in these ancient tongues would lie untouched until reclaimed through such a revival of learning as became the forerunner of the Renaissance.

In our time, the works of ancient China are positively threatened with that fate. Banned works in Russian will live on outside of the Soviet Union, under the care of interested scholars, and possibly such good fortune will fall to such massive works as the dynastic histories of China, in spite of destructive inroads into all established values of that country. Yet the profound and ancient thought of China, and of other countries, might easily in future time come to be dependent on the efforts of external scholarship. Great sectors of man's past can again become buried in the waste lands that have covered older civilizations in every quarter of the globe. We have not learned how to prevent wanton destruction, but only how to piece together again some of the recovered fragments of lost cultures.

Whenever such piecing together has been necessary, scholars have been called upon, to the limit of their abilities, to perform their reconstructive acts. In some cases they have tried for centuries; in others, they have tried more briefly in time and have failed to break through the barriers. With Greek, Hebraic, and Latin literatures their cumulative efforts have won rewards; yet of these three, as conceivably may be true of Chinese in later time, a neglect of studies can close the cultural and historical treasure houses partially or completely. Some later generation may be the solver of the mysteries of Mayan, but probably only in case the work of critical analysis steadily adds knowledge and younger scholars to carry on to greater knowledge. It is through these very obvious examples that one can realize this startling truth—that without the scholar the world around us would vanish and without the interpreter its fuller meanings would soon be dimmed.

This half century has had its ruthless demonstrations of that insolent attitude toward the history and literature of our world that would make all scholars into slaves of dictatorial masters. In this country, the scholar maintains his place and constantly increases his gifts to society; in turn, he is looked up to and is counted on for unprejudiced, highly prized contributions to human well-being. Yet even so, the public mind is too easily satisfied with the consequence and too forgetful of the conditions of its attainment. This may be said also of the scholar, with his spirit of specialization that blurs an awareness of other scholars about him. Equally true is it that the teacher who travels by signboards of critical dogma through the given textbooks of a literature, can be without feeling for his subject. Each must sense the intercommunication among linguists, historians of every kind, and producers of literary works; otherwise there can be no structure for continuing growth or conscious appreciation of the world behind us as well as about us.

VI

The future of literary studies is to be helped or hindered by the originality of those teachers who start younger students in their particular fields during the years of secondary school and college. No more resourceful and conscientious persons are to be found in educational service than those who guide the work in modern literatures. They have a particularly onerous burden in the general survey courses, more so in English and American literatures than in others. It is that exceptional demand upon each individual that raises a doubt on the dependence which they may show toward critical writings. As they prepare their lectures and arrange the topics for class discussions each day, year after year, the tendency may be toward absorption of ideas from criticism and a consequent neglect of reading in the original texts. The issue is not one of plagiarism, but of such absorption from the writings of specialists that the substances unconsciously fix one's point of view. The fault may carry on from imperceptible imitation to the point of complete adoption of points of view and a substitution of what someone else has thought for active thinking.

I know everyone realizes the ineptness of borrowed phrases; they are quickly recognized in the speech of others, if not in our own. This difference in our awareness of imitative speech leads me to the conclusion that a teacher may easily adopt phrases and ideas unawares, to use them as if his own. If this happens, the lack of original thinking behind the statements in which they appear probably is obvious. The well-wrought idea that is created from reflection is not marred by imitative sound or sense.

Here I am thinking only of work with literature. The faults of borrowing and of echoing conventional dicta are to be found in all other fields of humanistic study. All are open to imitative discourse and therefore to dogmatism. Abstract terms for art and philosophy may serve as substitutes for analytic thinking, while the nature of art almost invites to dependence upon descriptive phrases. The point of particular emphasis in reference to literature is that this is the master form and most significant, for good or ill, in all humanistic expression as in teaching. To avoid what may be thought an open charge of blame, I hasten to add that I have been discussing what is an evident danger to be guarded against. Terminology and general conclusions framed in descriptive phrases are of great help in defining characteristics of literary periods and of their significant writers. Many such practices are imperative if we are to raise discussion above particulars, but terminology and imitative thought can move into speech and writing as a substitute for individual analysis. This single fact is reason to fear lest the teaching of literature may become dependent on printed criticism and lose that essential originality of the teacher in his own interpretations from the text.

American practice in teaching of literature has been modified toward that kind of dependence by heavy enrollments in secondary schools and colleges. Demands for materials have been great, and supplies have increased enormously year after year in measure to satisfy them. A danger has come from this mechanical sufficiency of production, not to the student but to the teacher. Critical histories of English and American literature are of such excellent quality, and selections in matching anthologies so neatly dovetailed into their critical estimates, that large classes can be held in equilibrium and by their assigned reading be well prepared for lectures and discussions. The effect upon teaching will be good, or the opposite, according to the originality and initiative of the teachers themselves. There is a possibility that, in extreme cases, the critical history will become an alternative for individual interpretation by the teacher of those greater bodies of literary materials in English prose and poetry to which anthologies and histories are only introductory.

The less heavily burdened departments of German, French, and Spanish have equally dependable works that combine critical interpretations with annotated texts, ample anthologies, and general literary histories. Newer fields, and the older ones that now have a moderate following among college students, are being similarly supplied with textual and historical backgrounds. Every literature that colleges offer for serious study is brought to easier and finer interpretations through such applied values from scholarship to the arts of critical editing and historical survey.

As now practiced, these are unquestionably arts, based upon long experience of scholars, teachers, and critical historians. Rapid and coherent development of programs in modern literatures has led to the production of excellent materials for students from their earliest years of secondary education through the last of undergraduate study. The sole danger—if it be one, in the opinion of others—lies in easy acceptance of what is well done. The mechanics of mass production can overpower and drive out natural creativeness in reflecting on literature and so stop individual interpretation in teaching. We hear a good deal of the danger to imaginative expression in youth from excesses of visual exposure, and we know that they therefore read much less, in quantity, from longer works of prose and poetry. It may prove to be true, therefore, that in the study of literatures the critical authority of the printed page will seem an easy substitute for independent analysis of original texts, first for the teacher and next inevitably for students who have never learned to read, with conscious effort in thinking, through verbal symbols.

This unguarded generalization is left for later analysis. The intention here is to emphasize how important is the integrity of teaching of literatures. They stand midway between their own sources (and so of all the other humanities) and the expressive arts that rely upon literary materials for their being. From the one side, a literature draws in the essential words and symbols, ideas, beliefs, and ideals for its own existence. On the other, it sends its transmutations of human experience to workers in all the other mediums of cultural expression. Literatures stand at the crossroads of civilization. If diligently studied by those fitly trained, they will yield an understanding that can be had by no other means of the life of men in other times and from other origins.

Appreciation of what literatures have to tell us can be enhanced by the suggestions for original thinking that are to be found in critical writings, but suggestions cannot stand as substitutes for what the authors tell. Critical writing is not like the original texts that it represents. It is subject to destruction by new evidence and is usually dated by the outlook of its writer. For example, the writings of Stopford Brooke tell us little today about either Shakespeare or his works. For a knowledge of their author, I should go to the recent study of Miss Chute[5]; and for Shakespeare in every other meaning, I should go first to the plays and poems. It is so in the study of all literature. Teachers and critics are guides to sources of knowledge and designers of critical appreciation, but neither can give what we must get for ourselves or stand in our stead as interpreters.

Students should be sent to critical writings and asked on return to tell what they found. But since all critical studies are as removed from actuality in literature as are secondary sources of fact in literary history, they likewise are open to misuse by both teacher and student. Criticism can give easy answers that pass as substitutes for direct responses to what is in the literary work itself. It can make a dependent mind, and therefore an uncritical one, defeating in the end the learner's powers to criticize or to create new works of his own. As preventives for such losses of originality, the experienced teacher will direct the student toward his own most important source of critical judgment—personal experience, as modified by other teachers and critics and by his own reflection.

At any time in the course of his literary studies, the student or the mature teacher finds profit in such self-examination to discover the sources of his opinions. This retrospective review should show him how he came toward, if not into, the domain of English literature—or of any other that holds first place in his mind. He will find how much he is attached to the views of particular critics, and how far he has gone beyond what he learned from those who taught him at successive points in his studies. He will remember, too, when and how often he has read the works on which his opinions have been formed—how well he knows truly original sources. Such an introspective turn of thought will prove indifferently useful to those who have never come under the lasting influence of great works of literature. It is, on the contrary, invaluable to any who confidently believe that somewhere in the world of words they will find a permanent interest.

That backward look can be most valuable to teachers in secondary schools. By it will be recovered recollections of certain turning points in an education that took form during hours of free reading in literatures, from the requirements of courses, and out of influences of personal nature. Some or all of such positive advantages, known by experience, can be multiplied in one's teaching. They may have been unrecognized as advantages during their happening. That fact is in itself proof of the necessity to repeat, in the practices of teaching, what unquestionably were significant aids toward a developed interest in literatures. We know now what they were, and can apply them wisely to the benefit of those who likewise long after will realize their shaping influence. My own experiences with books and teachers, briefly summed up, signify something of the way in which practices of teaching are first formed in the years of secondary school.

Entering into imaginative experiences through printed pages began with the discovery that they could give freedom for distant travel, without effort, into all of time and place. It was unusual, fifty years ago, to read a magazine, and all of American letters seemed to be in schoolbooks or those ornamented volumes of Whittier, Longfellow, and Emerson used as gifts. They were known from cover to cover, but the real mass of reading that waited for hours out of school was from British authors. There was leisure to complete all the titles in every set of their works before a study of foreign languages opened the way into the literatures of Greece, Rome, France, and Germany. Our prescribed books were then illuminating or wearying, according to the teachers who brought them before us. The classics of Latin and Greek literature were for me as vividly alive as any books that I read in English, because that was the way they were taught. Long after, in graduate school, the modern literatures of continental Europe came into easy understanding; even then, Italian, Spanish, and German made slow going when the whole of English letters was being opened almost simultaneously for serious, and satisfying, study. I should have had reading in one or all of their literatures as an undergraduate and constant exposure to new writing in the English of my own and all other countries. Latin, Greek, French, German, and Spanish did not bend attention toward contemporary literatures in any language as then taught, though all made secure the symbols and ideas of the westward tradition.

I am conscious of the strict limitation on reading from any contemporary authors that was put upon me by the rigors of exact study in graduate school, but grateful for the chance to try for a grounding in the classics before rapid reading in works written after 1600. Today, it is my speculative guess that advanced students do much better with modern writers and much less than we did with the ancients. It is to this point that I have been coming in a roundabout way, namely, How does a teacher relate his own background to that of younger students? What are their common grounds of knowledge and how much regard have they for one another as intellectuals from whom to derive standards of critical judgment suited to these times as well as to absolute standards of value? Particularly, can a teacher, in an older tradition of learning, make his knowledge lively in the minds of persons of a different outlook on taste and meaning in letters?

These questions are answered, for me, by examples out of the minds of better critics of literature and of teaching. The workers with literature in formal education have left us a store of wisdom on their profession; here there is room for only two views on the relationship between the scholar and his students and readers. The first of these touches on the thesis that, particularly in literary studies, the teacher must know himself if he is to understand his students. His approaches to their ways of critical understanding must be by what he represents in their eyes and what they literally are in development and in outlook.

A few years ago Grierson and Smith graciously submitted their judgment to that of younger men. They did so in the prefatory note of their *Critical History of English Poetry,* with this offhand allusion to their background: ". . . We are well aware that critics like us whose taste in poetry was formed in Victorian days, may fail to do justice to the poetry and the criticism of the present generation, between which and the Victorian Age a 'shift of sensibility' has occurred comparable to that which took place between the Age of Pope and the Age of Wordsworth."[6] One can think of no happier prelude to a critical discourse in print or in the classroom. It exemplifies the spirit of scholarship at its best by warning the reader or hearer to be on his guard against what may be less true for his formative period than that of the writer who lives with the minds he is criticizing. By accepting such warnings, and by remembering them as he travels through all critical works, every reader gains catholicity and tolerance in his own approaches to literature. He learns also the honesty of independent judgments and emulates those who make them. In short, he cannot become an imitative critic or teacher, repeating what others have said and written.

The other example is effective only with advanced students of critical writing. It reveals what two critics, the one writing and the one written about, believed regarding the aims of literary study. In his recent chapter on "Literary History" Wellek writes of "Oliver Elton, whose *Survey of English Literature,* in six volumes—the most remarkable achievement of recent literary history in England—frankly professes to be 'really a review, a direct criticism,' and not a history."[7] This brief quotation stresses the distinctive belief of each, that "history" is made in the mind of the critic, and that his subjective responses to literary materials surpass in effect all factual and analytic reporting. Elton and Wellek are as one in stating that everyone determines for himself what his approach is to be; whatever he then writes or says is vital and real, because his own responses have been of that order of values.

It cannot be too often repeated, that to be dominated by fixed theories of criticism would be disastrous to any teacher and to the students under him. It is necessary for them, in due time, to know what others before them have thought about great works of literature. They should begin then to restock their minds with fresh impressions out of the works themselves, as they do comparative study in critical writings. These two procedures should be followed by student and teacher, and always as a means to personal reflection and personal expression. When such habits of critical analysis are established, there will be no more question concerning the importance of literary study or the quality of American production in literary forms. The ideal of individual responsibility for what each produces in his art is an old one. It is accepted as being fundamental to originality. That same spirit of individual responsibility must control the processes of critical interpretation. When teachers subdue theory to their own uses and rely on themselves more than on professional critics, they make their profession an art and themselves producing artists.

VII

Other demands now being made on American teachers of literature are created by foreign and domestic needs. These reach to the lowest level of elementary education and to the end of advanced study in graduate schools. They are being asked insistently to help in the interpretation of American life. Under a good many plans of the government, the teacher is going abroad and all too often without a preparation in the essential backgrounds of life here or in the country to which he is going. Materials for interpretation in both directions are wanted, for use at every level of learning. Since literatures are among the primary forces toward bringing understanding of peoples, there must be better planning of teaching our own and also of learning from the literatures of other countries. Part of that learning will be by translations, and a part through the services of foreign teachers in producing finer interpretations of their own cultures. Yet both of these ways to understanding are less enduring than a personal ability to read in the literature of one or more cultures in addition to our own.

The teaching of foreign languages, therefore, is forced upon our attention. A review of what is being done today shows that American schools are giving too little work in any foreign language during the earlier years. Not only is it commonly lacking in primary school, but decreases have been great at the secondary school level. In the reforms of the curriculum these past twenty years, languages have fared badly. There must be a change in timing and in method, so that American youth will start their study of foreign language at the best period of life for ready learning and will continue it to useful applications. Meanwhile, every means must be used to enlarge the control of students, in school and college, over their own language, that as a nation we may possess the ability to communicate through a general appreciation of the myriads of meaning that are waiting to be exchanged in words. We shall increase in understanding of all things as we gain control of our own vocabularies for reading, speaking, and writing at all levels of thought and interpretation.

The true answers on ways of teaching literatures are to be found in the state of maturity attained by the society that is to be taught. Other answers are probably good, but theoretical until tested by this applied method. It is useless to offer students the refinements of literary study until they know the rudiments of effective communication. So of a total society. The maturity of its arts will depend upon its own power of understanding and on the ability of teachers to improve that ability from its existing level. For generations, the teaching of languages and literatures in this country has been conditioned adversely by an uneven control among its citizens of the resources of their own language. That condition is changing rapidly, with better schools and an older, more stable society to be served by them. American scholarship, like the American people, is ready for productive service and appreciation of what is to be given by that service through literary studies based on surer use of language. The nation has arrived at a stage of readiness after its long period of colonization and continental conquest of physical resources.

All our study of language and so of literature has been related to that westward movement of peoples out of Europe and western Asia. Until recent years they were coming in great numbers to scatter without plan over the entire country. That has been the true "westward movement" of all history. By comparison, the successive waves of change, economically, from our Atlantic coast to the Pacific, were continuous and almost predictable. At least some of its economic contours are easily charted, now that the moving forces have subsided. But not so of this scattering of people, caused by every human desire, to give us in close contact groups of foreign-born citizens having all varieties of linguistic background. Slowly they learned to use two or more languages. This central land mass of the continent contains today the descendant generations from immigrants of a hundred and fifty years. Stabilization, culturally, is on the way with them now. Their mental and emotional habits are becoming parts of the American unity, and languages that once were resistant to American schooling in our form of English are now enriching its speech and writing.

The schoolmaster in America carried on his struggles with foreign idioms during several generations. A part of his difficulty was his own, for he too usually came from somewhere else bringing with him the marks of another background. Therein is the explanation of what has been the obligation put upon departments of English in the American college—not the shortcomings of secondary education, whatever they may have been, but the unfinished transformation from foreign language patterns into English patterns, and so of every process of thought.

The teacher in college, over the years, has had only a sublimation of what the schoolmaster and schoolmistress have worked in. All have had the duties, familiar in this country and accepted as important ones, of making foreign languages understood by reading, by listening, and conceivably by writing them. This third stage of accomplishment had its place in our study of Latin long before the decline of American concern with this most fundamental language for all literary studies, but the writing of Latin prose was the weakest educational device for developing understanding or appreciation. Modern languages now are taught, with a laboratory approach, in every way that one uses normally for the learning of his mother tongue; at last, through sounder procedures, the American teacher of any modern language has resources of method lacking when Latin, Greek, and the more customary modern languages were being taught for use in silent reading or in oral translation, but rarely for speech and writing and scarcely ever for the purpose of reading widely in contemporary materials.

These are in themselves facts of common knowledge. Their implication, in past decades, for the advancement of appreciation of any foreign literature, was by no means so obvious. The simplest comparison of what the American college was endeavoring to do, until recently, is of one who tries at the same moment to accomplish two physical operations that are flatly contradictory in processes. Demands in learning were made upon foreign-born students by English-speaking teachers who knew no modern language idioms except their own and those of British literature. They could not surmise what mental struggles were going on in the minds of their students as they endeavored to think in foreign vocabularies and to translate their thoughts into a strange language across the intermediate barrier of British idiom.

Today the American systems of school and college education have students of fairly uniform ability in English. They can enter into studies of modern foreign languages on equal footing, and with few hindering idioms or odd grammatical structures from their family backgrounds. Their faults are rather from a lack of wide reading in English and ignorance of any other language that will open the way into another modern literature. These are slight handicaps compared with the advantages from better textbooks, unequalled stocks of materials in print, and teachers with broader and deeper understanding of other cultures. A population that is linguistically and intellectually responsive to higher education as never before, will, in consequence, bring to this country its finest periods of cultivation through assimilations from old and modern literatures. These benefits irresistibly will increase the American power and desire for all the benefits that literatures in the past have brought to other peoples whose languages have developed to maturity and whose outlook on life is cosmopolitan.

If we are to justify such abundant hopes, we shall of necessity bring back into the American consciousness some of those literatures that have been permitted to languish. Greek, Latin, Italian, and the transferred and changed European tongues of Latin America are known sources of cultural interchange. They must have places in schools and colleges alongside the more commonly taught languages that for generations have introduced students to the literatures of French, Spanish, Dutch, Scandinavian, and German origin. On the other flank of customary languages for literary interpretation, is a new group from Asia and the nearer boundaries of the East and West. The demand to discover what these unaccustomed materials of higher education contain, of old and contemporary meanings, is an insistent one. Those who know the potential power in any literature to reveal the ideals of a people, are pressing for production of better interpretative studies. These—like the best of translations—are immediate aids toward developing original insight. Both are produced through intense study by the few and subsequent preparation of those who are being inducted into appreciative understanding of other cultures.

The greatest new freedom for finer accomplishments has come to departments of English. As they are being relieved of routine instruction in the rudiments of grammar and of oral and written expression, they are gaining new cultural potentials by opportunities at higher levels in these same areas of learning. Speech, drama, and more mature expression through writing, have become important phases of advanced work in English. In "language-and-area" programs, English has its most striking effect upon all within university and college staffs, and through them upon the total cultural outlook of American society.

VIII

One of the issues that teachers must deal with promptly, is the extent to which those who study language and those who study linguistics cooperate, from lowest to highest levels in education. Nothing in my reading of three years past impresses me so greatly as the necessity to define the terms that, as workers in humanities, we agree upon for the study and applied uses of words. What I should wish to have adopted as an ideal of all humanists is in the often quoted sentences of Sapir, in which he says, "Languages are more to me than systems of thought transference. They are the invisible garments that drape themselves about our spirit and give a pre-determined form to all its symbolic expression. When the expression is of unusual significance, we call it 'literature.'" To these sentences he added the other significant and disarming remarks, "I can hardly stop to define what kind of expression is 'significant' enough to be called art or literature. Besides, I do not exactly know."[8] His positive statements of faith and of ignorance can be of help as we estimate the value of what is being written today regarding the needs and purposes of work with words.

Persisting calls for attention to word meanings come from those who talk and write of semantics. The materials that they offer us under that heading are plentiful today, being the accumulations from popular writing as well as from formal inquiry into procedures for learning and application. Few persons within universities realize the extent of interest among business and industrial groups that search after ways to impress the minds of others by skill in the selection and arrangement of words. They are endeavoring to bridge at once all the historical, psychological, logical, and associative origins of word usage.

So far, in literary studies, we have proceeded from the assumptions that the study of foreign languages and the reading done in them and in English would open the way to expression and understanding. It is now required that the processes of development be restudied, in order to find whether or not a simpler and more quickly responsive approach to the meanings in verbal symbols can be defined for formal education.

The study of semantics has now passed a milestone in higher education. Having long been a subsidiary of all literary studies under other names, its potential usefulness as science or theory should be open to an objective assessment by all professional humanists. Those specialists who have devoted their lives to philology, in whatever form, and linguists, through their varied approaches, can give us the answers. Advocates of semantics as a defined field of study ask for constant observations on variants in meaning. They look to the differing circumstances of impression as of expression, not merely for changes through time; in fact, my notion is that they are scantly interested in anything more than the "present," a vaguely definitive word unless set in the reference of first hearing and use by someone. These concerns with meaning, by comparison with those of professional academicians, may seem without difference, but they are not. The seventh international congress of linguists, held in 1952 in London, devoted all its sessions to issues raised by these protagonists of a new faith in the uses of words, with some implied doubt on their part of a need to proceed historically. That formal recognition by scholars was given in a manner unpredictable by anyone ten years ago.

The simplest way of work with words, as words, is presumably by the study of synonyms and antonyms. From such beginnings many school and college aspirants for literary honors have gone into further investigations. I have known them to buy and to use Roget's *Thesaurus*, with the laudable idea of improving their vocabularies. Some have discovered the *Oxford English Dictionary* and the *Dictionary of American English*. These have often become fascinated by their tracing of words, through dated examples, over the centuries. Such massive works of scholarship can illustrate how man, for his changing purposes, has made words do his bidding. They make clearer to us of what persons were thinking when they wrote in former days. But to believe the historical dictionary to be more than a resource for the mining of ideas from words in older contexts, would be to delude oneself. Every incentive that arouses people to increase their appreciative recognition of words, phrases, and idioms in any language will profit all study in literatures. That recognition may go beyond the limits of study to create a wider usefulness for communication. At present, semantics as a "science" of language has something to gain from the research and practice of academicians in exchange for its undoubted power to arouse inquiring discussion.

Scholars are well aware of the issues involved in the meanings of words, as all know from their allusions to such works as *The Meaning of Meaning*[9] by Ogden and Richards, Sapir's *Language*, and the increasing stream of significant titles since the appearance of these earlier books on functions of language. Allusions to the part that words play in all thinking are to be met everywhere, as in the common remark on how difficult and complex are the problems raised by the literary and philosophical uses of words, and in Chinard's oral urging that moral and intellectual profit through literatures begins with a distrust of vague words. Such comments ask us for refinements in use and in definition, mentally, as much as on the printed page. One observation that comes from Cornford, as he writes on the intangibility of philosophy, is that "philosophical discussion, all the way through [has] rested on tacit assumptions, which were enshrined in the ambiguities of language."[10] The awareness of the scholar toward such difficulties needs no heightening. It is the teacher who is called on, in school and college, first to sense a need to strengthen in variety and depth his own use of verbal symbols and next to point the way for students toward developing their capacities for thought and expression.

Urgent attention being given by American scholars to semantics appears in many formal actions that carry into the classroom the issues that were raised at the London conference in 1952. The announcements of courses in semantics for undergraduates and graduate students multiply. As a single source of such interest, I have noted the following, from a 1950 catalog of the University of California at Los Angeles, on work being offered under staff men in philosophy. Semantics, in their program implies the study of the philosophy of language and of meaning, with special reference to all the implications for logic, theory of knowledge, and theory of value. The sources of discussion are indicated as being in the writings of Frege, Russell, Tarski, Carnap, Morris, Quine, and others. This list of persons who have given their thought to the implications of semantics for philosophy implies by their eminence something of the extent of interest in American universities. The same claims could be made for the uses of semantic discourse in pressing outward the existing boundaries of mathematics, law, aesthetics, and every literature by analytic studies of symbols.

It is in this last relationship that semantics, as a means to analysis and deduction, arrives at formal applications to literary study in the research of Spitzer. His lectures on linguistics and literary history gave a basis for his published collection of essays in stylistics.[11] In these he draws on relevant resources in the work of several other scholars to enlarge the scope of linguistic studies and to produce conclusions on appreciation aesthetically, psychologically, philosophically, and historically. Stylistic knowledge is so to be based upon proved principles having a scientific quality, not as individually produced in and through the personalities of critics. It is as though minute analysis of a text, after a reduction of its parts to atomic elements, is counted on to reconcile scholarship and criticism and to yield clear definitions of literary style that are free of personal bias and partisanship.

These scantly understood statements on method and aim are, for me, significant in ways that the inquiring scholar from any department of literature must accept. After a studious examination of what is in the writings of Spitzer and his allies in such research, he will agree with the three obvious judgments here passed upon some types of literary criticism now found in this country. It is concluded that classifications of literature by periods can be grotesquely oversimple; that the study of individual influences can be misleading, turning particulars into erroneous general conclusions; and that continuity of growth is not demonstrable.

Earlier writers on stylistics have dealt with concepts on the margins of this matter. They have brought out interesting parallels to the asserted realities of results from scientific methods in interpreting literature.

In contradiction of the Darwinian thesis as used by analogy to explain evolution in kinds of literary forms, some have shown that the Mendelian laws of heredity are equally applicable. The inference follows that literatures follow no predictable or demonstrable lines of ancestry, either slowly regular or irregularly recurring. Also, stylistic analyses of individual writers have been used toward the identification of anonymous works, or for more involved studies containing substances from a particular literary period or school of writers. How exact and therefore how useful they have proved to be, is not clear; apart from opinions of the critics, they still are in a twilight zone of credibility. Yet accepted or still to be so, such approaches to literature are to continue. They may raise intellectual detachment to a level where theory outruns sensibility, and remove literary studies of their kind into a separate compartment of knowledge. In that case, there will again be raised the doubt that analytic processes are wholly applicable to literature without destructive consequences for its supreme value as an art.

IX

The remaining topics for comment are teaching and research, as these terms stand day after day in the mind of the scholar. Before taking up that of research, in some detail, I may succeed in bringing out reasons why essentially these two functions are closely related and often are identical. Here is an instance in which outlook, professionally, has its effect on definition. Instead of that immediate and personal approach, a surer and more satisfying way is by stating the ultimate cause for choosing a life of scholarship. If this derives from one's philosophy of life, as I believe it should, the first need is to have one that bears examination. That, fortunately, is made easily possible for the worker in literatures, provided that thought is taken in time to obtain an adequate exposure to philosophies in general.

Upon his entry into serious work with any literature, every student finds himself promptly turning to the sister disciplines of philosophy and history, searching for explanations of his texts. Should he proceed toward teaching as a career, he will soon have borne in upon his mind that he never will know enough in either field. His increases of knowledge serve only to encourage him toward deeper inquiry, particularly into world philosophies and religions. It would have been fortunate for him to have had basic outlines of these presented as requirements among his undergraduate studies. Though philosophy is essential to the advanced training of all humanists, and most surely for those who deal in literary materials, it is not counted among those subjects to be definitely required of them.

As matters now stand, the student of literatures usually learns his philosophy through familiarity with the concepts of particular writers. In that way he gathers up the most essential fragments of meaning for interpretation, but not enough to give him a fair perspective of the thought in that period of time for which a particular work was written. He finds his philosophy through literature. In such manner he discovers deism, in the works of Pope and Dryden. He finds in Milton a blend of Christian, pagan, and formalized doctrines of the Renaissance. If he reads deeply in Spenser's poetry, he meets many of the symbols of philosophical thought that have animated the imitative writings of other poets. Working backward, in time, he comes upon all that the Renaissance sent onward throughout Europe—Italian scepticism, variants of Platonism, and the full flow of all that is in Greek, Roman, and Hebraic philosophies. These he can scarcely come to know. They demand attentive and continuous study, something that as a student of literature he is by then giving elsewhere in full measure. When he is once engaged in preparing for his profession, any serious work with philosophy, history, or religion will seem to him impossible.

His induction into the prevalent philosophies of the sixteenth to the nineteenth centuries, however, will eventually be accomplished. By the end of undergraduate studies he may be able to draw out of memory enough fact to make surface interpretations of an author's allusions and symbols. Should he progress satisfactorily through comprehensive examinations on his studies during four years in college, he is ready to venture on higher levels in a graduate school. There he meets, on admission, the requirement of training in methods of research. At once he will relinquish all thought of philosophy and of any free reading as being avocational. For a term of years his course will be charted by obligations that are put upon him by plans for his career.

That experience in methodical preparation for research is a long-range benefit. It is not imposed by chance or simply as a test of staying powers. While going through such necessary stages of training in method, the students themselves are discovering their personal aptitudes for various kinds of specialization. The faculty, in still greater degree, are learning these same facts about their students. No effort is made to indoctrinate them with an unquestioning faith in any single system of intellectual procedures; the purposes are rather to make clear the sources of learning and the appropriate methods for progressive development throughout a lifetime of study and teaching.

The student, in consequence, is guided into narrowed paths of investigation for definite purposes that will appear clear in due time. The literary faculties in any large graduate school have a great deal of experience in planning the work of advanced students. Every assignment of a thesis subject toward a higher degree requires a decision on the progressive development of an individual. Understanding and careful advising are developed in the process of making hundreds of such assignments over the years. An effort is necessary, on the part of both students and faculties, if critical judgment through reading and exact analysis of research data are to develop simultaneously. This compulsory strain to learn more of method and material while developing a thesis on an untested theory, creates a temporary confusion of purposes in the minds of many. If it is not overcome, the residue is a belief that teaching and research are opposites. Temporarily, even permanently, that notion may persist, to produce the assumption that close attention to one or the other is demanded for a successful performance in the judgment of the profession.

That assumption is from the old fallacy that research and teaching are opposed in nature and in purpose. The notion persists, in some quarters, that literary studies are particularly marked with this divisive formula, whereas precisely the opposite is the case. The nature of this old error is fully stated by Garrod when discussing the creative and the critical worker. He wrote in his *Scholarship: Its Meaning and Its Value,* as follows:

The two activities are conceived as antithetical. We pit Imagination against Knowledge, Letters against Science, the Poet against the Scholar: and in the very act of doing so we are fighting against the cause for which these contrasted causes exist—the unity of the human spirit.[12]

Another and positive statement on how the worker with literature is to free his mind from doubts on how to proceed, is in the simple solution of Hanford, as he tells how historical background, not historical criticism, prepares the mind to interpret. He tells the reader that the way to know an author and to find his place in the history of culture is by discovering why he thought and wrote as he did. So, for illustration, he writes, that

the indispensable aids to Miltonic study are a well-indexed English Bible, a Homer, a Virgil, an Ovid, a Horace, a Tasso, a Spenser, a Shakespeare. The Scriptural and other references in the notes [to his edition of Milton] will be valuable in proportion to the diligence with which they are employed. For the "good" student of Milton may be defined as one who reads, or at least desires to read, the Bible, the ancients, and the greater moderns as he read them.[13]

As a beginning of wisdom, the teacher may well follow this prescription—to read, "as he read them," those works that formed the thinking and framed the expression of a significant writer. That practice, if followed, will solve many questions on expenditures of time that might be taken from literature for philosophy, for science, and for history in pursuit of ideas essential to critical interpretation. The originals for his own thought, if known, give that background. On any author or any period of literary history, such source reading is practicable during the years of teaching and research in a long professional career. The lines of reading are not too easily marked, and the declared ends of such reading may be turned into searches for analogues and literal sources. It would, however, be a pity to have these common dangers of the road deter from travel. They are of the same sort, in different guise, as are hidden in the more accessible printed pages of literary criticism.

When the minutiae of parallelism are made final objectives in research, some benefits may be gained, but not many. The spirit of the searcher will determine. Finding minor likenesses in literary documents that are a year, or two centuries, apart in time of writing, is as apt to be unsatisfying as running down presumed biographical evidence by allusions in an author's works. Interpretation is to rest upon awareness of the writer's philosophy of life as developed out of known intellectual and emotional experiences, but background from an author's reading, as of his life, must be used with the same care as literary criticism of his works. Original and reflective thinking is asked of the scholar in both cases. He is to find why an author wrote as he did by discerning that writer's philosophy through what he learned from his own present time and out of the writings from all earlier pasts of history. He is to create his own philosophy in the same way, by turning to study; when he adopts the meanings in works of other men, passively, he will know no literature.

X

We shall do well to keep alive our definition of literary criticism as a process within the realm of art. It is not a science, with systematized schemes of operation under laws or rules applicable in every situation. This distinction is not challenged, so far as I know, by any who are now making criticism a subject of intensive study in the American university. Yet it would seem that a prefatory statement on the nature and uses of criticism might precede my general comments on American scholarship in the fields of literature as now to be found in the graduate schools of representative universities.

The beginner who enters upon a course of work in any literature as an undergraduate, is fortunate in being free from any rules of critical authority. He has some such impress of individual points of view from his professors, but that is never definitive in the sense of destroying initiative of thinking. Nor is the profession hampered by dogmatism in instruction that might make that effect possible. Fortunately, unless inbreeding has become a rule of practice in his institution, the varieties of professor he encounters will stimulate a sense of current differences in critical interpretation. It is during his years of wide reading, under moderate guidance, that the student is assembling the matter for critical judging. He is also maturing personal characteristics to give a particular quality to his own later interpretations. In lectures and class discussions he will be having that impersonal treatment of his capabilities that is, itself, a first course in critical judgment. Views of teachers and his reading in critical writings will form habits of mind that will be brought to use in graduate studies. Then he will learn more precisely what are the techniques by which critical writing is brought to its high levels as an art. That planned exposure to forms of practice will raise his individual standards through emulation, not by imposition of any dogmatic rules or routines. Full induction into the varieties of approach possible for him to follow in his teaching and research cannot lead to indoctrination.

Whatever the state of advancement to which a student or teacher arrives, at any point in his career, he benefits from examining the significant issues raised by specialists in the history of criticism. In doing so, the scholar realizes that he is to use the impressions drawn from others only by the same selective process as serves creatively in any other art. Instead of turning over all the critical writings of the past to find the judges who seem to us most just, we do better by holding our own ideas at arm's length occasionally for renewed inspection. The danger of imitation is always present, because imitation is easy and implies a kind of sponsorship.

What I have in mind here concerning the art of criticism is well expressed in the remarks of Creel introducing his study of *Confucius: The Man and the Myth*. These two excerpts are brought together, in order to stress emphatically the dangers of imitative work in criticism as in all other forms of art. He writes, "Among a large fraction of mankind, Confucius has for many centuries been considered the most important man that ever lived. His philosophy has played a part in the development of some of the most basic social and political conceptions of the modern West," and then, this observation, ". . . he believed that no creed formulated by another person can excuse any man from the duty of thinking for himself."[14] I know of nothing better suited to the needs of every student of literature or of philosophy. His sweep of inquiry should be as wide as he can reach, and his freedom from imitative thinking as real as that of the producing artist who follows his own patterns of thought, feeling, and design.

One sign of the intellectual freedom of American criticism is to be found today in the interplay of working critics between public and academic audiences. The practice is illustrated by the lives of many writers and teachers. These persons have become effective interpreters to all capable and interested readers and listeners. They have achieved this by conscious, individual application to their materials. The responses prove that American judgment in literature has improved in recent years, both outside and within academic environment. The contrast between the influence of criticism now and in the times of Stuart Sherman, Spingarn, Woodberry, and Thorndike is the same as that brought out earlier on changes in the nation-wide reading public. In spite of book clubs and a lack of bookstores, the people of this country steadily improve in independent judgment of what to read and how to arrive at wise choices. They rely on critical reviews and on their academic preparation for selective decisions.

The changing influence of critical writing over the years can be shown statistically, no doubt, if one would total up the evidence of several years that is registered in book sales by types of title. It is shown also in the nature and number of journals and magazines that carry original articles, reviews of current books, and comprehensive studies of the works of one or several authors. As a trial of such evidence, I have scanned the issues of the *Sewanee Review* for the years 1900, 1925, and 1950. This choice was dictated by the even, unbroken record of publication maintained by this semi-popular journal. As a quarterly, at the opening of the century Trent made the *Review* a composite of original and critical materials; he also extended its scope to include some political and educational opinion alongside its literary studies. That was the year of Woodberry's *Makers of Literature*[15] and of Santayana's *Interpretations of Poetry and Religion;*[16] the accounts of them in Trent's pages for reviews show a rising interest in scholarly interpretation for the benefit of professional humanists. Generally, the materials in the 1900 issues deal with the declared interests of the editorial board, "in the domain of literary study, history, and criticism, and in the discussion of pressing economical and social problems." The scope was wide, but a beginning in critical appraisal had been made.

In 1925 the United States began producing literary criticism more widely, it would seem, as to sources and with respect to contemporary writers. During the late twenties men who today are influential in American scholarship were contributing their earliest reviews and critical essays. One issue of this particular year had from an older, well-recognized teacher in the University of the South, George H. Clarke, a review of Amy Lowell's life of Keats which is admirable in its comments on her sources, motives, temper, and patterns of poetry.[17] Alongside such recognition of contemporary Americans, there also was much on foreign writers, particularly French. Stress was laid on the desirability of more comprehensive studies in comparative literature, and other signs prove an increasing vigor and widening of academic work at higher levels. A further shift toward universality of subject interest, here at home, appears in the issues of the *Review* for 1950. The editor maintained a careful survey of all important scholarly volumes, as the twenty-four titles brought under review illustrate; research and critical appraisals by American scholars had excellent recognition. Also, in unusual measure, the *Review* made place for original writing; such contributions were mainly from persons outside academic life. The list included seventeen critical essays, four pieces of prose fiction, twenty poems, and one study of films. The total of pages for 1950 reached seven hundred and forty, more than two hundred in excess of the number in either of the other years.

Records of other journals, magazines, and newspapers would be equally useful to demonstrate that critical writing has now become a constant outlet for academicians, that the uses of criticism by the public are increasing, and that production beyond metropolitan centers is in good part due to universities and colleges that sponsor new journals. As examples of this third point, moving westward from institution to institution, I might name many more than the ones issued regularly from these centers: Yale, Cornell, Kenyon College, Minnesota, New Mexico, Oklahoma, Stanford, and the University of Oregon. A detour into the South would bring in others, such as the *Virginia Quarterly*, that have maintained their regional and national places of influence over a considerable time.

A more scholarly process, possibly, is reflected by the record of the English Institute, whose annual sessions in New York City for several years have drawn into two-day discussions representative writers on many periods and many forms of literature. Their general topics have

opened the way toward constructive criticism of papers by participants, who later have developed their ideas into definitive form for
publication in the annuals of the Institute, or as trade books. In such
occasional conferences and in the annual meetings of scholarly societies, assurance is given of freedom from dogmatism in critical thought
and writing for the future. There will be no need of warnings against
the dangers of discipleship, which in older and more narrowly restricted scholarly environments has proved to be almost overpowering.
The final proof of this freedom is in the printed records of symposiums
in which every man has had his say among persons of very different
views. One writer, in 1952, posed the question of "intellectuals" versus
academicians, to conclude that today the academic critic is in suprem-
acy; this personal observation of Kronenberger in the *Partisan Review*[18] could be matched by contrary opinions, and both sorts by many
in which such contrast never arises. One may conclude that here, as
in Great Britain, the metropolitan and university concepts of criticism
as an art are coming toward closer harmony in theory as in practice,
and that the qualities in American criticism are known abroad.

A sign of such recognition, with a few justified comments upon the
relation of national temperament to critical tastes, appeared in a 1952
issue of the *Times Literary Supplement* under the title "The Function
of Criticism."[19] The article discusses critical writing in this country
and, with additions of references to British personalities and interests,
defines certain major tendencies. There are submitted two brief lists of
names that signify different kinds of work. For concentrated technical
analysis, at its best, credit goes to Ransom, Winters, Blackmur, Burke,
and Cleanth Brooks. For wise and sophisticated comment, the writer
directs his readers to the writings of Matthiessen, Wilson, Trilling, and
Kazin.

Starting from this British appraisal of persons, one might go on to
increase the list, first from faculties of colleges and universities. Again
moving westward, noting some who work with theory and others
mainly in production of criticism, I should begin with Jones, Richards,
and Miller at Harvard, and move on to Stewart at Brown, and to
Wellek, Williams, and DeVane at Yale; to Mizener at Cornell, and
Warren at Michigan; to Crane at Chicago, and Smith at Minnesota.
Three of these—Wellek and Warren, and Crane—have brought to
print recently two major works that illustrate the seriousness of cur-

rent interest in method. The earlier of the two, Wellek and Warren's *Theory of Literature,* is a comprehensive statement of views which in the brief period of five years have had wide acceptance. *Critics and Criticism, Ancient and Modern*[20] has been under scrutiny only since 1952; its general thesis and essays by several persons have an inner relationship identifying the whole volume.

These few critics, recalled almost spontaneously, are among scores who are remembered for single articles and clusters of papers issued over many years and for their far-reaching influence as teachers.[21] Equal place should be given in any summary to those who have worked within university and college environments and almost equally in public affairs as editors and professional critics for the weeklies, newspapers, and the monthly journals. Stark Young is a fine representative of those who have had wide public attention in both ways of life, and Van Wyck Brooks of that sequence of independent writers wholly devoted to major projects in their writing. From all these quarters and over the years of the past decade, the United States has had a list of major and minor works that are the final answer to any who doubt the importance of literary scholarship or its pervasive influence in American life. These are the devoted workers in literature who are creating a better balance of judgment on the story of human culture and increasing the desire of readers to see a constant lengthening of that story.

XI

Literary research depends on two essentials—an unbroken supply of materials and of people, at levels of quality and of quantity to meet the contemporary and predicted needs. In order to arrive at any calculation of need, one should discover what this country has in resources, what are the priorities to be met in supply, and how new processes of production might be set in motion. These questions apply to men and materials of writing equally, to non-academic conditions as well as to the state of the public potential in reading and in production of services to meet that demand. We should do well to have, for example, a popular discussion of our national ignorance of foreign literatures, in order to get attentive concern from the American public for the necessities of scholarship. Our national responsibilities toward the scholar are as real if less obvious than those toward the industrialist and the farmer. His share in national welfare is as positive as the services of those who maintain various parts of our physical economy. He too must have his raw materials and support in order to turn out finished products. The present difficulty is to make sure our national aid to the scholar unless emergency dramatizes his importance. What this country has learned in such matters through wartime exigencies can be made equally evident from the services of scholars in times of peace. Universities must maintain essential staffs, and now must add permanently to the number of specialists for the humanities. We cannot interpret foreign cultures without fine scholarship, nor have that kind of scholarship without constant, intelligent support.

In this setting, examples must serve to imply the quality of what now is produced by the American scholar and the reliance placed on his contribution. The great undone services are barely suggested by surmising what is required to insure true contact with a single Near Eastern culture. That calls for many types of inquiry and interpretation, not occasionally but constantly maintained. Multiply the number for one culture by the number known to be needed around the world and the nature of this task begins to appear. Positively, we have evidences of success in humanistic endeavor on a national scale. On these one may develop a pattern of increase. The national service of our greater libraries is unexcelled. Proof of that fact can be had from any humanist; yet that primary resource is incomplete in strategic places and can easily be weakened by interruption of its supplies. Less widely known resources are the strength of our national societies and of our university presses. Brief statements on these subjects will give some idea of other necessary but slightly known agencies serving the scholar in the nation.

Under the limiting name of a charter granted it more than fifty years ago, the Modern Language Association of America serves the interests of its members in modern literatures, languages, and aesthetics. The span of its interests in point of time is indeterminate, for the very nature of its subject matter draws into perspective countless items having historical relationships to the matter under inquiry. Studies have been mainly in Germanic, Romance, and English materials and in derivatives from these main stocks. Their range increases, however, at each substantial addition to university programs for the humanities. Today topics of African, Asiatic, and Slavic origin have recognition in the publications and at the annual meetings. The Association is enlarging its old interest in methods and aims in teaching, particularly of foreign languages. These causes and a flow of reports on defined questions modify the distinguishing outlines of planned effort within the main bodies of modern literatures.

Publications are restricted by financial possibilities. The Association now issues yearly six large numbers of its journal, totalling over two thousand pages, and likewise basic bibliographies and occasional larger works in book form. Each year it awards prizes for the publication of a few manuscripts through trade outlets under gifts from a few publishing houses.

The devotion of staff members and of the various committees appears in the effective work done day by day and for the annual meetings. During the first half of 1952 two hundred forty-seven manuscripts were submitted for reading and possible publication. Of these 61 per cent were on British literature, 14 per cent on American, and in descending order with slighter totals those on French, Germanic, Spanish and Italian; those in comparative literature followed in percentage those in French, those in linguistics the total in Spanish studies, and a few fell outside any formal classification. These figures probably reflect accurately the levels of American production. At the annual meetings of three days' duration, over fifty group sessions draw together specialists in as many different matters, and general congregations of the members bring all into attendance four or five times. Fourteen smaller national societies in related fields meeting with the Association enlarge the total of over three thousand persons out of a membership reaching every college and university to the total of over seven thousand persons.

The Association of American University Presses has one member whose records go back to 1869, but it was much later than that date before the Association became influential in support of scholarship. By 1900 the number was great enough and sufficient support was given in total to these presses to accelerate scholarly publication. That rising influence is dramatized in these figures on production: since 1878, they have issued 16,524 books, and of that total 5,824 appeared during the ten-year period ending in 1949. The increase has gone on yearly. In 1948 the total was 727 new titles. Here are works that with the best of good will the trade publishers could not print and hold for slow sale. The thirty-five editors who manage the affairs of their subsidized institutions rely on lack of overhead, earnings from sales, and the steadiness of understanding among the trustees in their universities. Like the scholar, every university editor makes sacrifices for his ideal of work to advance the professions of learning and science. Among those benefited, the humanities and social sciences are high in favor, by reason of the quality of their production and the call constantly for such titles as none but scholars can produce. Without that confident faith in the uses of scholarship, the student of literature would be lacking something. He must find, somewhere midway between his institution and his national societies, a publisher who will encourage him to years of labor in masses of new material until he has a manuscript close to finished production.

How distant still is the goal of these editors, is shown in the comment of Savoie Lottinville, a prominent member of the Association and, as editor of the University of Oklahoma Press, known to all who are involved in publishing professionally. He wrote, five years ago,

. . . if the universities of this country are doing a satisfactory job, they are turning out yearly several thousand young men and women of serious intellectual interests. Failure to exhaust every effort to put university-made books into their hands, when their interest has been stimulated, is not only unbusinesslike but unscholarly. Our experience . . . is as follows: on an average we sell not more than 300 copies of a book to libraries, 300 to 500 to scholars, and from 1,000 to 2,000 to laymen. To me this means that American education is not achieving its goal of an intelligent citizenship.[22]

Every commercial publisher would support this view, with the added qualification that "trade-made" books be counted in with those produced under university sponsorship with little hope of financial profit. Both sides of the industry annually make substantial contributions to the increase of cultural interest and to the requirements of productive scholars that their abilities be brought into the service of the country.

These are important functions. The spirit that makes their realization possible is prevalent throughout the humanistic faculties of our universities and colleges. Its productivity is marked clearly in a recent essay entitled "Is English Scholarship Advancing?"²³ The author, Robert A. Law, reviewed our progress in his own branch of humanistic studies to the year 1950. In thirteen closely packed pages he pointed to such facts as the number of scholarly journals to be founded since 1920; to the growth of interest in American cultural history since 1917, the year of issue for the first volume of the *Cambridge History of American Literature*; and to the widening curiosity of scholars that drew them toward research in the nineteenth and twentieth centuries.

His most effective evidence came from the publishers' lists of major works, such as definitive editions of important literary figures and the indispensable works of reference on which popular and scholarly appreciation of humane letters depends. The guides to literature, the encyclopedias, the dictionaries, the language studies that bring comparative cultures into realization, the greater histories (such as the *Cambridge*) and the composite *Dictionary of American Biography*—these have set the standards for future accomplishment high. Accurate notice is taken of the rise of American studies since 1913, when they were barely respected by many who observed the first award of a doctorate in our own literature by Harvard University. Today the ending of Law's account would be modified by others who talk of excessive attention to American studies, even while they admit the importance of what has been accomplished in seven short years at Harvard, Minnesota, and other institutions to make the production of composite studies of American life a respected aim of higher education. Further comments of Law are addressed to our increased concern with other cultures and other genres that were barely recognized in the scholarly world forty years ago; the rise of periodicals; and the entry of expressive arts into the curricula of universities. Trends in drama are noted as illustrating a widened and sharpened attention to what literature is in relation to the other arts and to society, in a period of rapidly changing perspectives on life and learning.

Then we have the often-cited work by Wellek and Warren on *Theory of Literature*, whose approach is as far removed from the formal bibliographical verities of forty years ago as it is possible to conceive. They gave us, in 1942, forty pages of highly useful bibliography, to which the ensuing ten years have added a good deal. The directives in these lists are toward factors of change and of theory—

such as nature, function, evidence, form, psychological relations, ideas, social forces, the other arts. The entire text and its apparatus stress the importance of those procedures in research that rest on theory rather than on fixed historical data. The younger student will learn quickly what to anticipate in his later training as he reads the chapter on "The Study of Literature in the Graduate School." Mature scholars will find in its pages some topics to dispute and many more to accept. This is a work of counsel toward excellence, either by dissent or agreement, all done insistently and wisely. As commentary for our time, in regard to modes of literary scholarship, the book is noteworthy for acute judgments on the meaning of "history" and "criticism" in the work of the literary scholar, and for comprehensive proposals on how to assure ourselves of greater consequences from literary studies.

Again the reference to an influential document must be barely by title. The thirty-six pages of a report from a committee of the Modern Language Association fully justifies the elaboration of its description: "The Aims, Methods, and Materials of Research in the Modern Languages and Literatures."[24] The wide distribution given it in October, 1952, was warranted by its sound and mature counsel to the uninitiated and its informing value for the general reader. There are many valuable assertions in its observations on lively and important issues in current discussions concerning the function of the scholar.

Finally, from the many possible works of recent years to guide the mind of the younger scholar and to arouse interest in his future, there is the book by Chauncey R. Sanders, *An Introduction to Research in English Literary History*,[25] a work justifying its title by careful exposition of the needs of the future decades and the processes through which the humanists will meet them successfully. Sanders points backward to those who have produced similar guides, and thus gives a quick review of American progress in method and in critical work with texts, literary forms, and relationships.

There is no conclusion short of book length to what might well be written on the subject of literary scholarship and its relationship to people as well as to the record of human culture. But a contrast of what is today in our universities for the humanities with what was lacking in the days of the youthful Gilman, can be drawn on as alternative to piled up details. In Thwing's *Guides, Philosophers, and*

Friends are given the incidents which Gilman reported to him concerning his personal experiences during the first few years following his graduation from Yale University with his degree of bachelor of arts. That autumn he reëntered as a graduate student. His own mind was unclear as to purpose, and the help given him scanty. He had touched lightly on twenty different subjects during his senior year, probably in search of some answer to his inner doubts as to what he should do, but in the autumn his mind still was not made up. President Woolsey advised that he might read a recent work on political economy and then return to discuss it. This Gilman declined to do. He next asked Hadley if he might read Greek with him, only to have the declination come that time from the opposite side of the desk. Subsequently he had some aid from Porter in reading German, a few talks with Dana, and ended his year convinced that it had been wasted.

The next autumn he was at Cambridge and still searching. There he was advised by President Sparks to make his own choice, either to hear Agassiz or to read Dante with Longfellow. Though this catholicity in counsel had its merits, it was of no greater aid toward a firm decision. Gilman went away as before unhappy and uncertain, saying, "I did not find at Cambridge any better opportunities than I had found at New Haven—but in both places I learned to admire the great teachers, and to wish that there were better arrangements for enabling a graduate student to ascertain what could be enjoyed and to profit by the opportunities."[26] Conceivably his brief term as librarian of Yale College subsequently gave the essential time for reflection as his alternative for guided studies.

Such experience close to books is the constant source of growth for the one who would follow literary pursuits after any fashion. It is possible today to turn all advanced study toward fundamental familiarity with literatures of the world and the languages that contain them, or to follow the courses of intensive inquiry set by scholarly patterns of progress. In any search for guidance the student in America today will find someone competent to point out the way toward the necessary resources in men and materials for help to a career in literature. Those humanists who follow any of its many paths agree that work with literature demands the longest and steadiest effort and has possible outcomes commensurately rewarding. These are the persons to amplify and to emphasize the topics lightly touched on in the pages of this chapter. They are furthermore the qualified guides to point toward wrong turns that may be made in the road.

NOTES

1. William Dean Howells, *Literature and Life* (viii+333; Harper, New York, 1902), p. 186.

2. *Ibid.*, p. 183.

3. Ashley H. Thorndike, *Literature in a Changing Age* (318 pp.; Macmillan, New York, 1925), p. 18.

4. Joseph E. Baker, *The Reinterpretation of Victorian Literature* (xii+236; Princeton University Press, Princeton, 1950), p. 7.

5. Marchette Chute, *Shakespeare of London* (xii+397; New York, 1949). A source of ideas on Elizabethan backgrounds admirably supplementing the book of Miss Chute and giving the general reader a fine conspectus of social, political, and cultural circumstance is A. L. Rowse's *The England of Elizabeth* (xv+547; Macmillan, New York, 1951).

6. H. J. C. Grierson and J. C. Smith, *A Critical History of English Poetry* (viii+593; Oxford University Press, Oxford, 1946), p. v.

7. R. Wellek and A. Warren, *Theory of Literature* (xii+403; Harcourt, Brace, New York, 1949 ed.), p. 264.

8. Edward Sapir. *Language. An Introduction to the Study of Speech* (vii+258; Harcourt, Brace, New York, 1921), p. 236.

9. C. K. Ogden and I. A. Richards, *The Meaning of Meaning; a Study of the Influence of Language upon Thought and of the Science of Symbolism.* (1st ed., 1923; 8th ed., xxxi+359; Harcourt, Brace, 1946).

10. F. M. Cornford, *The Unwritten Philosophy and other Essays* xx+140; Cambridge University Press, Cambridge, 1950), p. 43.

11. Leo Spitzer, *Linguistics and Literary History; Essays in Stylistics* (vi+236; Princeton University Press, Princeton, 1948).

12. H. W. Garrod, *Scholarship: Its Meaning and Its Value* (79 pp.; Cambridge University Press, Cambridge, 1946), p. 12.

13. J. H. Hanford, *The Poems of Milton with Introduction and Notes* (lxxxviii+582; Ronald Press, New York, 1936), p. viii.

14. H. G. Creel, *Confucius: The Man and the Myth* (xi+363; John Day, New York, 1949), p. 1.

15. George H. Woodberry, *Makers of Literature* (viii+440; Macmillan, New York, 1900).

16. George Santayana, *Interpretations of Poetry and Religion* (xi+290; Scribners, New York, 1900).

17. George H. Clarke, "Amy Lowell's Life of John Keats," *Sewanee Review*, XXXIII (July-September, 1925), 335-50. Also, as representative of early work from a prominent present-day academic critic, one would choose among the many on this same book the essay of Samuel C. Chew, "Miss Lowell's Biography of Keats," *North American Review*, CCXXI (March, 1925), 545-55.

18. *Partisan Review*, "Our Country and Our Culture II," XIX, No. 4 (420-50 pp.; 1952), p. 441.

19. *Times Literary Supplement*, No. 2642 (September 19, 1952), p. 612.

20. R. S. Crane *et al.*, *Critics and Criticism, Ancient and Modern* (647 pp.; University of Chicago Press, Chicago, 1952).

21. The topic of "new criticism" had a discursive and inconclusive review in a forum reported in *The American Scholar* for 1950-51, Vol. 20, pp. 86–104 and 218–31. Among the participants were William Barrett, Kenneth Burke, Malcolm Cowley, Robert G. Davis, and Allen Tate. Other practicing critics directing their attention constantly to particular subjects instead of toward theory, and with distinguished results, are T. H. Johnson, Adrienne Koch, William Charvat, Carlos Baker, Leon Edel, Babette Deutsch, F. J. Hoffman, John Ostrom, Leon Howard, and William Irvine.

22. Quoted in Chester Kerr's *The American University as Publisher: A Digest of a Report on American University Presses* (31 pp.; University of Oklahoma Press, Norman, Oklahoma, 1949), pp. 30–31.

23. R. A. Law, "Is English Literary Scholarship Advancing?" *University of Texas Studies in English* (1949–50), pp. 271–84.

24. Report of the MLA Committee on Research Activities, "The Aims, Methods, and Materials of Research in the Modern Languages and Literatures," PMLA, XLVII, No. 6 (October, 1952), pp. 3–31.

25. Chauncey R. Sanders, *An Introduction to Research in English Literary History*. With a chapter on research in folklore by Stith Thompson. (vi+423; Macmillan, New York, 1952).

26. Charles F. Thwing, *Guides, Philosophers, and Friends: Studies of College Men* (x+476; Macmillan, New York, 1927), pp. 60–61.

SIX

New Areas of Research and Teaching

I

As the universe has expanded physically in the mind of man, so has the intellectual orbit of the scholar. His universe, however, is in one world—our own. For him, stars are mainly a means to wonder. The humanist and social scientist are concerned with man, not matter. Now their increasing curiosity about people individually and socially is breaking down old barriers of tradition in higher education. They are beginning to study a global world, in efforts to solve its total needs.

By accident, or intuition, the humanists and social scientists in university work have adopted the word "area" to describe their new approach to knowledge. In many geographical or cultural segments of physical or abstract forms, they have gathered knowledge according to their particular disciplines. Western Europe is such an area; our own country, another. Yet even where most has been done and over the longest periods, a coordinated examination of past and present is needed; in no other way can the scholar explain the characteristics of a people, or of peoples, that have been bound together by religion, language, customs, or even mere geographic space. In some areas, most of the work remains to be done. The ignorance of the American scholar concerning certain parts of Asia is almost notorious; analytic research followed by unifying definition will be necessary to bring into common understanding the meanings of life in much of the Near East, as well as in Southern and Northern Asia.

There is nothing literally new in area studies except this decision to work cooperatively, in order to extend more rapidly the boundaries of present knowledge. The newness, beyond that, is in the necessity that forces on us a search after the means to global understanding. Asia, Latin America, and many parts of Europe and Africa are being brought under review in American universities and research institutes. We are finding where are the lacks in our traditional practices. Other nations can supply much in which now we are lacking, but essentially this is an American problem. We ourselves must know what we need and what we intend. The geographical or linguistic definition for a particular area may mean much or little; both are helpful in setting up limits, but religious and traditional beliefs are equally valid. The end in view is precisely that of our programs for "American studies" as these are being developed in several universities—to coordinate and, if necessary, to create, what the various disciplines should give to a balanced plan for comprehensive coverage of the values and possibilities for change within a given area of culture.

The humanists have two relationships to every such effort of penetration into the history and life of a people. One is of function. They have services to render which condition every other kind of study. The other is that customary and innate concern with all that relates to man as an individual. On the ground of function, humanists are drawn into every program for work in undeveloped areas. These demand help of linguists to every other group of scholars. The humanists also must bring to effective usefulness not only languages, but also histories, philosophies, and literatures wherever scholarship has neglected to perform its functions in the past. These are the four wheels on which all searches after meanings must travel. Once the search is well under way along new paths of learning, the humanists will devote themselves intensively to interpretation within their separate disciplines and to the possibilities for cultural development. They then leave to the social scientists the description and improvement of conditions under social or political definition. So, for example, the humanists would do little with central Africa, once the languages and basic dialects had been tamed. The linguist now about to record the manifold differences in speech among the unlettered tribes of Nigeria, in the end hoping to reduce the differences to a few and thus bring unity to planned instruction, will need years for that pioneer work and for the production of teaching texts. He then leaves to others the work of instruction and cultural interpretation. Other linguists will find similarly complex problems in highly developed languages of India, but these will be partly from our own ignorance. Culturally, India will detain the humanist for a lifetime of study. His followers in every discipline will return, generation after generation, as they have to the cultural content of the Mediterranean and Western worlds.

Experience in restricted and intensive study has given American humanists a full understanding, within limits, of the processes needed for comprehensive work in any area. They always have worked by that total approach. Though this country has its specialists in every aspect of Greek and Roman culture, all are aware of the broad outlines of their general field. They look on Greece and Rome as entities in human tradition. If they stop at the outer limit of contemporary affairs, it is because matters of the immediate past and present are within the interests of the social sciences; the humanists are ready when needed, as now, to help with contemporary interpretation from their knowledge of language, history, philosophy, and literature. No one, in fact, can deal with the derivatives from classical or less significant cultures without some help from the humanists. No one can go far, without them, to understand the ideas, idioms, and attitudes of any people. They explain the minutiae of evidence and supply general concepts. What the humanists have demonstrated, by their mastery of the classics, is that they possess the practical ability to open any contemporary culture that is beyond the easy reach of men by virtue of linguistic and other hindrances to comprehension.

The attack upon any untried area, therefore, is at its only vulnerable point, language, and by methods of analysis that the humanists have applied for centuries. They have been setting up the patterns steadily since the beginning of the Renaissance. Without them present to unravel the difficulties of a language, an entire group of area investigators will come to a dead halt. For example, some years ago an international committee elaborated plans for exhaustive studies in Africa. Its members were ready in 1933 to begin work with native tribes that they expected would yield many mutual benefits for trade and local administration. The consciousness finally dawned on the members of the planning committee that they spoke only German, French, and English and lacked any control of native dialects. Therefore, it was obvious that they would be unable to communicate directly and efficiently with the native populations. For the first time, they recognized their dependence upon the linguists, and soon saw the need to postpone their plans until these helpers had solved the riddles of a few African dialects. They learned also that they should wait still longer, until teaching texts could be produced under scientific application of discovered linguistic laws, and until native and Western minds had been trained to operate with printed as well as spoken words. Then, and only then, were the stages of the original program developed steadily and fruitfully.

This example is elementary in that it touches on only the obstacle of unanalyzed language. Language is only the key for studies of all that their traditions mean to living peoples. The tasks are enormously increased when, as now, Western schools are trying to penetrate into the traditions of highly developed and old civilizations that they have virtually ignored for centuries. What the workers with the classics attained by processes of steady evolution, is being attempted in unfamiliar areas at a rapid pace. Fortunately, we have resources that now help that hastened procedure. Scholars from various disciplines are working together with advanced methods for doing what can be done by practical application of rules. They also are being aided by administrative officers who support humanists and social scientists, as has not been customary hitherto with that consistency and generosity which are essential to productive results. All now realize how greatly each depends on the other in solving problems in human thought and conduct. The pity is that discovery of that fact has come late.

Staffs of universities and institutes are now being drawn from their traditional fields of scholarship, where they have learned the ways of profit-taking research in order to enlist in profit-sharing operations elsewhere. They will not all be useful, nor can older scholars all leave off what they are doing, but they can train other men in methods and can urge them to enter vigorously into the new fields of study. Hitherto the humanists have held themselves too much within areas where the soils of human culture are deep and made familiar through centuries of cultivation. They probably merit generally less violent censure than this from a recent critic of the American attitude toward China: "We have always known too little about China, and even when we thought we were most knowledgeable we were blinded by the grace and dignity of the Chinese and forgot the seething passions and the hard core of irony, the violence beneath the skin. Yet all the time the evidence was there, if only the scholars had gone to work."[1] Though the humanist may have been slow to see his obligation, in the challenge of Chinese culture and life, to be man's interpreter to himself and other men, his sense of urgency in present affairs is real now—toward Asia as a whole and toward many other undeveloped subjects in the humanistic disciplines.

II

The current vogue of area programs within American universities started back in 1933, from an increasing curiosity among scholars regarding our own cultural origins and growth. They were looking toward the future. In that year my talks with many men in departments of history pressed into memory one general doubt—whether or not the history of the United States was to devolve into a mosaic of small patterns that would hide the proportions and outlines of its full meaning. Research was plainly doing its work in the trenches. Production, in writing and in teaching, was being restricted by the kinds of data brought to light where the digging was most fruitful. Specialization in the history of the United States was yielding results, but to the general disadvantage of scholars and students. Their horizons were disappearing as work narrowed their range of vision. Despite the skill of many generalists in interpretation, leaders were becoming conscious of being followed by crowds of learners, if not imitators, who seemed to be losing their long perspectives. History was becoming a method for reaching predictable results—so predictable that formulae for research seemed to threaten initiative.

At the same time I found that American literature was coming to a new place in departments of English, where for a generation it had been a subsidiary of work with British literary history. Not until the third decade of this century were studies in American life and thought well regarded, by comparison, in our graduate schools. Before that time, able men were at work but lacked followers. This was due to confinement of graduate students within the limits of cultural histories and languages presented by European and Mediterranean areas. By 1933, however, meritorious programs for comparative studies were bringing out the continental sources of our thought. Howard Mumford Jones had begun his studies of French-American cultural relationships. Other men were moving on from familiar figures in literary history to survey the entire country and to bring new places and persons from all sections into general recognition. These were the few who foresaw a future that now is being realized through cooperative effort. Social scientists and humanists are working toward a clearer interpretation of the variety of American life, and of the potential uses for all our resources.

Several universities now have well-organized programs of teaching and of research. Their faculties and soon their graduates will supply the materials and the teachers that will be needed in secondary schools and colleges. From overseas are coming demands for the interpretation of American history and contemporary thought; these cannot be satisfied by brief and occasional tours of our lecturers abroad or by temporary residence here of teachers from other countries. The foreign attitude toward American standards of thought and conduct will be formed partially by such personal contacts, but systematically and fruitfully by much more constant definition of the educational process. We shall need to produce satisfactory texts and reference works, and in several forms suitable for the ages and interests of readers.

Harvard, Princeton, Pennsylvania, Wisconsin, and Minnesota are five among twenty universities which now have general programs in American studies for undergraduates and graduate students to prepare the way for intensive specialization in any field of the social sciences and humanities. Nearly all of the twenty also have comparable programs on foreign cultures that can bring workers in American backgrounds into familiarity with the peoples of countries where they expect to work or from which they will later on have resident students under their care. This same interplay of inquiry and learning in two representative culture areas is practicable in every institution that maintains a strong program on a foreign country, for the student can be sent on to another institution for what is lacking in interpretation of American life.

Our own country is now being brought under critical review by social scientists and humanists in ways that illustrate the general and special approaches to values in all area programs. Regional and national patterns are clearly marked. The Southeastern states, for example, have been studied by Odum and his colleagues at North Carolina to define productive lines of research; the Southwestern states, by Cleland of the Huntington Library and others; the Upper Mississippi Valley, by Pargellis, Curti, and Blegen. These are a few representative scholars among the many who today are directing programs in American studies to engage younger scholars in particular regional aspects as well as in the total concept of what the words "United States of America" can mean to observers at home and abroad.

Good advice on preparation for specialization is to be found in the remarks of A. V. Kidder, who has devoted himself to the cultural history of both North and Central America and therefore appreciates the benefits from a comparative approach.[2] He lists as basic subjects for area studies, work in genetics, history, archeology, sociology, and the humanities. Under humanities, would come all that formal training and field experience can give on the essential languages and arts. In his case, that has meant an understanding of these humanistic expressions as developed under Mayan and Spanish civilizations in Central America and in our own Southwest. This prescription of primary subjects is as a beginning. Its acceptance would lead to decisions on general studies related to one or more areas, and on special subjects for intensive work at later stages of advancement.

III

As a preface to comments on programs on areas beyond the United States, I shall list in two classifications those that are important to our future as a nation with increasing international obligations. "Security" is not a familiar objective for humanistic scholars, but is now added to their properly directed and traditional interests. To discover and to disseminate new knowledge while improving interpretation of that which is old, are still their declared purposes, and they can be influential in opening up those fields previously slighted or studied partially. Each new area is bound into a unity by linguistic and other determining forces in its evolution. One such may be merely geographic, as where a land mass has been inclusive and repellent to outward influence upon its peoples. Or religion may have bonded together races of men living apart in several geographic locations, as over the Arab world. The most familiar definition of area, more so even than the geographic sign, is that of a civilization with an unbroken record of existence over centuries in time. There the growth of language, tradition, and customary outlook on life has produced a fine pattern, with interrelationships among all its parts. At best, one must admit, many named areas for scholarly investigation are illusory because too inclusive in implication, as will appear from any list of announcements in the catalogs of a representative American university, but that will not hinder a sound and productive approach to the meanings of life and culture.

On a descending scale, in order of relative importance, I have placed the usual names of the areas under present study in either a first or second list. Each list has a definite importance in itself, the former one being intended for those who are entering into general studies and the second for those who are ready for specialization. In the first list the general programs to consider are on Russia, China, Japan, India, Latin America, South Asia, the Near East, and Europe. Special study, for defining a closer interest after one of these unfamiliar provinces of knowledge has been explored, is by either discursive or intensive attention to something more difficult and more significant than general overviews. There should emerge, therefore, two kinds of specialists in the end, those who are almost unique in ability to solve problems and those who are genuine generalists in one of these fields. The second stage in advancement of learning for each individual would be by his selective entry, under guidance, into one of these areas, loosely designated as Slavic, Far Eastern, Indian, Arabic, Persian, Turkish, Latin American, East European, Scandinavian, and African. For each of these possibilities, some American university has a strong or steadily developing program to offer the student.

The present specialists who scan these two lists will have some doubts that may lessen under explanatory additions. Importance, in my definition, is determined by national and international need. That is primary, by reason of world conditions and the position of the United States, its ignorances, and its opportunities to use the educational and field experiences of men from other countries. Another factor in producing these two descending scales, under general and special purposes, is the probable rate of progress we shall soon attain in each field of knowledge, given the present state of American scholarship and the known difficulty of every area.

Briefly, therefore, I shall bring out what I have in mind from these two points of view. The student who wishes to begin Slavic studies is today fortunate. He will find matters in readiness for work on Russia. We now have in this country the staffs and the materials to teach the language, history, literature, perhaps the philosophy; but only on Russian, among Slavic cultures, is that chance open to the beginner. The language is difficult, but will not hinder early progress in easy reading unduly long. For work with Russia as an area, curiosity sustains patience, and scholarship has eased the approaches sufficiently to encourage systematic study.

In contrast, Japan and China pose linguistic requirements that will delay considerably any overreaching survey of their significant places in cultural history or their present movement in active affairs, culturally and nationally; therefore any comprehension of the broad aspects of their religions, arts, and thought must be postponed or derived from secondary sources. Japanese language is more difficult than Chinese. Fortunately, our country now has many who can move about mentally in either one. Teaching is maintained at high levels by persons of "bi-cultural" ability; they know the likenesses and conflicts of Western and Oriental backgrounds. Several possess that ease of transfer from both Chinese and Japanese to European and American-British concepts which is essential to success in teaching and in research. On this last point, we have an advantage lacking before the Second World War.

By long and painstaking study, American scholars have brought to ready appreciation the cultures and present life of nations within the more familiar parts of our world. With these the programs are to make familiar what is known. That in itself is a matter for specialists in exposition and interpretation. The arrears of our knowledge are increasing in even such parts of Western Europe as we believe we know best. American scholars must depend more, in many such cases, on the abilities of others to bring us better insight and a surer appreciation of values. India, in need of persistent and energetic study by American scholars, can be understood through help from its own nationals and from persons in Great Britain with long experience in particular phases of Indian culture. This same is true of Africa, where French and British scholarship excels and will long outdistance what this country now is doing admirably in but a few aspects. The countries of Eastern Europe, from Finland to Greece and Turkey, are vital for our knowing; yet there too the responsibility rests first upon those who have not all our handicaps of past neglect. With Turkey and other parts of the Near East, we are in better state. There the missionary educator has been our pioneer, as in Japan and China, alongside the archeological historian who has covered pretty near all of the ancient lands of the Near East and northern Africa.

With the best of support and of good fortune, this country will be long in attaining true maturity of learning in many of these outer provinces of our past scholarship. We must anticipate from ten to twenty years of steady effort before they will be near us intellectually and culturally, or we to them. For progress in scholarship is by accumulated wisdom, not in books but in men, and it is seldom that a second or even a third generation accumulates that wisdom needed for free interpretation and easy exchange of understanding between peoples.

IV

Our recent gains in knowledge of Japan and China show why we are to expect slower progress in area studies of other complex cultures. With these two nations, the United States has had many historical advantages that ought to be remembered. It is well known by all Sinologists, for example, that every American scholar who uses a book or art object from either of these countries is indebted to the international scholarship of a hundred years. Not all students of the Far East, however, realize that the late W. T. Swingle, a botanist, was the most active promoter of our largest library of Chinese texts and manuscripts—and what today is the most complete and useful anywhere in the world. Neither he nor Hummel, its curator, foresaw what that division of the Library of Congress was to become; but they knew what they intended to do, and what would be needed, for the future of natural science and of all scholarship. This same kind of unusual personal history is behind nearly every special collection of works on Japan and China; generosity and devotion to an ideal over long periods of time were needed to build up such exceptional ones as the Wason collection at Cornell, the Harvard–Yenching Institute library, and those at Columbia and the University of California at Berkeley.

Along with the record of service to learning by the creators of our Far Eastern libraries, should be enrolled the names of the men who selected and used their contents to train younger men. Among these were Latourette, Warner, Goodrich, Henderson, Tomita, Evarts Greene, and Hodous. Next in time, and representative of the oncoming generation, were the Reischauers, Creel, Kennedy, and Sickman. Other persons from private life were giving funds and indirect aid to Japanese and Chinese studies, by helping our museums, libraries, and those in need of financial assistance to continue their study. Much was done by Louis Ledoux for Japanese art, by Bishop White for the massive Chinese collections of the Royal Museum in Toronto, and by donors to museums scattered across the country, from Boston and Washington by way of Chicago and Kansas City to the larger cities of the Pacific Coast. As a consequence of what had been done by 1940 and now is being supported, the American scholar and his visitors from overseas are able to work effectively in these important areas of knowledge and of living culture.

Despite these large investments of time and of money, this country lacked at the opening of the Second World War a fair number of accomplished interpreters of these significant civilizations of the Orient. Maturity is not a product of haste or of quick financing to sustain a great many students working under a few slowly developing staffs of experts. Fifty years have not been enough, and could not be, to make this country adequate for its needs. Yet today the United States is farther along the road to that goal than with India, or with the complex of Slavic and other cultures along the East European frontier. Among the centers that are strong in personnel and in physical resources are Columbia, Harvard, Yale, Chicago, Michigan, Washington, and California. Many independent specialists are at work in our museums and libraries, but the solid and constant advancement of research and teaching is being done in the universities. The record made since 1934 is the more remarkable in the light of an American doubt, as late as 1910, that Eastern Asia was due for serious study.

It was in 1939, in Leyden, that Duyvendak was commenting on the probable future of Chinese studies throughout the world. He then had his own institute at a high level of efficiency, but he was serving only a restricted number of scholars. My remark on the contrast of potentialities and actual use drew out his prediction that the "total future" of Chinese studies lay in the United States, and for two reasons: a steady demand from schools and colleges for teachers guarantees employment to persons trained in such specialties, and the public mind of America is open and attentive to unusual subject matter. In the Netherlands, he pointed out, neither home demands nor duties overseas would ever warrant enrollments of more than a few students each year. That was his forecast at a time when this country had nothing to match the opportunities for training in Europe. The Netherlands, France, and Germany were attracting those determined on following industrial, political, or scholarly careers. After their study abroad they looked forward to more familiar learning of Far Eastern backgrounds by field experience and residencies in Japan and China.

Since 1939 the rise of British and continental centers has gone on, as here, more rapidly. Great Britain no longer will need to bring specialists from Germany or China to man its chairs of Chinese, admirable as have been its appointments. Materials are harder to secure than in 1936 for all these centers of work, but movement of scholars from one place of work to another is increasing in countries from Germany westward to Hawaii and Japan.

It cannot be too heavily stressed that the strength of Canada and the United States in these areas rests upon effort and interest of many people over a long period of time. Missionaries and their children brought us the needed insights and their own adaptable powers of teaching in cultures. Librarians have been second to these persons in experience, but not in tenacity and in vision. Third in order, only because few in number, are those scholars who have come for brief or lasting stays in our museums, libraries, and universities. Those from China and Japan have well repaid what aid went to their countries from the United States. Those from other origins, as Sir George Sansom and other appreciative interpreters of the Orient in our time, have helped in this transplantation of the spirit and meaning of Far Eastern culture in Europe and the Americas.

V

As Leonard brought out in his 1943 survey, Latin-American studies were then enduring the mixed consequences of a decided inflation. On government funds, all scholarly and artistic activities of the three Americas had been stimulated, to the advantage of institutions and many independent workers in the arts. Books and journals had been supplied to universities and to our foreign centers for cultural inter-change. In Mexico City a well-stocked open-shelf library for adults and children demonstrated one process of democratic education. More effective than material supplies were the impressions left by such persons as Lydenberg, while librarian of this unusual Mexican center, and by all who travelled north or south as visiting teachers and exchange scholars.

In such ways the Office of the Co-ordinator of Inter-American Affairs, Nelson A. Rockefeller, proved to our neighbors in Central and South America our readiness to cooperate. Within a few years interest was quickened in historical, linguistic, and archeological research; then in literary studies. All this steadily strengthened former bonds of mutual understanding. It was a time of discovery extending beyond the old limits of American field study in Mexico and Guatemala. These countries had long been familiar to our archeologists, anthropologists, and students of Colonial and diplomatic history. Through long stays for research into Mayan and Spanish cultures, our specialists had created good will toward the United States that was carried on to all their American successors. Throughout the other Americas, lecturers on literature and workers in other art forms, while on temporary assignments, had the benefit of a cooperative spirit created by earlier scholars on long-term projects.

Friendships, as well as scholarly increase, proved that the Smith-sonian and Carnegie institutions had invested their funds and personal services well. Years of field and laboratory work under Spinden, Kidder, Morley, and Redfield had brought native personnel to high efficiency for independent studies in their own cultural histories. An easy command of Latin-American Spanish and of English had put all on an equal footing. As broader plans carried others to countries further south, the demonstrations in Central America were cited as evidence of good faith and high competence on the part of all individuals on similar missions.

Planning had begun some years before 1943, under auspices of the American Council of Learned Societies. Men of diverse interests followed the lead of Waldo G. Leland, its chief officer, after his planned tour of the primary South and Central American states. His chief aides at first were from humanistic fields. On libraries, Hanke was markedly valuable; for languages and general cultural background, Berrien, Hamilton, and Zeitlin; on modern practices in museums and all developments in modern art, d'Harnoncourt and his comrade Covarrubias.

One of the more strategic decisions was to establish a permanent committee for producing an annual *Latin-American Handbook*, to report internationally all significant publications. This volume has become a constant help to all who are developing materials for teaching and for publication. Other committees fostered cooperative projects within our own country. Thus many scholars who had lived in intellectual isolation within their own disciplines came into touch with men in other institutions and in all subjects related to their own interests. By 1943 these temporary developments took lasting form under a national committee of the three research councils. This group was to care for the interests in Latin America of all our scientists, social scientists, and humanists. It was expected to assist all plans of separate institutions and of individual countries to their mutual advantage.

Without realizing the fact, our universities had begun to draw the profiles of international programs in which persons in a given specialty relied on one another, regardless of nationality or institutional affiliation. I doubt if any were then thinking of area programs on Latin America in their own institutions to cover all essential disciplines. Talk was rather of cooperation. The members of these central committees realized that as federal funds lessened, there would be need for replacement of aid to field trips and to research at home. More important still, there would be required additions to their budgets to bring younger men into their fields of study and to build up libraries to effective levels. The border states, California, and North Carolina had longer traditions of direct contact with Latin-American countries, but as in the Northwest and Middle West, there had been slight effort to spread local interests into less-developed fields. Archeology, anthropology, history, languages, and literatures had been sustained modestly under the independent direction of departments. Geography was represented well, but scantly. Such basic subjects as sociology and economics were least of all in condition to function in a planned program.

To this situation the Latin-American policies had brought excellent though temporary help directed toward improvement of inter-

American relations through scholarship and the arts. That support tended to do little for separate institutions here, but it laid the lasting basis for our present cultural missions. The consequence is that larger cities of the other Americas now have centers providing general information on education, courses in English, and supplies of recent materials in print bearing on world events and cultural advances under the sponsorship of any, or several, nations within the free world.

The gains in contact across old boundaries were still to be stabilized by support from private funds and by further aid of the federal government. Our Hispanic Foundation in the Library of Congress is one lasting evidence of the judgment shown in those years of change. State universities also were generous in creating new positions, that more subjects might be brought before undergraduates and graduates. This was advancement of substantial kind beyond the indefinite, enthusiastic promotion given to the teaching of Spanish in the heyday of educational innovation some years ago. Since 1943 the gains institutionally have been steady, by replacements and by additions to faculties. By constancy to their declared interests, many universities have, in consequence, made the humanities and social sciences more significant; they have not yet entered seriously some of the most essential fields for international cooperation through higher education.

For example, sociology is in primitive stages of development. Field study and training of foreign personnel for work in their own countries are undeveloped as scientific interests. By 1943 a center of sociological research at São Paulo had defined its aims and had won favor locally; above any other in promise, it has had some encouragement, but far too little. The humanists have shown a similar lack of planned action toward scientific analysis of languages, for teaching or for description of changes that are historically significant to scholarship of the future. Michigan has outdistanced the lesser efforts to develop methods of teaching English to Spanish-speaking nationals, and in the other countries—notably in Mexico—there has been a decided advance in teaching the elementary uses of English. Yet so far the results are less than could and should be attained promptly under adequate support.

In theoretical and historical linguistics the distinction formerly held by the Argentine has gone to Mexico, where the *Nueva Revista de*

Filología Hispánica is issued under the auspices of the Colegio de Mexico. The transfer of scholars to Mexico and the United States came when work was hampered in the city of prior location. Today the two continents are indebted to the late Amado Alonso of Harvard University and to Alfonso Reyes, the distinguished cosmopolitan humanist, for this enduring proof of scholarly vision in the three Americas. It remains with us in the United States to amplify our aid to Latin-American workers in the humanities and even more widely to those in the social sciences.

A pattern of area studies on Brazil, or on any other leading nation of Latin America, has not as yet been developed here by a group of our universities. That is a possibility which is feasible, whereas it is beyond the power of any single institution to deal competently with the social and cultural life of any of the countries of South America. The aim, therefore, must be to succeed by a division of duties. Purchases of books and journals for use in our centers should be paralleled, if not matched, by deliveries to sister institutions in other countries. Many have excellent leaders and all have potentially greater strength in candidates for higher degrees and services. The Northeastern states have abundant experience, personnel, and library resources to develop speedily a regional program. With the resources in Washington, at the Hispanic Foundation and the Pan American Union, more advanced students can complete major investigations: many from other countries have done so. In the South, Duke, North Carolina, and Vanderbilt are moving into cooperative effectiveness; Tulane and others may be readily added in divisions of duties favoring all, including the students. Texas can be counted on to nurture original studies in its rich collections, and the three westward states have their special advantages in Spanish and early American backgrounds. This leaves California at Berkeley, with the largest faculty and exceptional resources in material, to draw advanced students from institutions having like interests, primarily in Mexican subjects, but likewise in all Colonial backgrounds of the Americas and in geography. California and Stanford have probably the clearest future for cooperation in services to their regional population and to independent colleges, secondary schools, and to international interests of every description on the Pacific Coast.

This imperfect summary could be lengthened to detail the plans of other institutions and of particular scholars. Its chief usefulness is to outline the emergence of studies in an undeveloped field of international scholarship. Beyond that, the purpose must be to do tangibly what has been done in theory more than in practice for several past decades. The moral to be drawn from an examination of the American record in China and Japan must not be repeated in our Latin-American relationships culturally, and so basically. This country, intellectually and artistically, faced toward Western Europe for generations. No one can say how well today we know the life and thought of that geographical frame of cultural histories, but at least the variety and depth of previous interests is reassuring. As for China, now we are overdue to look for reasons why our trade interests outran understanding of unique characteristics in its people concealed in their history, religions, and patterns of thought. This will not be said of Latin America if through foresight scholars divide the cost and care of responsibilities for mutual aid in learning as is intended in trade, agriculture, and industry.

Samuel Putnam knew the literatures of Spain and Portugal. He was equally familiar with their descendant cultures in the New World. Probably this cosmopolitan critic of Latin-American writings did as great a service by interpreting them to readers of English as by his translation of *Don Quixote* and his biography of Cervantes. Since he also understood well the peoples of the three Americas, his views on their cultural relationships have merit. It is as foreword to my conclusions on the present topic that I shall quote what perhaps was Putnam's final statement on the matter. He would have been the first to welcome additions to this brief comment, which appeared in the preface to a survey of four centuries of Brazilian writing.

In *Marvelous Journey*, published in 1948, Samuel Putnam wrote concerning the cultural relations of North and South America, that there had been "a certain colonial attitude on our part, contending over a long period with a cultural isolationism that had led us to look more and more exclusively to the Old World for our importations and, consciously or unconsciously, to look down upon our hemisphere neighbors and their intellectual productions."[3] Other persons have said as much, and on less evidence. All are partially right. Yet it is probably true that they conditioned their thinking by the same influence as Putnam, or you, or I—by habit. His attachment emotionally to Latin-American cultures made him their useful partisan, as was Lowell in defending our country against foreign criticism. But he was so intent on this conclusion, or so casual, that he did not stop to state both sides of the case.

Latin Americans are like all other people in having deep-rooted attachments to the countries of their origin. Ours are too various to designate, but for that reason alone we understand the spirit of every Latin-American national toward Spain, Portugal, France, Italy, or Germany. Their law libraries contain the French codes and their bookstores imprints from France and Spain in quantities equal to those in English. Their schools are traditional descendants from Old World form. They know Europe better than they know the United States.

In 1941 a liberal arts college in Brazil had, in its faculty of twenty-five, nineteen nationals of other countries. The number would have been twenty instead of nineteen, I was assured, had the one from North America maintained a proper degree of political detachment. More intimately than in kind of personnel, higher education in Latin America follows the lines of inheritances from overseas. Languages, religions, traditions, and native customs are replicas or modified copies of older originals. Reading is therefore first by the easiest way, then by whatever secondary language the family, village or city uses freely in speech and in print. All the familiar languages of Western Europe have currency in Latin America, and it would be difficult to prove on any national scale of measurement that English is the one among them of widest influence. But language is less important in this context than the degree to which it conveys ideas concerning other peoples and their cultures. Certainly other nations in the three Americas do as we, in relying on familiar channels of communication and in going outside them only under the stimulus of some particular purpose.

The marks of intellectual laziness are on all of us about equally. Even in scholarship, where awareness of foreign productivity should be constant, we have been content with a limited amount of intellectual trading. We have counted more on exchange of views with Europeans than with Latin Americans, often for excellent reasons quite apart from ease of comprehension. So too have they. Yet these inclinations, as Putnam indicated, are not reasonable causes for any insensitiveness toward native growth in American cultures or toward critical work of scholars in the humanities.

The remedy for neglect is by repairing its losses through action. Today the humanists of both continents have reason to work for the dissemination of knowledge. This country needs understanding of all the expressive arts in nations south and north of our borders. Latin America still hampers democratic education by its traditionalism. All have need of something that the others can supply, and preeminently the universal need is to know what are the traits and motivating ideals of our nearest neighbors.

Today peoples of the three Americas are looking more and more toward mutual understanding and self-interpretation. They are placing ideas and ideals alongside, or above, the values in material possessions. Scholars cannot solve all problems, but they can help to make the solution of many much easier for other persons. They cannot interpret all that is in the culture of a foreign area, but they can maintain a contact that increases tolerance through understanding.

The United States has discovered Latin America along with other lands and peoples in the unexplored half of its world. The nations on these two continents have the unmeasured advantage of nearness to objects within their interest. Out of that accident of place can come a surer understanding, demonstrating the power of the humanities to give like benefits in more distant places and where hindrances are greater than in our own environment.

VI

The lands of the Near East facing toward the Mediterranean Sea form one area of intensified inquiry for our social scientists and humanists. Southern Asia—from Iran southerly and east to India, Indonesia, and the Philippines—is another, equally complex and equally important for Americans to know as promptly and as well as is possible. Granted that haste and excellence are never associated in any humanistic process, the confrontation of these contrasting words gives ground for consistent effort. The third, North Asia, means initially Russia rather than the Soviet Union.

Each of these major sectors of the globe is under study in the institutions of this country, more intensively and more inclusively than was thought possible ten years ago. Varying degrees of progress during the intervening period are to be explained by the strength of earlier programs and by the support now being found for further development. On each of the three, careful planning has been done with cooperative aid from countries in Europe and from the Near East itself.

Among our longest traditions in scholarship is that created by linguists, historians, and archeologists working in Asia Minor, on the Syrian coast, and in Egypt. Penetrations have been made further eastward into Iran and Iraq and to parts of the Arab world. All these field projects have continued, with brief interruptions by war, and under varying levels of support, throughout the half century. Even war has aided the discovery of sites and of lost or hidden records. The Near East area is, in consequence, as familiarly known among scholars of this generation as Greece, having had great numbers engaged in field operations and in studies within institutions devoted to the description of ancient civilizations.

The record of American achievement in the Near East is to be found in such centers as the Oriental Institute of the University of Chicago, in the American Schools of Oriental Research, and in museums and universities that have for years maintained research within some sector of the "fertile crescent." Such representative works as that of James H. Breasted have shown the general reader and the student the variety and the fascination of the history thus developed. Detailed reporting continues in the journals of learned societies. What is now in print and in process of completion, and the precious artifacts and manuscripts recovered for study and display, fully justify the large sums spent to extend the story of man in the area of the Near East.

A second, more immediate, justification is from the side of preparing our nation for action in every present circumstance. As in China, American missionaries to the Near East were for decades accustoming their minds to the conventions of contemporary life.

While archeologists, linguists, and students of ancient art were raising a background of historical interpretation, these men and women were working with living peoples from Turkey southward to the Persian Gulf. Many years of teaching and of living were invested, along with American funds, in their schools and colleges. Without the scholar they would have been less successful; together, the missionary and the scholar made the life and culture of the Near East accessible to Western minds, but, as contemporary events prove too well, inadequately for a meeting of minds. Their societies have had over a century of direct contact with our country through resident workers; as an Arab historian wrote, "the intellectual effervescence which marked the first stirrings of the Arab revival owes most to their labors."[4] That is today a fact unrelated to our own present need to know Islamic thought in the Moslem world covering all but Palestine in the Near East and the northern half of Africa.

From 1939 to 1945 our institutions maintained some field work, but the specialists were held in restraint by the war when not answering calls for advisory participation. The growth of another generation of scholars was retarded, in consequence, but had deflection toward modern studies. The demands for contemporary overviews of Turkey, Iran, and the entire Islamic world hastened that turn of interest. As forecast by Speiser in his review of Near Eastern scholarship of the war years, 1947 was a turning point; from old to modern subjects, the trend had begun and had brought in new programs for development. Columbia, Princeton, Pennsylvania, and California declared themselves for modern subjects. McGill began a general attack on problems of the Islamic world; that new center and the most firmly established older center, at Princeton, are now moving toward area work that should be brought to realization in all of these centers rapidly.

When Mortimer Graves summed up progress in 1949, two years after Speiser made his survey, he could point to solid gains under guidance of such men as Birge, Hitti, John Wilson, and Albright. In that year Walter L. Wright, a leader in the field of Turkish studies, ended his career; so more recently has Dean Birge, author of the Council's *Guide to Turkish Studies* and compiler of dictionary material during a lifetime of missionary duty. Younger men are coming on to take up their burden, and with the same slow process of advance will begin at a much higher level of developed knowledge than their predecessors. It will require heavy support, however, and constant protection of programs to bring to needed levels American competence in Persian, Arabic, Turkish, and Hebraic studies for present-day understanding.

These necessities recall an incident of 1939 in the Netherlands. Professor van Iterson, the noted Dutch botanist, was discoursing on his difficulties in retaining a particular member of his staff against the attractive offer of a powerful international industry to work in the Near East. He had won out, at length, by using the soundest possible argument. If permitted to keep this specialist in academic life, he could promise that soon many others could be developed under guidance to meet all demands for industrial research. This same argument needs application in many parts of the scholarly world, as American institutions have belatedly realized. Their leading experts in law, linguistics, religions, and cultural histories are being drawn away by insistent demands of trade, industry, and governmental agencies. The supply for the Near East cannot in any predictable time be made adequate for the triple needs of research, directed service, and interpretation at the levels of public and academic need.

Our own understanding of Near Eastern peoples, as of our neighbors in the Americas, can increase only by cooperative work with leaders of thought in those countries. That work must be at levels of local ability and aspiration, in order to succeed, and with confidence in foreign participants. The hope must lie within someone, perhaps a writer, to create in masses of population that desire for self-expression and growth that we too easily define as a democratic sense of human welfare. I know of no clearer call to the American scholar than to become adequate in his understanding of life in some part of the Near East, so that he can win the confidence of those who will work with their own people. No lasting gains are made without learning and experience, and none without a desire to help others by those who know them best.

More briefly, a comparable story can be told of South Asia. This area, it will be recalled, is defined by American scholars as extending in a long southeasterly arc from Iran across India to Indonesia and thence northwesterly to the Philippine Islands. The problems are equally varied, in comparison with those of the Near East, and dependent for understanding upon the same abilities in American social scientists and humanists.

Standards in linguistics and in literary scholarship have been high, but work has been confined within more traditional boundaries of scholarship. Particular attention has been given to the cultural history of India, under the guidance of such university men as Edgerton, Norman Brown, Walter Clark, and Mandelbaum, and Poleman at the Library of Congress. Recruitment of younger men is going forward according to plans laid down after the end of active hostilities in

1945. Today Yale, Pennsylvania, Columbia, Cornell, and California are building up area programs uniting work in older literary languages with modern forms. This is imperative before any free movement is made through the customary disciplines, by direct contact with people and documentation, on contemporary affairs.

Subjects being brought under cooperative study, with the aid of nationals from the several countries in the area, are modern languages, art, literature, and histories of culture. Writing of critical and original kinds is being encouraged. In social sciences, the disciplines indicated are anthropology, geography, economics, current politics, recent social history, international relations, and sociology. Field studies are relied on heavily, as are demonstrations of practical procedures. American scholars and social scientists are going out, to India particularly, for residencies in institutions and wherever field operations are essential for learning and teaching.

Other centers than these five are noted by the Council committee representing university interests in South Asia. They are in Chicago, Harvard, Hawaii, Minnesota, Stanford, and Washington—universities that have strength in special fields and probable increases ahead within defined sectors of this total land area.

In the next ten years this planning committee foresees a demand, from all sources, for American personnel to the number of seven hundred and fifty generalists and specialists for duty at home and in the field. It is not reasonable to hope for so extraordinary an outcome under current methods of operation. That total cannot be even approached if our mature teachers are to be drawn away by insistent calls to temporary duties. First the gaps must be filled, and meanwhile assistance must be borrowed from centers in Europe and in the South Asia area. We shall be needing all possible stocks of printed material and constant advice. Of necessity, the peoples of those countries will follow the guidance of their own educational leaders, for they are in need of that help and no other can equal it. Any added assistance from abroad must be on their invitation and toward a mutual benefit. It is in that mutual return, of human and of cultural values, that other sectors of the world have deep interest. It may well be so, for they are thinking about the well-being of six million people, more than one-fourth of the world's population now living in the islands and on the mainland of South Asia.

VII

In 1936 a determined student desiring to learn Russian went from the United States to London, where he entered the School of Slavonic Studies. His decision was easily understood in the light of past events. For years the foreign centers of Slavic studies had held their place. London had Pares, Wallace, and Maynard. France, with the parent institute of Western Europe, had Denis, Leger, Mazon, and Boyer; Germany, Vasmer and Brückner. This country had at Berkeley what was to become a powerful center; apart from the work of Wiener at Harvard and of Harper a little later at Chicago, the United States relied during the early part of this century on George R. Noyes of the University of California. He there built up by normal processes well-rounded programs in Slavonic languages and literatures—first with one, then two, then three staff men to cover the areas, and himself always producing literary translations to draw untrained readers into the first stages of appreciation. Elsewhere, the American interest in Russian culture was perhaps not such as to deter a student from going abroad.

Yet in that same autumn of 1936 this traveller to London could have enrolled with twenty-one other mature students in the first year-long intensive course of Russian studies. George A. Patrick, one of two unusual early workers in Slavic subjects developed by Noyes, conducted that program at Berkeley. Three intensive seminars in summer sessions at three universities had prepared the way for these intensive courses of the academic year 1936-37 on language, literature, and backgrounds of Russian life and thought. Patrick by then had produced the first of his excellent language texts. He had the help of his colleague Alexander Kaun, of others as well, and above all the counsel of Noyes himself. But had this particular student wished, at the end of that year, to have gone on with his studies, he would have been compelled to go elsewhere, probably to Yale along with three of that select group. The shift was due to withdrawal of Patrick's courses because he was to have the next year free for preparation of advanced texts urgently needed in many centers at home and abroad.

Such incidents show the limited scale of Slavic studies then more graphically than statistics on students or books in our libraries. Yet our library holdings are the best index to our rapid increases in strength.

Exactly opposite to our rise from negligible collections to impressive ones, in a reckoning of the books we held then and have now, is the decline in all cultural relations with Russia. Our libraries have secured their large holdings by well-planned and constant effort of their directors and of the faculties in the universities. The growth of our primary centers has been due to financing by private and public funds since the beginning of the century. In background of preparedness, we have had with Slavic studies something comparable to that in Japanese and Chinese; our universities and libraries had small but excellent and early beginnings on which to build. Yet since 1947 no benefits have come to them through any channels that Russian officialdom controls.

In 1901 the Library of Congress had 569 books in the Russian language. Six years later, by purchasing a single library it added 68,000 selected volumes in Russian and 12,000 others that aided in the use of that collection. This library had been collected during the lifetime of its owner, Gennadius Vasilievich Yudin of Krasnoiarsk near Lake Baikal. He had written, in 1904, "I would, in my declining years, give my books, after a Russian custom," and went on to express the desire to make his gift to the United States "with the sole idea of establishing closer relations between the two nations."[5] His purpose was as laudable in 1907, when he accepted a moderate sum for the five hundred cases of books. The appeal of President Theodore Roosevelt and Herbert Putnam to Congress had been successful. Yudin had acted to the advantage of both countries, for he had started here an appreciation of the finest literature in Slavic tongues that will lead to mutual understanding regardless of all delays.

The second advance comparable to that at Berkeley was at Cornell, where in 1939 President Day sustained the wise plans of resident and visiting specialists to start a year-round program of Russian studies. That support gave to Simmons and others, with help from Sir Bernard Pares, their chance to develop the first area program. With them the American Council continued the national planning started by it in 1933. The Council went further later on to perfect such projects as the translation of important and badly wanted works and its publication, *The Current Digest of the Soviet Press.* No others match these two projects thus far in lasting and informing value.

The primary work of the Council, as always, had been to make clear the need for operation in a new field and to support with funds and guidance the first stages of a national development. That had been done during the war, when the government asked more of the universities than they could do, and all relied on the Council and its officers. As the universities took on the maintenance and development of their local programs, they began regional cooperation and a national design under guidance of the Council and the Library of Congress.

It was natural that in the period of rapid expansion some staff members should move from one institution to another. Before 1947 the most rapid and consistent growth had come at Columbia, following the arrival of Simmons, Mosely, Hazard, and Abram Bergson, and the return of Geroid T. Robinson from war duties. Today the department and the institute enroll a hundred and fifty students in Slavic studies, with a combined faculty of thirty directing research, teaching and publication. Cross and Karpovitch stayed on at Harvard, the other center doing exclusively graduate work, with research on international issues of social and political importance. Vernadsky stayed on at Yale, and the group at Berkeley remained as before; with additions to their staffs, these two are counted today among the five major centers. The latest of these in time of development is the University of Washington. Equally significant is the Hoover Institute and Library on War, Revolution, and Peace, by virtue of its priceless documents and the aids given to advanced scholars from all parts of the world. Its director, Harold H. Fisher, commands the regard of all in the field and works closely with the faculties of the other centers and with the national research councils.

Many other universities and colleges have one or more exceptional workers in Slavic subjects. A recent study of undergraduate area programs[6] on Russia has brought out the merits of nine institutions far advanced in service to undergraduates. They are California at Berkeley, Dartmouth, Fordham, Indiana, Michigan, Stanford, Syracuse, Washington, and Yale. Deming Brown, its author, adds a note on the strong assembly of courses at Wisconsin that are not, under departmental agreement, drawn into formal unity but readily arranged to meet individual needs. The subjects discussed by Brown show how closely an area program can be fitted to the other activities of departments. He lists languages, literature, history, art, government, economics, geography, anthropology, and sociology. It is under these headings that he has developed his individual descriptions of the nine undergraduate colleges.

All the conclusions of this survey are encouraging. The small number enrolled at each college, year after year, gives chance for a close review of student and faculty opinion. Each year—in one college over an eight-year period—there has been careful planning for the next year ahead. There has been chance to make a case study of student accomplishment, to train new staff members, and to advance the slow tasks of preparing materials for schools and colleges. That dissemination of ideas waits on the teaching and writing of persons trained in centers for advanced work. Some of the output in print is having the necessary support of national organizations for distribution; among the best known are the books and manuals issued by the Institute of Pacific Relations, by the Foreign Policy Association, by Columbia University in its Slavic Series, and by the Harvard University Press. Our colleges and public-interest groups have also the corollary aids of films, general lectures, and panel discussions. Dramatic productions and open reading rooms now supplying stocks of current magazines and newspapers for students of French and Spanish in several universities, may be the means later to increased familiarity with contemporary life in Asiatic countries.

It appears that the year 1947 was a significant one in the cultural relations of Russia and the United States. The report of the President's Commission on Higher Education appeared with a carefully developed statement of methods to advance Russian studies in schools through initial effort in at least two hundred colleges. It had a reference to the list of books, five hundred of them, that had been drawn up as essential for any college intending to carry on such a program. The statement concluded with this remark: "But these books cannot be bought; they do not exist; it will take a major publishing enterprise to make them available. And the same obstacle to serious scholarship exists in many other areas of non-European culture."[7] It was in that same year that Russian purchases of printed matter in this country totalled 174,000 items and our receipts from Russia as shown in the customs record were six thousand titles. The contrast is deceptive, however, in that we had then started plans for two excellent alternatives for slow importation and distribution. One was *The Current Digest of the Soviet Press*, which now appears weekly; the number for January 31, 1953, was a closely printed folio of fifty-two pages. The other aid to everyone is the Library of Congress *Monthly List of Russian Accessions*. The issue for September, 1952, had 174 folio pages giving in miniature the catalog cards of all new accessions by the associated libraries participating in the national scheme.

Emphasis today is not so much on resources of material as on the interpretation of American life abroad and on giving to citizens of the United States a fair understanding of Russian affairs. Obviously the greatest need is where hindrances since 1947 have been the greatest, depriving masses of people of the truth. These are the citizens of the Soviet Union. They should know of such incidents of the year 1947 as the offer of Koussevitzky to tour their country, giving all the returns from concerts to Russian War Relief; of the proposal from the American Council of Learned Societies to arrange residencies in American universities for twelve or more Russian scholars; of its despatch to Moscow of Simmons for this and similar purposes; and of the offers of the Library of Congress for exchanges of materials in print and the gift of certain desired works in the Russian language. A summary of such efforts by government and private agencies is in the volume issued in 1951 by the World Peace Foundation, entitled *Negotiating with the Russians*.[8] Despite the delays and present blocks to exchanges that affect our endeavors to act to mutual advantage, the American scholar continues to produce works of special and general character. Such a survey of Russian literature as recently was issued for Struve by a university press,[9] and the excellent list of translations brought to trade channels by the American Council of Learned Societies will have constant and beneficial effects on American understanding. The scholars have their *Slavonic and East European Review* with new articles and current reviews of books, and their programs of purchase and national distribution. Cooperation among ourselves and with other nations of the free world has been productive and will continue to be so increasingly.

Yet no one will leave consideration of area studies, as they are termed, without his thought turning to the spread of interests to be sustained by this country. Division of funds, as of labor, must be on a schedule of need and value. The two are not identical. Where the soils of culture are deep and lasting in strength-giving power, the scholar will incessantly work to find more and to interpret better than did his forebears. Much value lies in those fields insufficiently tested by previous humanists, and that will be won to our use. But insistent demand for national emergencies may best be met by considered plan and by division of labor. Expense is a formidable item, of libraries and of manpower devoted to lifelong service. We shall do well to make our old investments secure and to enter into new ones to the degree of wise provision for sudden need and lasting value.

NOTES

1. *New York Times Book Review*, February 1, 1953, p. 7.

2. Quoted in J. H. Steward's *Area Research: Theory and Practice* (xx+164; Social Science Research Council, New York, 1950), p. 118.

3. Samuel Putnam, *Marvelous Journey: A Survey of Four Centuries of Brazilian Writing* (xvii+269; Knopf, New York, 1948), p. viii.

4. W. R. Polk and W. J. Butler, *What the Arabs Think.* (Foreign Policy Association, Headline Series No. 96, New York, 1952), p. 47.

5. *Annual Report of the Librarian of Congress for the Fiscal Year ending June 30, 1946.* (538 pp.; U. S. Government Printing Office, Washington, D. C., 1947), p. 196.

6. Deming Brown, "A Report on the Undergraduate Area Programs of Nine American Universities" (Manuscript copy, Columbia University Department of Slavic Language and Literature).

7. President's Commission on Higher Education, *Higher Education for American Democracy* (6 vols.; Harper, New York, 1948), I, 19–20.

8. R. Dennett and J. E. Johnson, *Negotiating with the Russians* (xi+310; World Peace Foundation, New York, 1951).

9. Gleb Struve, *Soviet Russian Literature, 1917–1950.* (414 pp.; University of Oklahoma Press, Norman, 1951).

SEVEN

The Balance of Studies

I

The humanities experience changes that are as remarkable as those in the sciences. These are less easily discernible in their academic surroundings, and in immediate social consequences less important; yet in time their effects will be as far-reaching and as important for human welfare. That venturesome statement is supported by facts less arresting than earth-shaking discoveries or distance-destroying invention. Sciences operate in space and in matter: the humanities are within us. Their benefits are given and received at every level of need above that of simple physical existence. They have, too, the power to make physical burdens and deprivations tolerable to man as they increase his inner strength.

Manner and substance of learning are both involved in the changes now actively effective within our colleges and universities. They go deeper than surface definitions of method, and are more important than those recent additions to the substance of learning from unfamiliar world areas. New and more refined methods for humanistic study have been developed by analytic investigations. Finer critical appreciation and expression have come out of an improved understanding of the processes of human growth and development. We know better how to teach languages by going from classrooms into laboratories and we similarly have taken the arts into studios and studies where the individual can apply what he knows and feels. Also, humanists today see many opportunities lying beyond academic boundaries which had not seemed to be their moral, spiritual, and aesthetic concerns. They know that intellectualism is not enough, and more than ever before possess the means to demonstrate their beliefs by making their academic world a working part in this total one.

232

For that service, humanistic studies will need a definition that today is lacking. A balance is wanted, between means and values, that the undergraduate may see where he is going and the graduate student discern his own clearest opportunity in accord with his known talents. That balance will restore a sureness of purpose that was lessened by the inroads of the elective system, and faculties will regain that sense of direction which failed under the constant revisions of liberal education.

Every change in patterns of study for undergraduates should have had a compensating one in every course and sequence of studies. Often new staff and new materials should have been supplied; possibly there was needed a re-training of personnel to carry on the modified programs in languages, histories, philosophies, and literatures. In some places more thought should have been given to the "whole man" and less to the wholeness of a department. That habit of conserving student enrollment was possibly aided under the "concentration" procedures of recent years, but today far better planning of divisional committees is freeing students to work in accord with declared interests in several related fields. The humanities are coming into a closer unity, consequently, under two changes in their routines. The survey courses of the first and second years unite them, to give students a perspective on their further studies, and the final concentration, or honors, programs, again bring about a general unity of values for a review in the comprehensive examination.

Renewed constrictive control of individuals, teachers and students alike, can be developed in these survey courses precisely as was true of fixed routines in separate departments. Even the finest survey course may fail to show the way toward personal responsibility in matters beyond sheer learning. The humanities decline wherever faith in method displaces freedom of personal inquiry. A mechanized application of the survey principle can also scatter attention to so many slightly known subjects that the student loses his sense of direction. It is still useful to recall the remark of Gilman, that introduction to twenty fields of knowledge during his senior year at Yale left him curious about all and decisive in purpose toward none.

In their formal practices every field of the humanities and every subdivision of each field relies upon the same requirements for progress. These three essentials are found in every evolving process, and therefore in the growth and development of the individual. History, theory, and practice are to be provided him in all subjects of higher study. He will himself create a balance of values from applying all three in proper measure to the subject in hand and so in all his program.

The story of humanistic studies is of overemphasis on one of these three requirements and of attempts to correct such unbalanced treatment of traditional subjects. Excesses of historical inquiry have kept out theory and practice. Critical theory has produced at times a spirit of dialectic discourse instead of interpretation; hence our histories of criticism, offsetting and then hindering work with literary texts. Every humanist has his own definition of method, but not always of his aims. If he examines his activities, he may re-establish the three processes in use and reaffirm his own faith in what the humanities can do, as he determines what his constant aims should be.

That effect is to be made first in the individual, as he learns the uses of fact, theory, and practice. To apply himself, he requires resources, guidance, and a chance for active experience in one or more of the humanistic arts.

Not all who are called follow. Only a few undergraduate students become members of the profession. They may do so as teachers, research workers, or librarians in colleges and universities; they also have opportunities as curators and as specialists in other services of museums and art galleries. They may become interpreters of humanistic values to the public mind at any age level and in any part of the world, or they may be more fully expressive of self as practicing artists. Probably no person can follow successfully more than one or two of these pursuits, but he can direct others toward all of them. His place of vantage in a college or university is an extraordinary one. It is his responsibility to show what are the outlets of his subject into life, and to answer unasked questions among those who follow his teaching.

Of all practitioners in the humanities, the scholarly librarian has possibly the widest range of experiment. He may try any form of humanistic activity, for he lives at the center of all their resources and at the place of meeting for specialists and students. He knows the state of scholarship in many fields and their needs of personnel. He in consequence comes to know the uses and values of all work in the total field and can direct others toward them. Since humanists must rely on the foresight and influence of the librarian, the beginning of definition is with his role in making the humanities consistently and constantly effective.

II

Libraries belong to the entire academic community, but are the special possessions of humanists. They use library materials more regularly than other scholars, and for the widest variety of purposes. It follows that the faculty for humanities determines largely what shall be the stock of books and journals in any college library to sustain general interests as well as their own. The stacks, consequently, become in time an excellent index to the activities of faculty members and their success in each field. The growing and changing collections of a college library reveal also what are the relationships of people within the institution. Students, teachers, librarians, administrative officers, and trustees are all concerned. A break at any point in the chain of supply and demand can follow from the acts of any person in these five academic groups. The cause of breaks may be a waste of funds or false economy. It may come from excessive support of one subject, or from a lack of interest in a vital field on the part of the faculty. It may even follow from misuse of good library resources under lax administration. The evidence is there, for praise or for blame, and the effect on the progress of humanistic work in the college can be demonstrated under the old laws of supply and demand. Happily, a college library also shows where vitality is greatest and what departments are under excellent direction that enlists constant support.

Signs of life or of inactivity are less easy to find in the bookstacks and journal files of a university. They often contain "dead" collections built up by specialists who brought together admirable bodies of material, only to move on to another institution or to end their work without leaving successors in their particular fields. Collections in university libraries, moreover, are too varied and too great for any valid deductions on the place held by humanistic studies and on the consistency of support given them by the administrative officers. Budgets, rather than stacks, are the revealing sources of data on library policies in a university. If the administrative officers repeatedly make unfavorable reductions, they lose their library specialists and defeat their faculties. On the other hand, university librarians are aware of the active needs in a faculty and can secure support, with help from committees of trustees and faculty members. They themselves are experts in judging the constant and rising demands, and they furthermore have as their aides persons who know each field intimately. Their resourcefulness in finding and in borrowing books is constant, saving funds in their own budgets and aiding the scholar more efficiently than he can himself.

Though the size of a library may show its particular uses and types of service, size is no index to values for the typical undergraduate college; one must examine carefully its collection of books and periodicals. Balance of kinds of material, and constant care in choosing the works to buy and to remove are the important factors. Since the quality of humanistic studies is determined during the years of college study and depends on the nature of library resources, the first test of quality of work is rightly made in the stacks and in the office of the librarian.

A count of the number of volumes in a college library is no longer a basic test of the right to accredit admission of advanced students to the graduate schools. That test missed the mark badly, for it ignored the merits of librarians and the judgment of faculties. Useful values give the true answers. The 168 institutions of higher education in Canada possess, all told, fewer volumes than are in the Harvard Library. That fact in itself has no bearing on the question of relative efficiency in serving the needs of undergraduates. Advantages at Harvard at that level of learning are probably unsurpassed, but a small college may have certain distinctions in its service to smaller numbers. This largest university library in the world is, first of all, a storehouse of learning. Its potentials are increased by the routines for prompt loans among all the greater libraries and from every open collection. The New York Public Library reference collection, the Library of Congress, and many other major bookstocks are as easily accessible for aid through photographic copying of their materials. Increasingly, the American scholar is given access to whatever is in any catalog.

Knowing where to find a particular work is as good as owning it, for occasional use, and economically far preferable. This service of location is done for the scholar. He soon learns that he likewise can discover through help of librarians the titles and authors of works on his special topic that are found only by indirect methods. Catalogs and bibliographies are effective but incomplete. Librarians are the final resource of the scholar. They are his means of guidance to unknown, as to known books, enabling him to surround his field of learning. No favored-nation clause in any international treaty is clearer in its promised advantages than this understanding between the American humanist and librarians at home and abroad. They know what he desires to know, and have made preparations to answer direct or unexpressed questions on his field of inquiry.

The special guides to long-recognized areas of humanistic study are described in the bibliographies of bibliographies—those master keys to lesser doors of humane studies. We know, from the study and writing of scholarly librarians, where to find such concentrated holdings on hundreds of particular areas of knowledge. The most recent report of this sort, by Robert Vosper, is also an index to much that was written in ampler detail by earlier writers. His essay on the "Resources of University Libraries,"[1] printed in 1952, is an admirable guide to printed matter and to the theory of acquisition of books now governing library practice.

A comparable review of art holdings is in Walter Pach's work, *The Art Museum in America*,[2] giving an historical account of their growth and a guide to the location of special collections. It would be as difficult as it is needless to make a descriptive list of similar works covering the total area of humanistic studies. The scholars in each field have made it their responsibility through their societies to provide such general helps. Their journals keep up the current record of works as soon as new titles appear, thus reporting steadily the new data to be found in reference books, library catalogs, and special bibliographies. The wealth of such information is the most enduring asset of the humanist, whether in this or any other country, and its easy accessibility is making this country the center of world scholarship.

III

The beginning of balanced training appears when language is recognized as basic to all learning, and as the three fields of history, philosophy, and language become interrelated in the minds of teacher and student as basic to work in literature; when taken together they can create a new unity. Overemphasis on historical method is injurious, but the disappearance of historical perspective would be disastrous not only to history as a subject but to every recognized field of learning. It is the danger of such losses in perspective that the humanist guards against in behalf of all people. Within the humanistic definition of history are all the values that have affected man, or can affect him, in his two worlds of events and of personal experience.

The spirit of history is in a remark of Anne O'Hare McCormick, made shortly after the end of the Second World War, concerning the people of Italy. She believed that they looked with confidence toward the future because they possessed a sense of historical continuity. Her comment placed Italy in contrast to nations that temporarily had lost that kind of faith. In 1949, Levin Ludwig Schücking, the venerated Shakespearian scholar, was teaching at the University of Erlangen, living in a security that he had lost at Leipzig. He was helping to restore the standards of German scholarship. Materials were scanty, but in time could be partly replenished. The obstacle was in the students; they lacked a sense of intellectual self-reliance and that spirit of inquiry which physical security and freedom of thought engender. Schücking was less concerned over the future of his own studies, in English, than for the future of history. He feared that Germany could not raise up many older men, as leaders, who would be capable of attracting younger men into careers as historians. He saw few giving such promise; yet he held to the hope that history might again become the "arsenal of democracy" for all of Germany.

That state of affairs has its parallels. Germany has had opportunity and some aid toward the recovery of historical perspectives. Russia, meanwhile, has lost beyond return a school of historians that was notable for the variety and high quality of its production. In 1950, as Mosely pointed out, in his address before the American Philosophical Society, Russian political theory had turned the minds of scholars backward into the remote past; as early as 1942 the historical scholar had retreated from reality, still held by the fear that even in his studies of early historical documents he might fall under the charge of disloyalty for encouraging "outmoded" views.

We have other examples of such erasures from human records and living minds. Each illustrates the closeness of historical sense to that faith in values which is at the center of all humanistic progress. A homely summary of that is in Ellis Arnall's quotation from a Georgia circuit rider, who said to him, "You know what I think? I think that everything you do, or I do, affects not only what is going to happen but what already has happened, years and centuries ago. Maybe you can't change what has passed, but you can change all the meaning of what has passed. You can even take all the meaning away."[3] These words have in them all one needs to know of the dangers from dictatorship and of the values in historical perspective, through knowledge, to overcome those dangers. All who give increase to that knowledge and disseminate it are guarantors of intellectual freedom. They guard against the attacks of ignorant and willful men, for they know that ideals also are weapons and that these are found only in a free society.

Today there is need of more positive action to keep history and all other humanistic studies free, in school and in college, lest the extremists inflict on students their partisan views of what should or should not be taught. There are many Americas in one. All must possess something of the sense of continuity and of faith in the future which history and literature constantly bring. The humanities are not for propaganda. Nor are they to be tried by the tests of propagandists. They are to give understanding and expression of the beauty and variety in lives of individuals. Their free survival is the first requirement of intellectual and spiritual integrity in institutions, in the nation, and in the life of the individual.

IV

Before surer balance comes to humanistic studies, place must be made among them for the newer studies opened to undergraduates. These are in the expressive arts. The academic history of some began soon after the turn of the century. All have come to recognition in college programs since 1925. The reasons of that late acceptance are to be found in the attitudes of humanists toward the three essentials of history, theory, and practice, particularly in the humanities. Their tendency has been to postpone the practice for their students, and often to attend only to the claims of history and theory. Many years have passed since such views were dominant; an extraordinary change has come about since 1925. The arts have been welcomed, and are today being developed in many graduate schools as well as in the colleges.

First of the practicing forms of art to be well established in higher education was critical and original writing. Students of evident talent were given opportunities beyond the routine requirements put upon all entering students. Today colleges and universities provide the formative training of the future poet, dramatist, novelist, essayist, or newswriter. We are told of the temporary disturbance at Harvard, in 1912, when Baker started his 47 Workshop in playwriting, answering his own rhetorical question, "How can anyone interested in humane tradition say that the making of drama does not fall within the scope of a university's legitimate concern?" Forty years ago writing of plays was the most suspect of the types of writing for academic consideration; today playwriting is practiced and plays are being staged in university and college playhouses across the country. Many civic and academic centers are sources of new plays for regional and metropolitan theatres, and of talented actors. There is confident hope that unawares the public is maturing to support the drama nationally as in music. By the addition of staff members who are themselves literary craftsmen, our institutions have increased the range of their influence in drama, as in the forms of literary composition that are less subject to experimental testing. Through wide use of the arts of writing as accompaniment to historical and theoretical study, they have made personal experience a normal expectation of those devoting themselves to the humanities.

For fifty years the history of art has had standing in university faculties. This is easily understood, for much of classical and later learning entailed a familiarity with sculpture, architecture, and painting. Independent unity, with practical trial of these forms, undoubtedly was delayed by the prestige won by specialists in historical studies, possibly also by uncertainty over the success of untried American activity in any form of cultural expression. At any rate, records of the development of art education in our universities and colleges show that it was not until 1925 that broader patterns began to grow around the established style of historical definition.

One critical comment that is often repeated is that in 1925 three aspects of the arts were being stressed in this descending order—art history, art appreciation, and aesthetics. Theory held sway eastward, and practice first came to general favor west of the Mississippi. When the elective system changed all the restrictions on subjects and order of courses, chance finally came for more complex treatments in the arts as in all other humanistic subjects. Architecture, design, painting, and sculpture were presented with relationship one to the other, and in studios as well as in lecture halls or museums. By 1930 original work was being accepted for advanced degrees. The universities of Iowa, Ohio, Minnesota, and Michigan were among the earliest institutions to develop the arts in three dimensions. The balance of history, theory, and practice had begun to appear.

The strongest native impulse toward art education in American colleges came from the secondary schools.[4] There the theories of progressive education had proved their merit. A high point in that acceptance was established in belief, if not everywhere in action, by the appearance in 1934 of Dewey's book *Art as Experience*.[5] Visual arts were then proved to possess intellectual qualities and spiritual values wherever they were related directly to life through acts of the individual. Experiment, practice, and finally artistic performance followed. Trial of method was granted elsewhere than in the scientific laboratory or in the professional art school; it was offered to students as a factor in higher education. Dewey's work gave formal statement of what the progressive movement had done throughout the country in many schools, and so raised to college scrutiny what by 1934 was a demonstrated fact in American education.

Though foreign influences in this field have been too varied and constant for any but expert commentary, the widespread effects from one source are so well known as to need only the briefest mention. The Bauhaus group had its end in Germany during the confused years before the Second World War. This country had the good fortune to receive its émigrés, who immediately identified themselves with their new country and were welcomed in American institutions. In their new environment they demonstrated again that craftsman and artist are alike in approach and in purpose, both belonging to the age in which they live. Their ideas of design and of function, as craftsmen and artists, are to be led but not controlled by conditions of a machine age. Materials are to dictate variety in design and in treatment, and utility is to guide theories of form. So much is briefly the unity of theory and of practice to be applied to our teaching.

Walter Gropius was the primary force in this transformation of the study and experience of art in educational institutions. Kepes, Moholy-

Nagy, Albers, and Giedion are other familiar names in the developing story. When Moholy-Nagy published his *Vision in Motion*[6] in 1947, the academic processes of the Bauhaus group were stated for the American mind very much as those of progressive education had been stated by Dewey thirteen years earlier. Design had been given a new reference, in relation to each usable material. The results have been made evident in American painting, sculpture, architecture, typography, ceramics, metal work, still photography, and moving pictures.

The formative stages of a new American art education have been passed, if one may judge from the writings of the specialists. They see ahead a greater freedom from fixed routines of learning that now hinder students from gaining philosophical and technical independence. The uneasiness which they show comes from the quiet prevalence of administrative injunctions against teachers without higher degrees—a proper device in times when standards were ill formed in every academic field and difficult to establish in the humanities by any except expert judges. Yet the appearance of the practicing artist in colleges is in itself a salutary change in American ideas of learning. The practice of literary composition was more readily accepted by virtue of its relation to critical and literary studies. The arts had a similar advantage, historically and theoretically considered, through their bearing on classical tradition in every form. Musical composition, fortunately, has made its way without academic hindrances, and largely because brilliantly exemplified and taught by persons of widening professional influence. Thus the artist in residence of only a few years ago has become a permanent member of the academic community.

Drama has an academic history more distinct than any of the other arts. One reason lies in its variety of means for individual expression. Another, less evident, derives from the fact that a college or a university is the only secure place economically for all the elements of dramatic writing and production to mature. A third reason, entirely clear to all who think and live in this medium, is the fraternity of feeling among its professional and noncommercial followers. This has been true from the early days of the Drama League down through those of the Theatre Guild and its subsidiary parts. The American theatre of today is a national product. Its identification with the universities and colleges is about as common in men's minds as Broadway, the street, is with New York City.

Too much stress is put on profitable performance of plays for this to be easily believed. That is because of forgetfulness. Art is not created for any reason, intrinsically, except to satisfy an individual compulsion toward fine use of one of its forms. If this were not the case, the leaders of theatre work in universities and community centers would not have spent their lives in the field nor have prepared equally disinterested successors. George Pierce Baker was only one of many who joined hands with idealists in the commercial theatre. The list of names is long, as is demonstrated in the works of its master historian, George C. D. Odell, in his account of the New York stage. Generosity of spirit in this field of art has always been a topic of admiring comment. It is a natural by-product of unstinted devotion to artistic purposes which university and community have helped to live and increase.

The earliest meeting of note in the contemporary history of our university drama occurred in 1925. Then Baker and a few others from the universities met with Arthur Hopkins and equally interested producers. The list of participants had six names still heard wherever the growth of American drama is being discussed. They were B. Iden Payne, Thomas Wood Stevens, Edward C. Mabie, Kenneth Macgowan, Frederic McConnell, and George Pierce Baker. Out of that beginning came the National Theatre Conference to give academic leadership down to this present time, the representative American Educational Theatre Association, and the American National Theatre and Academy. The continuity of contact between the educational and the professional groups is to be seen in these and other bodies having a national objective.

What began in 1925 as the conviction of a few, by 1935 had grown into a reality. That was the year when the Federal Arts Projects began experimenting with the people. Men and women from academic life guided the drama, with constant support from community theatres. They went on from that national service into the war effort. The full account of the ten years from 1935 to 1945 is still to be written,[7] but a few names bring back the recollection of types of assistance given by hundreds of individuals. Hallie Flanagan Davis, Barclay Leathem, Paul Green, and George Izenour typified the quality of direction and of invention going into the structure of the Federal Theatre Project.

By 1939 drama and all the visual arts were being united under academic direction. The process has been continuous since, with the theatre as the coordinating force. Robert E. Gard has made it so in the state of Wisconsin, with the aid of his university colleagues in art and music. Smaller institutions have been leaders in the movement to make all the arts fundamental elements in a liberal education. Among the earliest to do this was William and Mary College. In the Northeastern states, Wesleyan University now requires every student to make at least one serious trial of his artistic capabilities, while Sarah Lawrence has been constant in its devotion to the principle of art in higher education since the time of its foundation. In the autumn of 1952, the latter college dedicated a new arts building, with addresses by persons whose professional and academic experiences gave their remarks real significance. Two speakers pointed to the social and the personal values within the arts as they now exist and grow in the American college. Agnes de Mille said, ". . . if you do not know the difference between good and bad, I promise you there will be no good or bad anywhere in America fifty years from now, as there was none fifty years ago. . . . You will, . . . I hope, from time to time open your doors to the veterans. We need sanctuary; we need to communicate with you; we need to collaborate with young, fresh minds; we need to talk and mingle with educated audiences, educated in our trade and in our art.[8] And Archibald MacLeish, addressing the student who puts herself on stage in any academic theatre, said, "She will be part, from that time onward, of the only community which ever has endured or ever will."

These are brief and vivid insights. Longer views of values from the arts in higher education were given to the assembly at the University of Bristol, in 1951, when an international conference on academic drama considered the responsibility of the university to the theatre. The speakers were reported in a volume that included among others the address of Sawyer Falk on "Drama Departments in American Universities."[9] If writing today, he would lengthen the story of only a few years ago. He would say more of television at Western Reserve, Iowa State, Syracuse, and at perhaps ten other university stations that are well beyond experimental stages in a form that depends heavily on dramatic performance for existence. He would remark too on the musical dramatic forms evolving at Stanford, on the sharp increase in original writing, and on such composite programs as those of Frederic McConnell in Cleveland and of Gilmor Brown in Pasadena. These two names are among the oldest and best in point of service and constructive experiment in newer forms of dramatic art.

Many other reasons support the view that drama and theatre now flourish in American institutions under circumstances that promise well for the future of many phases of the humanities. Size of investment is a poor argument for importance; yet the expressed desire in form of capital expenditure is not confined to our zeal for athletic stadiums. Between 1920 and 1950 the records of the National Theatre Conference show that thirty-seven community theatres and twenty-eight college and university theatres were erected at a total cost of fourteen million dollars. This was without benefit of federal subsidy, something not desired or apparently needed. Some of these newer houses have a completeness unequalled in any urban professional structure, and all maintain their standards of operation and direction with anticipated influences in education and in the profession outdistancing their present excellent records.

It is fitting that academic drama should be last under review among the expressive arts. The outlets from this source into every kind of human circumstance are unlimited. We shall be seeing the unity of the arts giving to the humanities a clearer purpose in all their procedures, and a demonstration of the interdependence of history, theory, and practice in everything from archeology to literary criticism. The expressive arts are bringing into higher education a better balance of studies for students and therefore to society. Music, visual art, and drama are today practiced by more persons than at any earlier time in our history, and this in an era of mechanized distribution and presumed spectator and auditor dependence on film, radio, and television. Facts on participation show a desire to work in the arts at every age level and in every region of the country. The issue is before the humanists in colleges and universities, whether or not they will enter these fields with the purpose to elevate standards. It is accepted by many of them that training through experience in the arts belongs in the pattern of individual development. Colleges are demonstrating through them what the humanities need, in every subject of higher studies, to give experience as well as learning. With the increase of participation in languages, histories, philosophies, and literatures, the student today has prospects of different kind than his predecessors twenty years ago. In every subject he finds the opportunity to unite experience with material and theory of learning; those possibilities are enlarged wherever the expressive arts are offered as additions to the pattern for individual development.

V

The position of the graduate school in all matters of humanistic nature is improved when useful changes are made in the colleges. We may therefore anticipate constant increase in usefulness of research and teaching at advanced levels. The admirable programs being devised for the undergraduate are responses to demand. For variety and relationship of fields these are of greater significance for the humanities in graduate schools than for either the sciences or the social sciences. This is the case because universally the changing programs of undergraduate education are built more solidly on humanistic studies.

The present need is that society at large gain a better understanding of the place of the scholar in every phase of contemporary activity. True regard comes from understanding that leads to recognition and support. It is therefore useful to give, in conclusion, examples of the ways of scholarship in the humanities in meeting incidental obstacles to the achievement of its social and personal objectives. A few examples of the evil effects from interruption of humanistic effort would prove how society loses whenever the individual worker is delayed or stopped in his program of scholarship. Yet a more serviceable description of the humanist can be found in examples of long-continued, intensive devotion to a single purpose.

Eight years ago, in 1945, comparative quiet on the international scene made it possible to bring back the books to the greater libraries here and in Western Europe, and again to reopen museums for the practice of scholarship. The storehouses of the humanists were returned to them, except as some were damaged or destroyed. In the United States there were virtually no losses of material, but this country had other war damages to its work in the humanities. Deferments of book purchase, of travel, and of publication stopped many scholars and delayed their projects. Younger men were in the services and thus the stream of personnel to meet the rising enrollments of tomorrow diminished to the danger point. Much is said of the need for teachers in the public schools, but not enough of what the American colleges will require nor of the decline in graduate school admissions and granted degrees. Here are war damages at the most vital point, that of leadership in matters of every sort above the level of physical subsistence.

In 1944 the Oxford Press issued two volumes, of text and plates, on the subject of *Early Celtic Art*.[10] That such a work could appear in a war year proves the power of the university printer. It also was evidence of the desire for excellence that had sustained the author, Paul Jacobsthal, through years of intense study. I need not enlarge on what historical and linguistic knowledge were necessary for the background of investigation, or on the discriminating art in its preparation. No one else in our time, if ever, has been equally qualified for the further pursuit of this study. As significant for him and for society was the obvious truth that he was qualified for nothing else in comparable degree but might end a lifetime of preparation without completing his history. The war had not stopped the presses, but it had sent all rare books and museum objects into secure hiding beyond the reach of scholars. At length, after 1945, the essential objects were restored to their accustomed places in local museums and in the larger ones of Edinburgh, Cardiff, Dublin, and London. Work was resumed by the only specialist fully competent to carry forward this account of human history beyond the fifth century of the Christian era.

Every older scholar can match this account of intellectual recovery after interruption by war or other causes. Many truncated monuments of learning will never be complete because the men who began them have gone and have left no capable followers; others stand idle as their designers wait for the necessary funds and freedom to finish them. The experienced scholar knows also of instances in which planned and persistent efforts have brought full rewards.

Two examples of sustained scholarly devotion that will seem prosaic to all except scholars and bibliophiles are reported here because they are of the sort which humanistic scholarship must have in order to attain excellence. Studies in English and American cultural history will rely on these two new sources of information and guidance to materials of literary and historical importance. Recently the *Short Title Catalogue*[11] for the years 1641 to 1700 appeared in three volumes. The full title relates the origins of the printed works here listed as from presses of Great Britain and "British America." The contents are references to 80,000 books. What Donald Wing and his assistants have given us, through the aid of the Index Society, is a key to contemporary knowledge in every category for half a century of history. Twenty years were needed to complete this continuation of the earlier catalog covering the period from 1485 to 1640. A comparable gift to us is the third volume of the *Literary History of the United States*,[12] which is a critical reference guide to all manner of writings from the years of our history since Colonial times, with ample details on the prominent authors and on the critical studies made by later writers. One element in this work is a sequence of 207 bibliographies on individual authors, in itself sufficient proof of the varied and acute understanding of the author and compiler, Thomas H. Johnson. Here in consequence is something much more useful than a work of reference; it is a source of knowledge on every aspect of American life, from Colonial days to the middle of the present century.

Two recently finished contributions to our knowledge of literary and social history are soon to change our appreciation of eighteenth-century England. After thirty years of attentive care R. W. Chapman has published the collected letters of Samuel Johnson.[13] He has given all future readers in the field what cannot elsewhere be found, and what due to him need never again be searched after. These comments are equally true of the work that George Sherburn has done with the correspondence of Alexander Pope. Thirty and more years will be behind the pages of his critical edition, due to appear in 1954. Virtually simultaneous appearance of these important additions to literary history makes the future of eighteenth-century scholarship more clearly related to contemporary interests. From now on every student of the backgrounds of English life and culture will derive some of his conclusions from these two sources.

Our own history is being made clearer by the same kind of intense, long-continued study of individual leaders of American life and thought. The lost and strayed papers of Abraham Lincoln have been brought to print in the first definitive edition of his writings.[14] Roy

P. Basler and his aides have spent years on this task of assembly and interpretation. The nine volumes which they brought out in 1953 would, however, have been scanter and less significant in their values without the earlier work of scores of fine scholars on every particular of Lincoln's life and times. Another increase in American resources is coming out of the editing given the papers of Thomas Jefferson by Julian P. Boyd, to bring us a "first edition" and a definitive one in some fifty volumes now in production at the Princeton University Press.

It is out of such painstaking and constructive application of scholarly powers that we secure later on the plays, poems, and biographies that give the benefits of scholarship to the people. Without such scholarship the writings of Carl Sandburg on Lincoln and Stephen Vincent Benét's poem *John Brown's Body*[15] would never have come to paper; nor would audiences in eighty American towns and cities have heard the dramatic reading of that poem by Judith Anderson, Tyrone Power, and Raymond Massey. Always the cycle of creative interpretation starts with the scholar.

VI

Fair conclusions on the function of the humanities in a changing world are to be found in many contemporary statements on their present significance and their constant value. As a social justification of them in our own time, sufficient is given us in two sentences from George Sarton, who wrote: "The humanities are not useful, but they are necessary. They are essential to the good life even of the humblest people, who may be too poor in any sense to cultivate them, for the fate of these people will not be as pleasant if their masters, however just, are not humane."[16] His view is justified by history. Their constant value over the centuries and in every circumstance of life needs no written commentary. Their ways of bringing variety and beauty into the daily lives of people are as well known as their power to create confidence and faith. The protection of these benefits rests with society, in every age and in every country. They are lost where scholars and teachers are hindered and finally stopped in their research and interpretation, and where writers are the first among artists to be banned as warning to all the others. Wherever the individual is looked on as something inviolate, as entitled to the freedoms of thought and expression, the humanities will flourish. They likewise will change to serve the needs of each generation of men. This too is a belief justified by history.

NOTES

1. Robert Vosper, "Resources of University Libraries," *Library Trends* (July, 1952), pp. 58–72.
2. Walter Pach, *The Art Museum in America* (xi+300; Pantheon, New York, 1948).
3. Walter R. Agard et al., *The Humanities for Our Time* (159 pp.; University of Kansas Press, Lawrence, 1949), p. 27.
4. My comments on art education derive from the writings of Stephen C. Pepper and others in the *College Art Journal*, a manuscript by Fred Logan, and my twenty years of observation of Victor D'Amico's teaching in private and public schools of New York City and in the Museum of Modern Art.
5. John Dewey, *Art as Experience* (vii+355; Balch, New York, 1934).
6. László Moholy-Nagy, *Vision in Motion* (371 pp.; Theobald, Chicago, 1947).
7. Hallie Flanagan, *Arena: the Story of the Federal Theatre* (ix+475; Duell, Sloan & Pearce, 1940). This account is by the director of one of the five divisions of the project. A full-scale study has been in preparation for some time. The original records are still preserved in the Library of Congress.
8. *Sarah Lawrence Alumnae Magazine*, November 14, 1952, p. 9. The following quotation is from the same issue.
9. D. B. James, ed., *The Universities and the Theatre* (vii+115; Allen & Unwin, London, 1952). The quotation from George Pierce Baker earlier in this chapter is taken from page 12 of this work.
10. Paul Jacobsthal, *Early Celtic Art* (2 vols.; Clarendon Press, Oxford, 1944).
11. Donald Wing, *Short Title Catalogue of Books Printed in England, Scotland, Ireland, Wales, and British America and of English Books Printed in Other Countries, 1641–1700* (3 vols., 1,652 pp.; Index Society, Salt Lake City, 1953).
12. Robert E. Spiller et al., *Literary History of the United States* (3 vols.; Macmillan, New York, 1946–48). The other editors were Willard Thorp, Thomas H. Johnson, Henry Seidel Canby; also associate editors Howard Mumford Jones, Dixon Wecter, and Stanley T. Williams.
13. R. W. Chapman, ed., *The Letters of Samuel Johnson, with Mrs.*

Thrale's Genuine Letters to Him (3 vols.; Oxford University Press, New York, 1953).

14. Roy P. Basler *et al.*, *The Collected Works of Abraham Lincoln*. The Abraham Lincoln Association, Springfield, Illinois. (9 vols.; Rutgers University Press, New Brunswick, 1953). The other editors were Marion D. Pratt and Lloyd A. Dunlap.

15. Stephen Vincent Benét, *John Brown's Body* (376 pp.; Doubleday, New York, 1928).

16. *Isis*, November, 1947, p. 3-4.

17. Useful material on the individual scholar is found in Richard D. Altick's book, *The Scholar Adventurers* (1951), published by the Macmillan Company. Its chapters recount in narrative the stories of unusual discoveries and exceptional works of learning accomplished during this half century by research workers in British and American literatures.

The two long entries regarding the work of John Matthews Manly at the University of Chicago will gratify all who knew him and learned from him. Much more could be told of his power to inspire younger persons as well as to guide them unobtrusively toward their goals. The first to receive a doctorate in English from Harvard University, he soon made that sign of formal approval his least known distinction. The study of Chaucer's text through eighty known manuscripts could not have been attempted with his sureness of success by any other scholar of his generation. That task was completed with the aid of Miss Edith Rickert and a few junior members of his staff. Other recorded evidences of his breadth of knowledge and power of analysis are in the unpublished history of the cipher and code bureau of the Army from 1917 to 1920, and in the article that appeared in *Harper's Magazine*, CXLIII (1921), 186-97, on the Voynich manuscript; there under the title "The Most Mysterious Manuscript in the World," Manly related his adventures in tracing out the truth and error in the studies of other men in their fruitless attempts to unravel its meanings.

Appendix

The American Council of Learned Societies merits special description in any review of the humanities. It is the central body for all membership organizations serving the interests of humanistic scholars in the United States. The Council represents these societies individually and as a group, nationally and internationally; it also cares for requests from foreign countries in behalf of individual scholars or concerning any form of activity within the fields of humanistic study.

Organization of the Council is through equal representation of its constituent members. Two delegates and the secretary from each society participate in planning at each annual meeting, when temporary and long-term committees are appointed for specific assignments. An advisory board meets regularly throughout the year with members of the staff, to guide the existing program of awards and projects, and to share in their responsibility for the many duties of advice and planning that come to the Washington office. These duties include aid to individuals and universities here and abroad, to governments, and to international organizations.

On occasion, temporary additions to the staff are needed, in order to conduct enterprises over a considerable period. An instance of this sort was the project for protection (and, so far as possible, the return to their rightful owners) of all objects of art and other cultural treasures that were exposed to the destructive force of the Second World War. The Austrian repositories, for example, held 27,000 recovered possessions. Of that total, 13,000 were restored to Allied governments for return to their owners, 8,500 to private German sources, and 3,600 to the German government. According to a report in the *College Art Journal* (XI, 3, p. 195), only 3.5 per cent were still unidentified in the spring of 1952. Similar accounts are to be had from other collecting centers in Europe. Another project was to finance and to bring to completion the *Dictionary of American Biography*, which called for enlistment of an entirely different type of scholar and for support over a much longer period. One more recent program of the Council, during war years, was to establish training centers in modern languages that were not taught at all, or not in sufficient degree, to meet the urgent demands for linguistic specialists.

The usual functions of the staff and committees are the planning of long-range programs and administering funds allocated for fellowships, grants, and projects. Member organizations give token support, but the Council depends on voluntary contributions for salaries and the overhead expenses of its general operation. Such financing determines conduct of plans as laid down for each year. Examples of special delegation of duties under such aid have been given previously in this text. Two that originated in the central office are the current digest of the Soviet press and the production of a national register of social scientists and humanists. Advisory and consulting services are constantly required abroad (as for the work of UNESCO and the International Union of Academies), and at home for the varied interests of government, institutions, and its constituent societies.

Since its organization in 1919, the Council has rendered continuous service to persons and organizations concerned with humanistic values. One means to wide influence is through the united action of the four national bodies representing the disciplines and fields of the sciences, social sciences, and the humanities. The Council furthermore has constant contact with groups engaged in secondary and adult education, and with specialists in the production and distribution of materials for the scholar and for the general reader.

The following paragraphs show in brief form the structure and purpose of each constituent society. As members of the American Council of Learned Societies they have relied upon it for a wide variety of services over a period of thirty-five years. A detailed account of the assistance rendered them, and so to the enterprise of higher education in the United States, would be long and illuminating. A briefer but significant statement would show the influence of the Council in other parts of the world toward the unity of human knowledge and understanding.

AMERICAN COUNCIL OF LEARNED SOCIETIES (1919)
1219 Sixteenth Street, Washington 16, D. C.

American Philosophical Society (1743). 104 South Fifth Street, Philadelphia 6, Pennsylvania. Founded by Benjamin Franklin "for promoting useful knowledge," the Society has a limited membership of five hundred resident members and seventy-five foreign members. Primarily for research, it distributes grants in some thirty fields; from 1933 to 1952, its officers and committees made 1,370 grants totalling nearly $1,200,000. Its *Transactions* (1769– ——), *Proceedings* (1838– ——), *Memoirs*

(1935-——), and *Year Book* (1937-——) cover a wide range of interests as presented in the papers of its annual meetings and as developed under its grants. The holdings of the Society, in rare books and manuscripts and objects of great historical interest, are among our national treasures.

American Academy of Arts and Sciences (1780). 28 Newbury Street, Boston 16, Massachusetts. Its membership of one thousand Fellows is in four classes—mathematical and physical sciences, the natural and physiological sciences, the social arts, and the humanities. Publications, in two series, *Memoirs* (1785-——) and *Proceedings* (1848-——), are to "cultivate every art and science which may tend to advance the honor, dignity, and happiness of a free, independent, and virtuous people." Scholarly works of special character are the *Monumenta Palaeographica*, on Greek and Syriac manuscripts. Its central humanistic concern is expressed in the work of the Institute for the Unity of Science and the Committee on Science and Values. Four endowment funds provide income for projects of research and for special awards. Eight monthly meetings are held annually, and conferences are called frequently to advance inter-disciplinary relations among the arts and sciences.

American Antiquarian Society (1812). Worcester 5, Massachusetts. Founded to preserve and make available for scholarship the materials of American history, the Society has a restricted membership of two hundred individuals. Its research library is notable for books and pamphlets printed before 1821, and for special holdings in narrower fields of the nineteenth century. Its annual volume of *Proceedings* presents learned papers and valued bibliographies. In 1952 the Society completed the publication of volumes in Evans' *American Bibliography*, a work of great value, and has brought out other works of similar merit, such as Brigham's *History and Bibliography of American Newspapers*. The library is open to the public.

American Oriental Society (1842). Sterling Memorial Library, New Haven, Connecticut. The American Oriental Society was founded for the promotion of research in Oriental languages, literatures, and cultures, and the publication of books and papers dealing with these subjects. The 862 members in 1952 had the following advantages: (1) subscription to the *Journal* is included in the annual membership dues; (2) any of the Society's publications may be purchased at 20 percent discount from the list price, and often special discounts of more than 20 per cent are allowed; (3) meritorious papers and longer treatises may be submitted for publication to the editors of the *Journal* and monograph series; (4) members may participate in the annual meeting by the reading and discussing of scientific papers; (5) books are lent to members, upon request, from the Society's library of over 5,000 volumes.

American Numismatic Society (1858). Broadway at 156th Street, New York 32, New York. This is an endowed society having four classes of members: Fellows, to the number of one hundred and fifty; honorary fellows, to the total of fifty; associate members, unlimited in number; and corresponding members, persons having foreign residence and foreign organizations. Three meetings are held yearly. All lectures and exhibitions are open to the public. The building of the Society houses large permanent exhibitions of coins, a library, and rich collections from the ancient, medieval, and modern periods. Its publications are *Numismatic Notes and Monographs*, *Proceedings* (1878–1907), *Numismatic Studies* (1938–   ), *Hispanic Numismatic Series* (1950–   ), and *Numismatic Literature*, a quarterly guide to new publications in the field. Occasional awards are made to students for noteworthy papers; others are made to advanced scholars and to sculptors for excellence in the art of the medal.

American Philological Association (1869). 695 Park Avenue, New York 21, New York. The American Philological Association was founded for the advancement and diffusion of philological knowledge. Its activities are carried on through its publications: *Transactions and Proceedings*, the *Monographs*, and *Special Publications*; and its meetings. A volume of *Transactions and Proceedings* is published annually; this is distributed free of charge to members. The current number is Volume 82. The Association had in 1952 a world-wide membership of about 1,150. Membership is open to persons who desire to further the advancement of philological studies.

Archaeological Institute of America (1879). Andover Hall, Cambridge 38, Massachusetts. In 1952 the Institute had a membership of about 2,125, and a modest endowment fund to sustain cooperative programs with foreign centers in Athens, Rome, Jerusalem, Baghdad, Egypt, and in New Mexico. Its publications are the *American Journal of Archaeology* (quarterly); a nontechnical work, *Archeology*; the *Bulletin* (annual report of the secretary); and the *Newsletter,* an occasional issue. A lecture program and other aids to popular appreciation of archeology are sponsored by the Institute, as extensions of the research programs approved at its annual meetings.

Society of Biblical Literature and Exegesis (1880). Garrett Biblical Institute, Evanston, Illinois. The membership roll of 1952 included the names of 1,200 individuals. On nomination of any member others are added to this active list; honorary elections are by the same procedure. The annual meetings of the national society and of its five regional branches in Canada and the United States bring together advanced students, teachers, ministers, rabbis, priests, and others of like scholarly interests. The publications of the Society are its *Journal* and a *Monograph Series,* and individual members cooperate constantly in preparation of materials on Biblical and Oriental subjects to be issued through other channels in foreign countries.

Modern Language Association of America (1883). 6 Washington Square North, New York 3, New York. This Association exists to promote study, criticism, and research in modern languages (including English) and their literatures. Members receive six issues of *PMLA* (Publications of the Modern Language Association), almost 2,000 pages, each year. This journal includes, besides learned articles, an annual bibliography of work in the field, an international compilation of "Research in Progress," a list of members and other useful addresses, reports, news, announcements, editorials, surveys, and general information of professional interest. The Association occasionally publishes books in two series (Monograph, Revolving Fund), which members may purchase at considerable discounts. Annual meetings—with a three-day program of more than seventy groups, sections, and conferences—are sometimes attended by as many as half of the more than 7,000 members. There are standing committees on research activities, trends in education, book publications, photographic reproductions, international cultural cooperation, the New Variorum Shakespeare, and American bibliography.

American Historical Association (1884). The Library of Congress Annex, Washington 25, D. C. This Association has over 6,000 members representing all fields of historical study. With the Mississippi Valley Historical Association, it gives general coverage in subjects of interest locally, regionally, and nationally in this country. It is actively concerned with the teaching of history in secondary schools, in which service it cooperates with the National Council for the Social Studies. Annual meetings are planned around central themes, with added subjects, and are largely attended. A branch of the Association on the Pacific Coast also conducts a regional meeting.

Publications are a quarterly, *The American Historical Review*, distinguished by the quality of its book reviews, general articles, and minor notes; an annual volume, *Writings on American History*, and the *Annual Report*, with supplements. Other publications appear under the names of important committees, such as the Beveridge Committee, that on the Littleton-Griswold Fund, and another for grants from the Carnegie Revolving Fund. Prizes are awarded for distinguished scholarship. Active efforts are made to increase public interest in historical matters by the use of radio as an instrument of education, and by encouraging projects in local and regional history.

American Economic Association (1885). Northwestern University, Evanston, Illinois. The membership, in six classes, totals about 9,000. To this list are added the names of some 2,000 subscribers to its publications. Publications regularly issued are a quarterly, *The American Economic Review*, covering progressively the advances of economic thought, and annual volumes of *Papers and Proceedings*. At irregular intervals appear the *Directory* of members and the *Handbook*. The Association publishes monographs of timely interest. It maintains also a "re-publication" and a translation series. Much of its notable service is rendered in advisory roles of members designated to deal with international and domestic issues.

American Folklore Society (1888). University of Pennsylvania, Philadelphia 4, Pennsylvania. In 1952 the Society had a membership of 1,050, the largest in its history. The annual meetings bring out their wide diversity of interests, nationally and internationally, showing how folklore of any one people depends in many respects on interchange and adaptation. Publications are the *Journal of American Folklore*, a quarterly issued continuously since the founding of the Society; a Memoir Series of book-length studies, now in its forty-third volume; and the Bibliographical Series, which began in 1951.

American Philosophical Association (1901). Bryn Mawr College, Bryn Mawr, Pennsylvania. The American Philosophical Association was founded in 1901, although for more than a year before that date there was in existence a Western Philosophical Association. The original group had less than a hundred members; in 1952, 1,414 persons were enrolled in its three regional divisions. These function autonomously, giving their own programs at separate meetings, electing their officers, and collecting their own dues. There is a movement to make the Association more centralized, in part to simplify its increasing activity in international affairs. The Association is affiliated with the International Federation of Philosophical Societies in Paris. The Association also participates actively in the periodic meetings of the Inter-American Congress of Philosophy.

The Association does not support an official periodical, but issues annually in September a volume of *Proceedings*, which contains the three presidential addresses at the regional meetings, official reports, and a list of members. It also administers a fund to provide for the lectureship in the triennial Carus lecture series and to bring each sequence of lectures into print.

American Anthropological Association (1902). University of California, Los Angeles 24, California. A membership in 1952 of 2,900 included about 700 institutional subscribers and a large number of individuals and libraries in other countries. The annual meeting is held with seven or more similar organizations of local and regional origin. Publications are the *American Anthropologist*, a quarterly, in its fifty-fifth volume; the *Memoirs*, of which seventy-five volumes have appeared at unstated intervals; and the *Bulletin*, a quarterly established in 1947. The Viking Fund medals and the Kidder Award are presented at three-year intervals. A manual for Point-Four officers of the government recently was prepared by the Association as a continuance of the many wartime activities of its members. A fifty-year history of the work of the Association has been completed.

American Political Science Association (1903). 1785 Massachusetts Avenue N.W., Washington, D. C. The membership in 1952 totalled 5,900, a marked increase due to demands for public service and the growth of the discipline in universities and colleges. It is the largest and oldest society of its kind in the world. Aids are supplied to individuals and to groups, with a frequent reporting of outcomes from inquiries into governmental practice and on matters affecting the welfare of the profession. The meetings are similarly noteworthy for cooperation of persons in public and educational services. Publications are the *Amer-*

ican Political Science Review, a quarterly, and the reports of committees operating under special assignments from the Association.

Bibliographical Society of America (1904). P.O. Box 397, Grand Central Station, New York 17, New York. The Bibliographical Society of America, organized in 1904 and incorporated in 1927, has a membership of 1,300 and endowment funds totalling about $58,000. The annual meeting is held in May or June in a university town and the midwinter meeting in January, usually at the New York Historical Society, New York City.

The Society's publications in print include Sabin's *Dictionary of Books Relating to America* and *Incunabula in American Libraries, A Second Census*. The *Papers* of the Society, a quarterly, now in their forty-seventh volume, present scholarly articles, bibliographical notes, and book reviews.

Association of American Geographers (1904). The Library of Congress, Washington 25, D. C. The interests of the Association are extensive and varied in the fields of education, government, and private business. The membership of 1,750, in 1952, represented diversified activities in teaching, research, and exploration. Yearly meetings are conducted for the full membership and also in autonomous regional sections. Publications are *The Annals*, a quarterly, and the *Professional Geographer*, a bimonthly news journal. Bulletins giving reports on scientific matters are issued at intervals.

American Sociological Society (1905). New York University, Washington Square, New York 3, New York. The five classes of members enrolled in 1952 made up a total of 4,300 individuals, among them being a substantial number of undergraduate and graduate students. Annual meetings for presentation of papers and business transactions also receive the reports of planning and research committees. Publications are the bimonthly *American Sociological Review* and an occasional special issue devoted to a current concern of workers in the field.

College Art Association of America (1911). 625 Madison Avenue, New York 22, New York. The purposes of the membership, in five classifications, are to advance the teaching and research interests of all academic workers, and to extend the public appreciation and discussion of art on a national scale. The annual meeting is attended by educators, practicing artists, museum directors and curators, and collectors. Publications are the *Art Bulletin*, an illustrated quarterly, and the *College Art Journal*, a quarterly devoted to the interests of teachers and of art departments in museums and other institutions. The Association maintains a book-buying service for its members.

History of Science Society (1924). Brandeis University, Waltham 54, Massachusetts. A membership of 967, in 1952, had the services of an active editorial staff under the direction of George Sarton, the leading authority and most influential writer in the field. His international review, *Isis*, devoted to studies in the history of science and civilization, has the distinction of being equally notable for its scholarly and literary qualities.

Linguistic Society of America (1924). Box 1001, University Station, Charlottesville, Virginia. To promote scholarly and general interest in studies of language and languages, the Society holds two meetings yearly. Over eight hundred individual members and three hundred and fifty libraries receive issues of its publications. An aid to a general knowledge of linguistics is the enrollment of students at reduced fees, as in a few other national societies, with the effect of an early enlistment of interest in research and teaching. The publications of the Society are *Language*, which has completed twenty-eight years of regular issue, and two series of dissertations and monographs, totalling respectively forty-five and twenty-five volumes. Many important separate works have had the imprimatur of the Society, among them the Bloch-Trager *Outline of Linguistic Analysis*, which had an important part in American wartime plans for the training of personnel. The Society was active in every other phase of that program, which was directed by the American Council of Learned Societies. It conducts annual institutes and supports staffs for field operations here and abroad.

Mediaeval Academy of America (1925). 1430 Massachusetts Avenue, Cambridge, Massachusetts. The Academy enrolls in two classes of active membership, Fellows and Corresponding Fellows; additions to membership in these are made by election for distinguished scholarship in the medieval field. In 1952 there were 1,021 active members, and in all classes a total of 1,224. Two yearly meetings are held, in April and December. Publications are *Speculum*, a quarterly of which Volume 24 appeared in 1952, and notable separate works in the field now totalling some sixty titles. The Academy has an endowment fund. It cooperates in certain projects with the British Academy and the Royal Historical

Society, the American Academy in Rome, the Byzantine Institute, the Dumbarton Oaks Research Library, and similar institutions devoted to varied branches of medieval studies.

American Musicological Society (1934). Wellesley College, Wellesley 81, Massachusetts. For the "advancement of research in the various fields of music as a branch of learning and scholarship," the Society enrolls four classes of active members; the total of eight hundred and fifty names on its lists in 1952 was supplemented by those of two hundred and fifty persons as subscribers to its publications. The eleven chapters in various parts of the country meet independently and unite annually in a meeting of the full membership. Publications are the *Journal*, appearing three times each year, *Papers* (1936–1941), and *Bulletins* (1935–1947). Individual volumes also have been issued from time to time.

American Society for Aesthetics (1942). Cleveland Museum of Art, Cleveland 6, Ohio. This latest cooperating member of the Council has had a vigorous growth, in large part due to the work of Thomas Munro as its organizing force and as editor of its *Journal of Aesthetics and Art Criticism*. Some six hundred members represent varied interests of the social sciences and humanities in universities, colleges, and museums, and professional activities in music, theatre, dance, and other arts.

The Society represents a change from speculative philosophy as the primary concern of an aesthetics devoted to theories of beauty; its first interest is in descriptive, factual studies of all the arts in relation to one another, to human nature, and to social environment. Problems involved in its considerations are related to semantics, evaluations in cultural history, and processes of education.

The *Journal*, a quarterly, offers to English readers a constant supply of theoretical discussion of all the arts. Foreign contributions are frequent, and distribution of the journal on an international basis is to a steadily increasing number of subscribers.

Index

Abraham Lincoln Association, 251
Acton, Baron John, 90
Adams, G. P., 138, 148
Adams, Henry, 72, 89
Addison, Joseph, 158
Adler, Mortimer J., 148
aesthetics, 141
Africa: and area studies, 205; dialects of, 46
Agard, Walter R., 31, 250
Agassiz, Louis, 200
Agrarianism, 93, 94
Alaska, 102
Alberts, Josef, 242
Albright, William F., 223
Alonso, Amado, 218
Altick, Richard D., 251
American Academy of Arts and Sciences, 255
American Academy in Rome, 262
American Anthropological Association, 259
American Antiquarian Society, 255
American Catholic Philosophical Society, 143
American Council on Education, 125
American Council of Learned Societies, 30, 40, 56-58, 88, 215, 230, 253-262
American Diplomacy, 1900–1950 (Kennan), viii
American Economic Association, 258
American Educational Theatre Association, 243
American Folklore Society, 258
American Historical Association, 98, 104, 257-8
American Historical Review, The, 88
American Language (Mencken), 160
American Musicological Society, 262
American National Theatre and Academy, 243
American Numismatic Society, 255
American Oriental Society, 255
American Philological Association, 256
American Philosophical Association, 137, 258-9
American Philosophical Society, 238
American Political Science Association, 259
American Scholar, The (Emerson), 118
American Schools of Oriental Research, 222
American Society for Aesthetics, 143, 262
American Sociological Society, 260

American studies: 94 ff.; foreign interest in, 208; Harvard and, 198; history in, 79-81, 207; literature in, 172, 207; literature, early neglect of, 154; programs in, 204; representative centers of, 208; rise of, 159; textbooks on, 172; of typical areas, 208-9
American University as Publisher, The (Kerr), viii, 202
American writers, and regionalism, 156-7
Anderson, Judith, 249
Anthropology, and history, 96; *see also* Languages
Aquinas, St. Thomas, 145
Arab world: 222-24; American aid to, 223
Archeological Institute of America, 256-57
Archeology, centers of study, 256
Area studies: of Africa, 205; of Brazil, 218; of China, 206, 212-13, 219; and comparative literature, 207; definition of, 203, 209, 225, 228; English in, 181; expense of, 230; of India, 224-25; of Japan, 212-13; of the Near East, 221-24; new concern with, 207; relative importance of, 210; representative centers of, 213, 223; of South Asia, 224-25; strategic, 210
Arena (Flanagan), 250
Argentina, decline of studies in, 217; regard of, for France, 102
Army, U. S.: in Africa, 63; in Japan, 88; in Korea, 62; language needs of, 60; language school of, 58, 60; and philosophy, 127
Arnall, Ellis, quoted, 239
Art education, representative centers of, 241
Art as Experience (Dewey), 241
Art Museum in America, The (Pach), 237
Artist in residence, 242
Arts, expressive: the artist in residence, 242; in Canada, xiii; in colleges, 152, 240-46; cultivation of the, xii; design in, 241-42; and elective systems, 240; experiments with, 244; and the federal government, xiii; foreign influence on, 241; general bearing of, 245-46; general cultivation of the, 152; history of, 240; influence of secondary schools on, 241; in institutions today, 245-46; internationally, xii; laboratories for, 240, 244; museums and galleries of, 237, 253; music in, 242; and

263